MAKERS OF AMERICAN LITERATURE

Makers of American Literature

A Class-Book on American Literature

BY

EDWIN W. BOWEN, A. M., Ph. D.

Formerly Assistant Professor of English in the University of Missouri, Now Professor of Latin in Randolph-Macon College; Author of "An Historical Study of the O-Vowel in English," Etc.

New York and Washington

THE NEALE PUBLISHING COMPANY

1908

Discipulis Prioribus et Fidelibus Amicis

CONTENTS

PREFACE

The present volume is designed as a guide, in a general way, to the study of American literature. It is of course not a history of American literature. It purports simply to discuss and consider the literary achievement of our leading American authors,—those who stand out most conspicuously in a general survey of our literature and who are recognized among the foremost makers of American literature.

No attempt is made in the following chapters to assign the authors considered their relatively proper place in our literature. That would be a hazardous undertaking even for a thorough scholar and most competent critic, and the writer of this book is fully aware that he does not possess the necessary qualification for the successful performance of so difficult and delicate a task.

Each essay is followed by a selection from the writings of the author discussed, in order to illustrate his style.

Several of the papers comprising the following chapters have been previously printed in magazines. These papers, I need hardly state, have been revised and adapted to the plan of the present volume. For permission to use these I wish here to express my thanks to the editors of the following journals: the *Forum,* the *South Atlantic Quarterly,* the *Lutheran Quarterly,* the *Presbyterian Review,* the *Sewanee Review,* and the *Methodist Review.*

The selections from Nathaniel Hawthorne, Ralph Waldo Emerson, H. W. Longfellow, O. W. Holmes,

J. G. Whittier, and J. R. Lowell are published by
permission of, and by special arrangement with,
Houghton, Mifflin & Company, the authorized publishers of their works.

The selection from Irving is published by the consent and permission of G. P. Putnam's Sons, that
from Prescott by the consent and permission of the
J. B. Lippincott Company.

The selection from Lanier is published by permission of, and by special arrangement with, Charles
Scribner's Sons, the authorized publishers of his
works; and the selections from Bryant and Whitman
by permission of, and by special arrangement with,
D. Appleton & Company, the authorized publishers
of their works.

To all of these publishers I wish to express my
grateful thanks for permission to quote from their
respective publications; and also to Mr. Horace
Traubel, the literary executor of Walt Whitman,
I here express my hearty appreciation of his kind
consent to use the selection from Whitman.

No one is more conscious of the many imperfections of this little volume than myself, and I feel
that I must beg the reader's kind indulgence as I
send it forth on its mission into the world.

EDWIN W. BOWEN.

Randolph-Macon College, Virginia,
        November, 1907.

INTRODUCTION

The question is sometimes asked, Is there really an American literature? To this question the impartial and discriminating student of the literatures of the two great English-speaking nations of the world must surely make an affirmative reply. For American literature is as different from English literature as the typical American is different from the typical Englishman. To be sure, the literary product of the two countries is related, and there consequently exists a family resemblance, so to say, just as the two peoples are related and have much in common. But the two nations are separated by the broad Atlantic and differ essentially from each other; and this essential national difference is reflected in the literary product of the kindred peoples.

American literature, it need hardly be remarked, is centuries younger than English literature and hence less rich, less copious and less varied. It is also true that American literature sprang from English literature and, in its humble beginning, is not to be distinguished from the literature of the mother country. The first American writers were simply transplanted Englishmen, who wrote under the inspiration and stimulus of British literary traditions and ideals, until the physical conditions of climate and country coupled with the patriotic idea had their perfect work, and in due course of time a new nation was born. With the growth and development of the national independence there developed apace, like the child from the parent, a distinctive national literature. Thus American literature is to-day essentially and radically different from English literature, and this difference is increasing with the passing years. It follows therefore that American literature is much farther removed from English literature at the present day than it was a century ago.

It is a fact as interesting as it is unique that the United States and England, though speaking the same tongue, still have two distinct and independent literatures. Yet the explanation is not far to seek. It is simply the natural outgrowth of political causes and events. If the literature of a country is really the expression of the people's thoughts and emotions, their political, social and ethical ideals,— in a word, the people's life in the broadest and deepest sense of that term,—then it is perfectly natural that American literature should be distinct and different from English literature. For surely these two peoples have distinct and different ideals and aspirations and different national entities. These characteristic national differences are reflected of course in the literatures of the respective peoples. It is a mere accident that the two nations use the same language. And yet even the language is not entirely the same on both sides of the Atlantic. Horace's phrase, "the estranging ocean," seems especially apropos in view of the noteworthy differences in the use of our common vernacular in England and America. The language appears to have undergone some striking modifications on American soil, both in mode of utterance and in form of expression. These American variations from the British original are so decided as to serve as a shibboleth to differentiate American English from British English. No doubt time will accentuate these variations, and a century hence the differences between the two great branches of our common speech will be even more marked than they are to-day.

Literature in its broadest sense is the interpretation of life, national and individual, political and social. Just as British authors have interpreted English life in the successive periods of that nation's existence, so our American writers have endeavored, during the first century of our nation's history, to interpret American life, and our contemporary writers are essaying to do likewise. But it is no slight undertaking to interpret accurately and adequately the varied and complex aspects of our modern American life in terms of literature. The first attempts of our American writers in this direction were quite feeble, and naturally enough our early writers followed in the beaten paths of British authors and lacked originality and initiative.

American literature is mainly a product of the nineteenth century. Our Colonial writers were few and followed British models so closely in theme and method, and drew their inspiration so generally from that source, that they failed to produce any writings distinctively American. They did not portray American characters; they did not paint American scenes; they did not depict American life except in so far as American life was a reflection of English life. Being under the dominance and inspiration of British ideals and traditions, our Colonial writers naturally saw American life through British spectacles, which so colored their thought and emotion as to make their productions British rather than American. Washington Irving was the first American writer to make a departure from the beaten track and to blaze out a path for himself in literature. He was therefore a pioneer who discarded the old literary landmarks and pointed out a better way to Americans of his generation aspiring to be men of letters. The example of his success soon infected others, and at length American literary independence was established, not long after the establishment of our political independence. The time-honored literary traditions of the mother country shattered, American writers were thrown upon their own resources and were compelled to seek for themes and inspiration in our own American life and on our own American continent. So our literary independence followed in the wake of our political independence, and America has to-day a distinct national literature as a logical result of our distinct national existence. The rapid and rich flowering of American literature is a fit subject for felicitation, altogether creditable to our people. Nor has this matter failed to challenge the admiration of the foremost men of letters of the Old World, who view with amazement our phenomenal literary development quite as much as the statesmen of European nations view our marvelous political development.

In writing a brief history of American literature, it is necessary that a great many names be omitted which would clamor for mention in a more comprehensive treatise. A complete treatise would have to include all those writers who have contributed, in any manner, by their productions to swell the literary output of America. But such a volume would probably be more exhaustive than critical. For it would necessarily include contemporary as well as past writers, the living as well as the deceased; and no critic, however unbiased, can see and represent a living author in his true and proper perspective. Furthermore, some of our contemporary writers may have contributed far more generously to the making of American literature than any of our authors whose activity ceased in the nineteenth century. Yet the plan of this volume precludes special mention of any such writer, however important his work and influence may be in the history of American literature, simply because he is still living. In a treatise like the present which from the nature of the case cannot include all of our American writers, the principle of selection must be adopted and applied as wisely as may be. Representative authors must be chosen who are universally recognized as the literary leaders of America, the most prominent figures in the history of American literature.

It is not to be supposed that the critics are agreed as to the relative rank and merits of each of our prominent American writers. Nor is it to be expected that there should be unanimity of opinion as to what authors should be included in a compendium like the present. For, after all, it may be a debatable question just who are the makers of American literature, in the restricted sense of the term, and hence this seems a legitimate field for difference of opinion. However, there can hardly be any room for doubt as to the propriety of including all the authors here discussed. Some critics may be disposed to inquire what was our guiding principle in the matter of selection. The reply is, that, in the first place, we have aimed to include those authors whose productions are clearly of a high order of merit and have contributed in an appreciable and material manner to the enrichment of our literature; and in the second place, we have rigidly excluded all living writers. Of course it is an indisputable fact that some of our contemporary men of letters have greatly enriched American literature by their generous and enduring contributions. Yet, for obvious reasons, no living author may properly be here discussed since the lapse of time is, above all things, essential to furnish the true perspective, in order critically and accurately to weigh and determine any writer's accomplishment. It is true that additional authors who are not excluded by the latter principle might have been selected for discussion. But a line had to be drawn somewhere, and it seemed the part of wisdom to err on the score of exclusion rather than that of inclusion.

CHAPTER I

THE COLONIAL PERIOD

The first products of American literature, such as those of the Colonial period, were not literature in the strict meaning of that term. In the strenuous times of our early history the settlers were so busily occupied with the stupendous undertaking of developing their new country—clearing the primeval forests, cultivating the virgin soil and incidentally decimating the aborigines—that they found no leisure for the pursuit of letters. Whatever time the pioneer colonists had left over from these absorbing activities, the Puritans among them devoted to the study of the Bible and the cavaliers among them devoted to outdoor sports and social pleasures. Small wonder therefore that the few specimens of literature produced in the Colonial period of American history furnish but meager claim to be admitted to the dignity and rank of literature. Even the most enthusiastic and admiring student of American letters is embarrassed, not to say bored, by our Colonial literary productions; they are so insufferably tedious, insipid and inane—utterly destitute of life and interest.

The works of such writers as Captain John Smith and William Bradford make a dismal exhibit by the side of the brilliant productions of that galaxy of contemporary British authors who constitute the golden age of English literature. No American writer of our Colonial period deserves to be mentioned in the same breath with such English au-

thors as Dryden, Congreve, Milton, Addison, Steele,
Swift, Pope, Johnson and Goldsmith, to name only
a few of those whose classic productions adorn the
annals of English letters during that same period.
Over against these English luminaries we can set
only such feeble and sickly Colonial lights as Captain John Smith, William Bradford, Jonathan Edwards and the Mathers, who are in total eclipse by
comparison. It ought to be said, however, that
this comparison is intended not as a reproach (that
would be as stupid as it is unpatriotic), but only
as an indication how ill-adapted and utterly unsuited to the development of literature was the
American environ in those early days of our history.
Indeed, it is all the more creditable to American
letters and a source of justifiable pride that our
literature, within the brief space of a century, has
grown and developed from this insignificant and
unpromising beginning to its present established
place of distinction and prestige among the literatures of the world.

In our early Colonial period there were two well-
marked and distinct *foci* of literary activity, viz:
Virginia and Massachusetts. As early as 1624,
Captain John Smith published his "History of Virginia." A rover and adventurer, who relied more
upon his sword than upon his pen to win him fame,
Smith, after a two years' residence on American
soil, quit Virginia, in 1609, and returned to the Old
World, where his eventful and checkered career was
terminated by his death, in London, in 1631.
The romantic legend of his rescue by Pocahontas
and other thrilling adventures connected with his
name are so widely current that every schoolboy
knows of this daring explorer, although few have
ever read a line that he wrote. Critics have not

failed to question the authenticity of the famous Pocahontas legend and have demonstrated the falsity of not a few of the author's marvelous assertions. Smith's picturesque and vigorous narrative, while possessing only slight literary merit, is yet unquestionably on the borderland of pure literature. A singular interest attaches naturally to it for the reason that it is the first American contribution to letters. Of his rather voluminous productions the "History of Virginia" is Smith's most widely known work. But even this is far more valuable as a historical document than as a piece of literature.

Since the Southern cavalier found his entertainment and diversion in social life, not in letters, few of the Virginia colonists therefore continued the literary tradition established by Smith. The Colonial annals of the Old Dominion, the foremost Southern State, are not adorned with any names famous even in American letters. There is George Sandys, Virginia's so-called first poet, to be sure; but he was simply a bird of passage who happened to complete his translation of Ovid during his brief sojourn on the banks of the noble James. There is nothing in him that is Southern, in fact nothing that smacks of American soil, for the matter of that. Besides, the mere accident of the completion of a piece of literature in America could not surely establish the claim of a foreign writer to be classed as an American author. Those most interested in maintaining the traditions of letters in our Colonial period were college professors and clergymen. Stith, the third president of William and Mary College, then recognized as the fountain of intellectual life in Virginia, wrote an interesting and much prized history of the colony. Stith perhaps had implicit confidence in Captain Smith as a veracious

chronicler of the early history of the Old Dominion
and therefore did not deem it worth while to investi-
gate for himself and verify Smith's statements in
every instance. But the book is far from being a
reprint of Smith's "History of Virginia"; and Stith
incorporated into his volume much fresh and accurate information gathered from various sources,
making it the most important work of its kind produced in Virginia before the Revolution. After
Stith comes Colonel Byrd, the founder of Richmond, whose "History of the Dividing Line"
between Virginia and North Carolina, far from
being a dry-as-dust tome, is enlivened with imaginative touches here and there and possesses some real
literary merit.

It will be observed that the Southern writers of
our Colonial literature had a decided bias for history and descriptive narrative. But not so their
New England contemporaries. These latter drew
their inspiration from religious themes. Theology
is the dominant note in their literary productions,
prose and verse. Moreover, in New England the
transplanted flower of literature appears to have
taken firm root from the very first and to have
flourished more vigorously there than in the South.
Hence the long muster of such New England writers as Bradford, Eliot, Winslow, Winthrop, Mor-
ton, Hooker, Roger Williams, Anne Bradstreet,
Wigglesworth, Ward, Sewell, Prince, the Mathers,
and Jonathan Edwards.

This formidable array of our early men of letters
represented but little genuine literature. The poets
of the number are Anne Bradstreet and Michel
Wigglesworth; but their verses have long ago fallen
into a well-merited oblivion. Mrs. Bradstreet was
acclaimed the Tenth Muse by the uncritical colon-

ists and enjoys the distinction of being the first woman in America to join the craft of authors. It would be ungallant, though true, to say of her ponderous poems that they richly deserve the fate which has overtaken them—being a striking illustration of the dreary stuff which passed for poetry with our undiscriminating early colonists. Mrs. Bradstreet's "The Four Elements" and "The Four Monarchies" had their reward in their author's day. The Reverend Michel Wigglesworth's "Doomsday," however, even despite its gloomy and forbidding Calvinistic meditations, enjoyed a greater popularity than Mrs. Bradstreet's poetic reflections. But judged by present-day tastes Wigglesworth's effusions are little removed from mere theological doggerel and are without a ray of light to illuminate their gloom and dreariness. His verses are now interesting chiefly as a specimen of the so-called poetry of New England during the days of Milton and Dryden. To accept such drivel as poetry surely bespeaks a woeful lack of discrimination and taste on the part of our early critics, and is a gross reflection upon the judgment of our early men of letters.

The work of the prose writers is of a somewhat higher order of merit. The chief source of inspiration of most of the prose is religious interest, and the bulk of the work is sermons. Eliot, the apostle to the Indians, wrote a translation of the Bible for the use of the aborigines; and Hooker published a collection of his sermons for the edification of his readers. Winthrop's "History of New England" possesses a certain interest for the historian, of course, while his "Letters" are valuable as being the first collection of epistolary literature produced on this side of the Atlantic. Cotton Mather's voluminous *"Magnalia Christi Americana"* stands as

a monument to its author's unflagging industry and
pedantic learning, rather than as a signal literary
achievement. Mather's lack of accuracy and logical treatment and his prolixity withal contrast
sharply with the noteworthy love of accuracy, orderly arrangement and succinctness which are so
strikingly apparent in the diaries of Bradford,
Sewell and Winthrop.

The limits of space preclude a detailed consideration of this group of New England writers. But
simple justice demands that a few words be devoted
to Jonathan Edwards, that eminent divine whose
religious utterances impressed themselves so forcibly upon the heart and conscience of his Puritan
contemporaries. For Jonathan Edwards and Cotton Mather were far in advance of all the pre-revo-
lutionary writers in the field of philosophy and theology; and of these Edwards is generally conceded
to have been the greater in point of intellectual
grasp and actual achievement. Edwards's important contribution to our Colonial literature was his
famous treatise on the "Freedom of the Will," written during his presidency of Princeton College.
Upon this erudite Calvinistic exposition of the freedom of the will the learned author lavished his
ripest thought. Edwards also wrote a memorable
ordination sermon on the punishment of the wicked,
which exerted an abiding influence on theological
inquiry and discussion in New England during the
nineteenth century. As the foremost exponent of
Calvinism in the North Edwards was succeeded, in
turn, by Hopkins, Emmons and Dwight. Of these
Dwight was by far the most brilliant. He is favorably known to the student of our early literature as
the author of an epic poem "The Conquest of

Canaan," five volumes of sermons, and some descriptive writing on travels.

As the relations of the Colonies to the mother country became more and more strained, it was but natural that the stirring events of the Revolution should have called forth much political writing, and that the popular interest in philosophical and theological discussion should have consequently waned. The flood of political tracts and pamphlets therefore which issued from the press in the latter half of the eighteenth century soon engrossed public attention, dominating the thought and literary activity of the entire country. Those strenuous times dictated simple and practical methods of appeal to the people. Consequently those who felt the impulse to write paid but little attention to the art of expression or literary finish, their supreme aim being the practical effect. There are some famous names adorning the pages of American history during this period, but they are principally the names of our Revolutionary worthies, such as warriors and orators. Thomas Jefferson, the man of ideas and the author of our immortal Declaration of Independence, Patrick Henry, the silver-tongued orator of Virginia, and Samuel Adams and Otis of Massachusetts no less distinguished for their burning eloquence and patriotism,—these illustrious worthies, however great their services in the founding of our nation and in the making of history, really contributed very little of permanent interest to American letters. They were men who accomplished great achievements in the field of human activity; but they were not men of letters. The chief claim of Hamilton and likewise of Madison to mention here is their authorship of the *Federalist* papers, to be sure, an excellent production of its kind, but hardly deserving to rank high as literature. Thomas Paine exhibited a forceful style and rendered a good service to his countrymen by his vigorous pamphlets on "Common Sense" and "The Crisis." His "Age of Reason," however, is a rather shallow book which created far more consternation among believers of his day than its merits warranted.

The figures that stand out most prominently in the dawn of our literary history are John Woolman, Joel Barlow and Philip Freneau. Woolman's "Journal" possesses some real literary merit and elicited from Charles Lamb the eulogistic comment (in a letter to a friend) : "Get the writings of John Woolman by heart." Whittier thought so favorably of Woolman's beautiful diary as to edit it, in 1871, and confessed himself greatly moved by the serene and lovely spirit of its author. Barlow is worthy of special mention because of his well-meant, though somewhat abortive attempt at pure literature. His prolix epic "The Columbiad," has been quite accurately described by Professor Richardson as "the most stupendous and unmitigated failure in the annals of literature." On the contrary, Barlow's mock-heroic, entitled "Hasty Pudding," offers something to the reader to repay a perusal of its pages. It displays a lively humor and some imaginative touches here and there in the picturesque descriptions of its rural scenes.

Freneau is easily first of this trio of Revolutionary writers and, in fact, is the only poet worthy of consideration in our Colonial period. This New Jersey bard had a checkered career as patriot, printer, and editor during those troublous times of political struggle. Yet he produced more verse, good, bad and indifferent, than any contemporary singer, and deservedly won his distinguishing title,

"Poet of the Revolution." It is true that his facility led him to publish much that ought to have been suppressed,—mere doggerel rhymes—simply because, having caught the ear of the public, he felt that he must force his jaded muse, to retain his hold upon popular favor. He used to dash off his verses with astonishing rapidity, and he gave proof of his versatility by writing upon a variety of themes of passing interest and in a varying humor. He wrote not only political, satirical and humorous productions, but he also wrote descriptive poems of some worth, and even essayed society verse with a considerable measure of success.

Some of Freneau's lyrics are very good of their kind and offer unmistakable indication of the genuine poetic gift. The best of them are marked by originality, imagination, and real poetic feeling, and stand out clear and distinct amid the inane lifeless imitations, the jingling rhymes of our Colonial versifiers. His little song "The Wild Honey-suckle" breathes the true woodland note and is redolent of the breath of spring flowers. We venture to quote it in full:

"Fair flower, that dost so comely grow,
　　Hid in this silent, dull retreat,
Untouched thy honied blossoms blow,
Unseen thy little branches greet;
　　No roving foot shall crush thee here,
　　No busy hand provoke a tear.

"By nature's self in white arrayed,
　　She bade thee shun the vulgar eye,
And planted here the guardian shade,
And sent soft waters murmuring by;
　　Thus quietly thy summer goes,
　　Thy days declining to repose.

"Smit with those charms, that must decay,
  I grieve to see your future doom;
They died—nor were those flowers more gay,
  The flowers that did in Eden bloom;
    Unpitying frosts, and autumn's power,
    Shall leave no vestige of this flower.

"From morning's suns and evening's dews
  At first thy little being came;
If nothing once, you nothing lose,
  For when you die, you are the same;
    The space between is but an hour,
    The short duration of a flower."

Freneau's masterpiece was "The House of Night,"
a more pretentious poem and bolder in conception,
though not happier in execution, than his "Wild
Honey-suckle." It contains some palpable blemishes of versification as well as of expression, but
it is decidedly original and is the best thing done
in verse on this side of the Atlantic during the
eighteenth century. Sombre and bizarre in conception and weird in effect, the poem, in spirit at
least, is not unlike the genius which inspired Poe's
poetry. But it is a far call from Freneau to Poe.

Passing over Benjamin Franklin, whom we shall
discuss in a separate chapter, we would call attention next to Charles Brockden Brown. Brown was
a writer of such promise as to make the critic feel
that he would surely have achieved some rare literary distinction, had not death claimed him before he
reached the meridian of life. In Brown's tales the
American school of fiction struggled to find its first
expression as a new and distinct form of creative
literature. True, Brown did not succeed entirely
in freeing himself from the English traditions of
fiction, and his work is imperfect and, for the most

part, violates all the canons of literary art and good taste. Yet he deserves no little credit for his effort as a pioneer writer to break with the time-honored traditions which bound authors of his class and to portray in his novels distinctly American scenes and characters. In portraying, in his stories, American men and women, Brown made a noteworthy departure; and his example commended itself to the judgment and taste of his immediate successor, Cooper, who found in the American Indian a fit theme to engage his creative fancy and prolific pen.

Brown's genius is decidedly sombre. Critics have not failed to point him out as the precursor of that acknowledged American master in the domain of the grotesque and weird, to wit, Edgar Allan Poe. The two authors certainly have much in common, though Poe was infinitely more richly endowed with imagination and far surpassed Brown in the art of literary expression. Brown's "Wieland" is his best romance and, though far removed from such a harrowing, thrilling detective story as "The Murders in the Rue Morgue," it still gives evidence of a vivid and vigorous imagination and compares not unfavorably with the English fiction of its period. Aside from the promising quality of his work Brown is interesting as being the earliest example of an American who endeavored to eke out a livelihood solely by the support of his pen. He was the first professional man of letters in America, and truly his lot was a hard one; and as an author he saw few halcyon days in his all-too-brief years.

Yet Brown's pathetic example did not result in an abatement of interest in letters, on the part of young writers aspiring to literary fame. On the contrary, his self-sacrificing spirit inspired young Americans with literary aspiration to do and dare

likewise. Brown's age was, so to say, the chill,
gray dawn of our national literature, and our early
professional men of letters had more of light,
warmth and comfort to look forward to as time
wore on. For already by the hopeful products of
their pen Washington Irving and James Fenimore
Cooper were beginning to give no uncertain indication that the spirit of literature had not perished
utterly from our western shores with the untimely
death of Brown. Nay, in Philadelphia, Brown's
own city, there lived and wrought a contemporary,
a man of varied activity, whose reputation as
editor, diplomat, scientist and author was permanently established in the early history of our nation
and whose fame as an author especially entitles
him to the distinction of first place, in point of time,
among the makers of American literature. This
versatile and talented man was Benjamin Franklin,
whose literary accomplishments and importance as
an American man of letters are outlined in the following chapter.

CHAPTER II

BENJAMIN FRANKLIN

Benjamin Franklin is among the most conspicuous figures in the early history of American letters.
Indeed, in the strict sense of the term, there was no
American man of letters at the time when Franklin
flourished. The man who made the closest approach
to this literary distinction was the famous divine,
Cotton Mather; and surely he is not properly entitled to be called a man of letters. This fact that
there were no American men of letters at the time
Franklin lived but emphasizes the remoteness of
our Colonial history from the present. At the time
of Franklin's birth in Boston (17th January, 1706),
the American colonies were under the rule of Queen
Anne. At the time of Franklin's birth there was
but one newspaper in America, and there was not
a printing press south of Philadelphia.

Yet despite these unfavorable conditions Franklin early showed his literary bent. Franklin's
father took young Benjamin from school at the
tender age of ten and put him in his chandler's shop,
intending ultimately to fit him for the ministry. In
his father's shop the boy gave unmistakable evidence of his love of letters by eagerly devouring
the few books in his father's meager library. Only
a love of literature amounting to a passion could
induce a mere lad to read and re-read such dreary,
dry-as-dust theological pamphlets as were found
upon the shelves of Josiah Franklin's musty library.
Of the entire collection only one book—"Plutarch's
Lives"—would possess any interest for the average
boy. But young Benjamin was far from being an
average boy. For what average boy would save up
his few pennies, as Franklin did, in order to buy

Bunyan's "Pilgrim's Progress," and when he had read and re-read it, sell it, and with the proceeds supplemented by his scant savings, purchase a copy of Burton's "Historical Collections?" Though his father little realized it, young Franklin was rapidly developing a taste for a more profitable employment than that of molding candles or grinding knives.

When Franklin was twelve, he was apprenticed to his older brother, who was a printer. This apprenticeship, no doubt, had decided weight in determining Franklin's subsequent career. It was while setting type in his brother James's office for the *Boston Gazette*, the second newspaper published in America, that young Benjamin began to write, producing two ballads in doggerel verse. At that time the street ballad was the main source of popular information. Franklin, having written up a recent occurrence in this form, at his brother's suggestion hawked his ballads through the streets of Boston. His father, however, disliked seeing his son resort to this device for selling his literary wares, and so he dissuaded him from any farther attempt at ballad poetry by telling him that all such poets were beggars. Thereupon Benjamin gave up the manufacture of ballads and employed his leisure moments in voraciously devouring all the books that came within his reach. So strong was his passion for reading that, as his biographer informs us, he did not scruple to persuade a book-seller's apprentice, who was his friend, to bring him books home from the store furtively at night. These Franklin would read, sometimes sitting up all night in order to finish the book by morning and have it returned to the store without detection.

During this formative period Franklin was strongly influenced by whatever he read. It is interesting to observe what books exerted the greatest influence upon him. Under the influence of a book on vegetable diet which he read, he forthwith became a vegetarian. On reading Xenophon's "Memorabilia," he became a convert to the Socratic method of dispute and subsequently adopted it in discussion, of which he was inordinately fond. Influenced by Shaftesbury's and Collin's writings, he soon drifted into skepticism. But, beyond and above all of these, the book which bore most lasting fruit was a volume of Addison, which Franklin read again and again.

It is interesting to note that this remarkable book was the third volume of the "Spectator." This book Franklin literally read, marked and inwardly digested. Upon it he founded his admirable prose style which is a model of clearness, terseness and force. A mere lad, he was held spellbound by the wit, humor and charm of the "Spectator." Its beauty and grace of style sank into his mind and made a never-fading impression. All the leisure hours at his disposal he devoted to this volume. He set himself exercises from it. He would take some number that especially struck his fancy, jot down the substance in rough notes and, after a few days, reproduce the thought in his own language, imitating the style and manner of the original as closely as possible. He would even turn the essays into verse as an exercise designed to enlarge his vocabulary. Nor did he neglect the arrangement of the thought. He would separate the sentences, throw them together promiscuously, and then re-arrange them in the original order. In this manner Franklin became steeped and saturated, so to say, with

the Addisonian style. It served as the model for
that succinct, lucid, nervous and vigorous style
which Franklin elaborated in his own writings.

Thus equipped, Franklin addressed himself to his
literary work, though not yet out of his teens. He
contributed a series of letters to the *New England
Courant,*—a paper printed by his brother James.
The first letter was called forth by the discussion as
to the virtue of inoculation as a preventive against
smallpox, which discovery at that time divided the
Boston public into two hostile camps. Cotton
Mather was an ardent advocate of inoculation. The
Courant maintained that inoculation was an invention of the devil. When the discussion was at its
height, Franklin wrote an article and modestly
thrust it under the door of the *Courant* office
at night, in the vague hope that it might find its way
into the columns of that paper. The article was
published, and while there is no record of it pre-
served, it is reasonable to suppose that it was the
first of the famous Silence Dogood letters which
Franklin contributed to the *Courant.*

The authorship of the Dogood letters was not revealed at the time of their publication. They were
first ascribed to Franklin in Parton's biography.
Franklin, however, claims the Dogood papers in
some notes intended for his "Autobiography."
These papers are a noteworthy production for a
mere boy. They reflect the spirit and style of the
"Spectator" in a striking way. They exhibit the
same playful humor and grace of style. The papers
include a variety of composition,—letters, criticisms and even dreams.

Shortly after the publication of the Dogood
papers Franklin left Boston, setting out for New
York, and ultimately made his way to Philadel-

phia. Every one is familiar with the graphic sketch the author himself gives in his "Autobiography," of his arrival in the Quaker City, seeking employment, and with barely enough money in his pocket to buy him a loaf of bread for breakfast. From Philadelphia Franklin went on a fool's errand to London. After sore disappointment in his mission he found work in London as a printer. Here while setting type for Wallaston's "Religion of Nature Delineated," Franklin was inspired, from sheer disgust with the argument of that treatise, to write a refutation. The result was the trivial pamphlet, "A Dissertation on Liberty and Necessity, Pleasure and Pain." Franklin afterwards repented of this stupid effort and endeavored to suppress the pamphlet. It is an atheistic production and does not contribute a whit to its author's reputation.

While leading an immoral life in the great British metropolis Franklin set out for Philadelphia, at the instance of a quondam Bristol merchant, who engaged him as a clerk in his Philadelphia store. Upon the death of his employer he secured work as a printer and continued at this trade afterwards, till he made his fortune and retired from business. At first he was employed by a printing house; afterwards he set up a printing house of his own in partnership with his old friend Meredith. This event marked the turn of Franklin's fortune. He conceived the idea of publishing a newspaper in connection with his printing house. At that time there was only one newspaper in America outside of Boston. This was the *Weekly Mercury,* published by one Bradford, in Philadelphia. Franklin's plan of establishing a new sheet leaked out, somehow, and his rival Keimer forestalled his move in issuing, on December 28, 1728, the first number of the *Univer-*

*sal Instructor in All Arts and Sciences and
Pennsylvania Gazette.* To checkmate this new venture of his rival printing house, Franklin immediately began in the *Mercury* a long series of essays
under the pen-name of the "Busybody," written
after the fashion of the Dogood papers. The up-
shot of the matter was that, with the fortieth number of the *Universal Instructor and the Pennsylvania Gazette,* the paper passed into Franklin's
hands.

The Busybody papers are of the nature of satire.
They reflect, presumably, in an accurate manner the
character of the times, the foibles and failings of
Busybody's fellow-countrymen. The first paper
sets forth the purpose of Busybody, viz., to censure
the growing vices of the people, to lecture them on
politics and morality, and to lead them to an appreciation of good literature by giving excerpts from
the best books. The second paper is a diatribe
directed against those who sin against good taste by
indulging in excessive laughter on the slightest
provocation, or who are guilty of any other folly
equally offensive to good breeding. The third paper
elicited a spirited reply from his old rival Keimer,
in the form of a tract entitled "A Touch of the
Times." To this Franklin published a rejoinder
ridiculing Keimer. This was followed up by a
paper denouncing impostors and mountebanks and
exposing the folly of seeking the buried treasures of
pirates. This was probably the last paper from
Franklin's pen to the Busybody series. The rest
were mainly from the pen of Breintnal.

It is evident from a comparison of the Busybody
papers with the "Spectator" that Franklin took his
cue in these essays from Addison. To be sure, it is a
far cry from the Busybody essays to the "Spectator"

numbers, and the resemblance is only remote. Still, it is significant that there is a resemblance, however remote. In Franklin's essays, as in the "Spectator" papers, there is no excess of imagery, and the language is plain, simple, terse and direct. The words used are familiar Anglo-Saxon terms, such as are readily understood. The meaning is as clear as daylight and admits of no ambiguity. To this simplicity of language are wedded a keen wit and a racy humor and a certain vigor of style, which give peculiar force and cogency to these Busybody essays.

From the Busybody papers Franklin next turned his attention to the all-absorbing question of the hour, viz., the currency question. Franklin presented his views in a vigorous and cogent pamphlet, "A Modest Inquiry Into the Nature and Necessity of a Paper Currency." Judged by present-day notions this pamphlet was false political economy. Yet it carried conviction to Franklin's contemporaries and resulted in a large order for paper money to be executed by his printing house, which proved "a very profitable job and a great help," in the language of the "Autobiography."

After the *Pennsylvania Gazette* came into Franklin's hands, the moribund journal took a new lease on life and soon developed into a flourishing semiweekly. Franklin used the *Gazette* as the medium for his reflections and criticisms on contemporary doings and happenings, and contributed liberally to its columns. Occasionally, he even ventured into verse, discarding prose as inadequate to his purpose. The most notable example of verse he contributed to the columns of his *Gazette* is his long poem, entitled "David's Lamentation Over the Death of Saul and Jonathan." This is a close paraphrase of the Scriptural narrative and was written about the time when Franklin, abandoning his atheistic views, formulated a liturgy for his own use, founded the Junto and penned his famous epitaph.

In 1732 there came from the press of Philadelphia three noteworthy publications, all bearing Franklin's imprint. The first was the *Philadelphische Zeitung,* the first German newspaper printed in America; the second was "The Honour of the Gout"; the third was "Poor Richard's Almanac." Of these the last, being by far the most important from the point of view of the present study, deserves especial mention.

The "Poor Richard's Almanac" had its origin in the popular demand for almanacs in the American Colonies, as in the mother country at that time. This demand is indicated by the fact that the first piece of printing done in the Middle States and the second done in America were almanacs. The American almanac-makers followed the precedent set by their English contemporaries, of including a hodge-podge of irrelevant matter, in addition to the calendar and allied subjects which find a legitimate place in an almanac. Franklin conformed scrupulously to the traditions of the philomaths even down to the detail of heaping liberal abuse upon the work of rival almanac-makers. He chose for his *nom de plume* "Richard Saunders," a philomath who, for a long time, was editor of the *Apollo Anglicanus.* "Poor Robin," an English comic almanac which was so indecent as utterly to shock modern tastes, furnished Franklin the general plan for his "Poor Richard's Almanac." From this clue Franklin produced the first number of his world-famous "Poor Richard" in October, 1732. The venture proved a phenomenal success and the almanac went like wildfire.

It is the prefaces to the "Poor Richard Almanac" which arrest our attention especially. The prefaces, as they appeared from year to year, constitute an admirable piece of prose fiction. They are shot through with a rich vein of rollicking humor and with a vivacity that quickens the reader's interest and entertainment. It is here that we become acquainted with two characters of Franklin's creative imagination,—Richard Saunders and his wife Bridget,—whose portrayal is almost as artistic and complete as that of any two characters in the entire domain of English fiction in those times. The author shows a rare acquaintance with human nature in his conception of these characters and his execution leaves little to be desired in definition and distinctness of outline. The broad humor is perhaps somewhat too coarse for modern tastes. But it must be borne in mind in this connection that the standards of literature in the eighteenth century are different from those of the twentieth. It is, therefore, conceivable that Franklin's coarse humor, which perhaps offends modern tastes, was not objectionable to his contemporaries.

The humor of "Poor Richard," however, was not restricted to the preface. On the contrary, it appears throughout the whole book, everywhere relieving the monotony of the prognostications, eclipses, calendars, and so forth. For instance, on one page is found this diverting prognostication, for the edification of sailors: "August, 1739. Ships sailing down the Delaware Bay this month shall hear at ten leagues' distance a confused rattling noise like a swarm of hail on a cake of ice. Don't be frightened, good passengers. The sailors can inform you that it is nothing but Lower County teeth in the ague. In a southerly wind you may hear it in Philadelphia." Sometimes amusement is afforded by the witty turn given a maxim, as "Never take a wife till you have a house (and a fire) to put her in."

Franklin, like other philomaths, adopted the plan of inserting in his almanac pithy, striking sayings and maxims between the remarkable days of the calendar. In this manner he interlarded the calendar with bits of the condensed wisdom of the ages. These maxims he designed to encourage and inculcate principles of thrift, industry and honesty. He introduced this feature as a means of disseminating profitable instruction among the common people, after "Poor Richard" became so widely circulated. It may be worth while to quote a few of these proverbial sentences as illustrating Franklin's felicity at phrase-coining no less than his wisdom in inculcating principles of probity and virtue among the common people, many of whom read no other book than "Poor Richard." "It is hard for an empty sack to stand upright." "Keep thy shop, and thy shop will keep thee." "Fools make feasts and wise men eat them." "The rotten apple spoils his companion." "If you would have your business done, go; if not, send." "God heals and the doctor takes the fee." "Necessity never made a good bargain." "Marry your sons when you will, your daughters when you can." These pithy sentences, however, were not all the product of Franklin's own invention. Many of them he borrowed from other almanac-makers. But when he borrowed a trite proverb, he recast it in his own imagination and sent it forth with a fresh stamp upon it from the die of his own invention. Such maxims afterwards passed as new coins and formed not the least element in the success of "Poor Richard."

Moreover, "Poor Richard" contains some of the best short pieces of Franklin's writings. Here may be mentioned "Father Abraham's Address," a masterpiece of its kind. This is a homily which "Poor Richard" put into the mouth of a sensible old man, familiarly known as Father Abraham, and purporting to be delivered at an auction toward the close of the French and Indian War, when the outlook for the future was exceedingly gloomy during those memorable lean years. The effect of this brief paper on the sale of the Almanac was magnetic. It attracted hosts of readers to "Poor Richard." The popular demand for the Almanac was so great in consequence of "Father Abraham's Address" that, when the increased issue was exhausted, the newspapers published the "Address" again and again to satisfy the clamor. Franklin himself published it as a broadside. His nephew, of Boston, printed it in pamphlet form and sent it broadcast through the land. It crossed the Atlantic and was widely circulated in Europe under the caption, "The Way to Wealth." It has been translated into all the languages of the Continent, and been twenty-seven times reprinted as a pamphlet in England, to say nothing of the numerous times it has been issued as a broadside in that country. Under the title "La Science du Bonhomme Richard" it has been printed at least thirty times in France. It is, no doubt, the most popular piece of literature produced in the American colonies, if translation into foreign tongues is any test of popularity.

At the approach of the American Revolution Franklin was sent to England as a special representative of the province of Pennsylvania and sub-

sequently resided abroad most of the time.   He was
now deeply interested in politics and scientific research.   He had little time left for mere literature.
In fact, he never cared at any time of his life for
literary fame, and was so indifferent to it as never
to sign his name to anything he published.   Amid
his manifold duties as a diplomat he found time to
write pamphlets on the burning questions of the
day.   His undaunted courage in those dark days
of the Revolution inspired the drooping spirits of
the struggling colonists, and led them on to a successful issue.   While abroad, besides his activities
in politics, diplomacy and science, he undertook to
write a history of his own life, the longest and most
interesting of all his works.

It was with great diffidence that Franklin undertook his "Autobiography."   The five opening chapters were written during a visit to the Bishop St.
Asaph, at Twyford, in 1771.   The manuscript was
then put aside, and the author's attention was next
directed to political matters of a more pressing
nature.   When Franklin returned to America he
brought the unfinished manuscript home with him.
Here he left it, in care of his friend Galloway, when
he went back to Europe on his French mission, in
1776.   Galloway, meanwhile, turned royalist and
his estate being confiscated, the precious manuscript fell into the hands of a Quaker friend and
admirer of the author, who made a careful copy and
forwarded the original to Franklin, at Passy, with
the urgent request that he continue and finish so
delightful and profitable a piece of work.   Still
Franklin was loath to resume the "Autobiography,"
though glad to recover the manuscript long given
up for lost.   He was busy with affairs of state and
his health was now poor; and these reasons induced

him to postpone the task. At length, after being re-
peatedly urged and entreated by his friends, he took
up the "Autobiography" again, in 1788, but only to
bring it down to the year 1757. Here he left off a
second time and sent a copy to several of his friends
and the original to M. le Veillard and Rochefou-
cauld-Liancourt at Paris. Franklin died shortly
after this, and his "Autobiography" was of course
left unfinished. The manuscript met with many
strange adventures before the memoirs were published first in a French translation by Buisson, in
Paris, in 1791. This version had little to commend
it to public favor. It was fragmentary, many passages being omitted or garbled, and the whole work
was little better than a travesty upon the genuine
memoirs. Then after long reprehensible delay and
many vicissitudes the "Autobiography" was first
properly published in the Bigelow edition.

The "Autobiography," even in its incomplete
form, is by far the most important contribution
Franklin made to American literature. Upon it
reposes, in the main, his claim to a conspicuous
place among American men of letters. As an autobiography it is a model and has proved extremely
popular ever since its publication. An idea of its
popularity may be formed from the fact that in
America alone the work has been republished up-
wards of fifty times. It is the general verdict of
critics that it is the best autobiography in the language. As literature it deserves to rank with
"Robinson Crusoe."

Franklin was not a voluminous author. Yet his
collected works make a considerable bulk. Few
writers have suffered more at the hands of their
friends than has Franklin. The excessive zeal of
his editors has led them to include too much of mere

ephemera in his works. Buisson, Price, Temple, Franklin Sparks, Parton, Bigelow and all the other editors after them have been overzealous to make their respective editions all-inclusive and definitive. The result is, there is much included in Franklin's collected works which the author himself never entertained the remotest idea of having attributed to him. Much of what makes up the bulk of his writings is mere padding,—"remarks," "observations," "essays," "notes,"—which ought, in justice to the author's reputation, to be eliminated. In almost all the editions Franklin is made to stand father to many a brief note or essay which he would have been very reluctant to acknowledge in print. Some future editor would enhance Franklin's fame as a writer if only he would eliminate everything that is of a trivial and ephemeral nature and include such of his writings as are of merit and interest and are designed to perpetuate his name as a man of letters. It is true this plan would materially reduce the size of his collected works; but it would, at the same time, greatly enhance their value. Such an edition would, of course, include the "Speech of Miss Polly Baker Before a Court of Judicature in New England," "The Witch Trial at Mount Holly," "Advice to a Young Tradesman," "Father Abraham's Speech," "Remarks Concerning the Savages of North America," "Dialogue with the Gout," "The Ephemera," "The Petition of the Left Hand," "Martin's Account of His Consulship," "The Autobiography," the Prefaces to the Almanacs, the best essays from the *Gazette*, his Letters and the "Parables" and a few other selections.

Franklin was the pioneer of American men of letters. Literary fame, however, had no special attraction for him. As already intimated, so far was

he from aspiring to literary distinction that he
made it an invariable rule never to sign his name to
any paper written for publication. He was too
much occupied with making American history to
surrender himself to literary work, whether for his
own delectation or for the delectation of posterity.
Even his "Autobiography," the more is the pity, was
left half finished, as is well known. He contented
himself with essays and pamphlets; and in this field
he is without a peer in Colonial literature. His
genius was kindled by the passion for American independence which stirred the hearts of the Colonists, and into that cause he threw himself with all
the ardor of his soul. An Addisonian by literary
training, he made heavy draughts upon his wit, his
humor and his fancy, to approximate the happy
style of that great master of English prose. And it
must be confessed that in this he has succeeded as
perhaps no other pupil of Addison's school has,
though his imitators have been legion.

Franklin really produced very little that deserves
to live. His literary fame seems out of proportion
to his output of genuine literature. He wrote no
history that has not been forgotten; he wrote no
poetry that oblivion has not swallowed up long
since. He created no great characters that have
taken hold upon the popular imagination. Yet it is
but justice to add that he did portray several minor
characters which have contributed materially to the
enrichment of American literature. The roster includes Alice Addertongue, Anthony Afterwit, Patience Teacroft, Silence Dogood, Titan Pleiades,
Miss Polly Parker, Richard Saunders and his wife
Bridget, with all of whom students of our Colonial
literature are well acquainted. While not great
characters, to be sure, these are, however, all happy

creations and imply in their creator a skill and an
invention of no mean order.

It is questionable whether Franklin was willing
to pay the price of the creation of a really great
character, even granting that his genius was equal
to the task. The imagination he may have had.
But he lacked certain other essentials, such as
tenacity of purpose and unflagging industry, which
hold the attention upon the subject in hand, despite
all interruptions and distractions. Franklin, according to the French maxim, had the defects of his
qualities. He was a many-sided, versatile man, a
veritable genius, if we may use that much abused
term. His interest drew him alternately into business, politics, diplomacy, science, education (he
founded the University of Pennsylvania), journalism and literature. He signed his name to four of
the most important documents of his century—the
Declaration of Independence, the Treaty of Alli-
ance, the Treaty of Peace and the Constitution. His
versatility and facility induced him to attempt a
variety of things. He lacked the singleness of purpose which seems a prerequisite of success in certain
fields of human achievement. Consequently,
Franklin rarely finished anything requiring undivided and unremitting attention. An essay or a
pamphlet which could be dashed off under the inspiration of a passing excitement or a fleeting
emotion, a mere bagatelle which did not require continued mental concentration and effort,—this
Franklin could do as cleverly and gracefully as any
man. But to bestow long-drawn-out effort upon
any piece of writing was irksome to him. Therefore, he would abandon any plan of composition
which demanded constant, unceasing attention.
This is the reason why the Dogood papers were
never completed; this is the reason why the Busy-

body essays were handed over to another hand to be finished; this is the reason why "Poor Richard" was discontinued; this is also the reason why the "Autobiography" was twice begun and twice put aside and finally left only half-written. This same weakness of Franklin's character which, for want of a more suitable term, we may describe, in a negative way, as a lack of singleness of purpose is shown in his habit of shifting from one pursuit in life to another, and not sticking to any one pursuit very long.

This characteristic defect seems to warrant the inference that however great Franklin was—and great he surely was—he nevertheless does not deserve to rank with the very highest type of minds. As another limitation of our author may be mentioned his small appreciation of poetry, as attested by his dismal paraphrases of certain poetic portions of the Scriptures. He lacked, too, to a marked degree, the spirit of reverence. He was wanting in the highest forms of grace and taste.

But these few defects were more than offset by Franklin's many excellent qualities as a literary artist. He possessed an unfailing sense of humor, which permeates and enlivens every page he wrote. To this redeeming virtue he joined a keen wit that gave force and point to all his political writings. He had, moreover, the happy art of literary phrasing—of suiting the word to the thing, and expressing his thoughts in clear, concise and pointed language. He made himself a master of a vigorous English prose style which never failed to convey his meaning in words too plain and simple to be misunderstood. He stands unapproached in the pioneer days of American literature, and his achievement in the domain of autobiography remains unsurpassed even in the present time.

FRANKLIN

SEEKING HIS FORTUNE (AUTOBIOGRAPHY).

My inclinations for the sea were by this time worn out, or I might now have gratified them. But, having a trade, and supposing myself a pretty good workman, I offered my service to the printer in the place, old Mr. William Bradford, who had been the first printer in Pennsylvania, but removed from thence upon the quarrel of George Keith. He could give me no employment, having little to do, and help enough already; but says he, "My son at Philadelphia has lately lost his principal hand, Aquila Rose, by death; if you go thither, I believe he may employ you." Philadelphia was a hundred miles further; I set out, however, in a boat for Amboy, leaving my chest and things to follow me round by sea.

In crossing the bay, we met with a squall that tore our rotten sails to pieces, prevented our getting into the Kill, and drove us upon Long Island. In our way, a drunken Dutchman, who was a passenger too, fell overboard; when he was sinking, I reached through the water to his shock pate, and drew him up, so that we got him in again. His ducking sobered him a little, and he went to sleep, taking first out of his pocket a book, which he desired I would dry for him. It proved to be my old favorite author, Bunyan's *Pilgrim's Progress*, in Dutch, finely printed on good paper, with copper cuts, a dress better than I had ever seen it wear in its own language. I have since found that it has been translated into most of the languages of Europe, and suppose it has been more generally read than any other book, except perhaps the Bible. Honest John was the first that I know of who mixed narration and dialogue; a method of writing very engaging to the reader, who in the most interesting parts finds himself, as it were, brought into the company and present at the discourse. De Foe in his *Crusoe,* his *Moll Flanders, Religious Courtship, Family Instructor,* and other pieces, has imitated it with success, and Richardson has done the same in his *Pamela,* etc.

When we drew near the Island, we found it was at a place where there could be no landing, there being a great surf on the stony beach. So we dropped anchor, and swung round towards the shore. Some people came down to the water edge and hallooed to us, as we did to them; but the wind was so high, and the surf so loud, that we could not hear so as to understand each other. There were canoes on the shore, and we made signs, and hallooed that they should fetch us; but they either did not understand us, or thought it impracticable, so they went away, and night coming on, we had no remedy but to wait till the wind should abate; and, in the mean time, the boatman and I concluded to sleep, if we could; and so crowded into the scuttle, with the Dutchman, who was still wet; and the spray beating over the head of our boat, leaked through to us, so that we were soon almost as wet as he. In this manner we lay all night, with very little rest; but the wind abating the next day, we made a shift to reach Amboy before night, having been thirty hours on the water, without victuals, or any drink but a bottle of filthy rum, the water we sailed on being salt.

In the evening I found myself very feverish, and went in to bed; but having read somewhere that cold water drank plentifully was good for a fever, I followed the prescription, sweat plentifully most of the night, my fever left me, and in the morning, crossing the ferry, I proceeded on my journey on foot, having fifty miles to Burlington, where I was told I should find boats that would carry me the rest of the way to Philadelphia.

It rained very hard all the day; I was thoroughly soaked, and by noon a good deal tired; so I stopped at a poor inn, where I stayed all night, beginning now to

wish that I had never left home. I cut so miserable
a figure, too, that I found, by the questions asked me,
I was suspected to be some runaway servant, and in
danger of being taken up on that suspicion. However,
I proceeded the next day, and got in the evening to an
inn, within eight or ten miles of Burlington, kept by
one Dr. Brown. He entered into conversation with
me while I took some refreshment, and, finding I had
read a little, became very sociable and friendly. Our
acquaintance continued as long as he lived. He had
been, I imagine, an itinerant doctor, for there was no
town in England, or country in Europe, of which he
could not give a very particular account. He had
some letters, and was ingenious, but much of an un-
believer, and wickedly undertook, some years after, to
travesty the Bible in doggerel verse, as Cotton had
done Virgil. By this means he set many of the facts
in a very ridiculous light, and might have hurt weak
minds if his work had been published; but it never was.

At his house I lay that night, and the next morning
reached Burlington, but had the mortification to find
that the regular boats were gone a little before my
coming, and no other expected to go before Tuesday, this
being Saturday; wherefore I returned to an old woman
in the town, of whom I had bought ginger bread to eat
on the water, and asked her advice. She invited me to
lodge at her house till a passage by water should offer;
and being tired with my foot traveling, I accepted the
invitation. She, understanding I was a printer, would
have had me stay at that town and follow my business,
being ignorant of the stock necessary to begin with.
She was very hospitable, gave me a dinner of ox-cheek
with great goodwill, accepting only of a pot of ale in
return; and I thought myself fixed till Tuesday should
come. However, walking in the evening by the side of
the river, a boat came by, which I found was going towards Philadelphia, with several people in her. They
took me in, and, as there was no wind, we rowed all the
way; and about midnight, not having yet seen the city,

some of the company were confident we must have passed it, and would row no farther; the others knew not where we were; so we put toward the shore, got into a creek, landed near an old fence, with the rails of which we made a fire, the night being cold, in October, and there we remained till daylight. Then one of the company knew the place to be Cooper's Creek, a little above Philadelphia, which we saw as soon as we got out of the creek, and arrived there about eight or nine o'clock on the Sunday morning, and landed at the Market Street wharf.

I have been the more particular in this description of my journey, and shall be so of my first entry into that city, that you may in your mind compare such unlikely beginnings with the figure I have since made there. I was in my working-dress, my best clothes being to come round by sea. I was dirty from my journey; my pockets were stuffed out with shirts and stockings, and I knew no soul nor where to look for lodging. I was fatigued with traveling, rowing, and want of rest, I was very hungry; and my whole stock of cash consisted of a Dutch dollar, and about a shilling in copper. The latter I gave the people of the boat for my passage, who at first refused it on account of my rowing; but I insisted on their taking it. A man being sometimes more generous when he has but a little money than when he has plenty, perhaps through fear of being thought to have but little.

Then I walked up the street, gazing about till near the market-house I met a boy with bread. I had made many a meal on bread, and inquiring where he got it, I went immediately to the baker's he directed me to, in Second Street, and asked for biscuit, intending such as we had in Boston; but they, it seems, were not made in Philadelphia. Then I asked for a three-penny loaf, and was told they had none such. So not considering or knowing the difference of money, and the greater cheapness nor the names of his bread, I bade him give me three-penny worth of any sort. He gave me, accordingly, three great puffy rolls. I was surprised at the quantity, but took it, and having no room in my pockets, walked off with a roll under each arm, and eating the other. Thus I went up Market Street as far as Fourth Street, passing by the door of Mr. Read, my future wife's father; when she, standing at the door, saw me, and thought I made, as I certainly did, a most awkward, ridiculous appearance. Then I turned and went down Chestnut Street and part of Walnut Street, eating my roll all the way, and coming round, found myself again at Market Street wharf, near the boat I came in, to which I went for a draught of the river water; and being filled with one of my rolls, gave the other two to a woman and her child that came down the river in the boat with us, and were waiting to go farther.

Thus refreshed, I walked again up the street, which by this time had many clean-dressed people in it, who were all walking the same way. I joined them, and thereby was led into the great meeting house of the Quakers near the market. I sat down among them, and after looking round a while and hearing nothing said, being very drowsy through labor and want of rest the preceding night, I fell fast asleep, and continued so till the meeting broke up, when one was kind enough to rouse me. This was, therefore, the first house I was in or slept in, in Philadelphia.

Walking down again toward the river, and looking in the faces of people, I met a young Quaker man, whose countenance I liked, and, accosting him, requested he would tell me where a stranger could get lodging. We were then near the sign of the Three Mariners. "Here," says he, "is one place that entertains strangers, but it is not a reputable house; if thee wilt walk with me, I'll show thee a better." He brought me to the Crooked Billet in Water Street. Here I got a dinner; and while I was eating it, several sly questions were asked me, as it seemed to be suspected from my youth and appearance that I might be some runaway.

After dinner, my sleepiness returned, and being shown to a bed, I lay down without undressing, and slept till six in the evening, was called to supper, went to bed again very early, and slept soundly till next morning. Then I made myself as tidy as I could, and went to Andrew Bradford the printer's. I found in the shop the old man his father, whom I had seen at New York, and who, traveling on horseback, had got to Philadelphia before me. He introduced me to his son, who received me civilly, gave me a breakfast, but told me he did not at present want a hand, being lately supplied with one; but there was another printer in town, lately set up, one Keimer, who, perhaps, might employ me; if not, I should be welcome to lodge at his house, and he would give me a little work to do now and then till fuller business should offer.

The old gentleman said he would go with me to the new printer; and when we found him, "Neighbor," says Bradford, "I have brought to see you a young man of your business; perhaps you may want such a one." He asked me a few questions, put a composing stick in my hand to see how I worked, and then said he would employ me soon, though he had just then nothing for me to do; and taking old Bradford, whom he had never seen before, to be one of the town's people that had a good will for him, entered into a conversation on his present undertaking and prospects; while Bradford, not discovering that he was the other printer's father, on Keimer's saying he expected soon to get the greatest part of the business into his own hands, drew him on by artful questions, and starting little doubts, to explain all his views, what interests he relied on, and in what manner he intended to proceed. I, who stood by and heard all, saw immediately that one of them was a crafty old sophister, and the other a mere novice. Bradford left me with Keimer, who was greatly surprised when I told him who the old man was.

Keimer's printing-house, I found, consisted of an old shattered press, and one small, worn-out font of English, which he was then using himself, composing an Elegy on Aquila Rose, before mentioned, an ingenious young man, of excellent character, much respected in the town, clerk of the Assembly, and a pretty poet. Keimer made verses too, but very indifferently. He could not be said to write them, for his manner was to compose them in the types directly out of his head. So there being no copy, but one pair of cases, and the Elegy likely to require all the letter, no one could help him. I endeavored to put his press (which he had not yet used, and of which he understood nothing) into order fit to be worked with; and promising to come and print off his Elegy as soon as he should have got it ready, I returned to Bradford's, who gave me a little job to do for the present, and there I lodged and dieted. A few days after, Keimer sent for me to print off the Elegy. And now he had got another pair of cases, and a pamphlet to reprint, on which he set me to work.

*   *   *   *   *   *   *

CHAPTER III

WASHINGTON IRVING

Washington Irving is properly accorded the first place among the pioneers in American literature. Born in New York City, in 1783, shortly after the surrender of Cornwallis to Washington and being the first American writer to exhibit the real, vital spirit of literature, Irving may not inappropriately be called the father of the American republic of letters. Some few critics, it is true, claim this distinction for Charles Brockden Brown, but manifestly without sufficient reason. For the talented Philadelphia romancer never lived to fulfill the promise of his youth and is known chiefly to a few scholars and students of our early literature, whereas Irving's name is almost a household word in America, and his works are still eagerly perused by the great English-reading public and by the scholars alike. Had Brown not been hurried to a premature grave by that dread scourge consumption, he would have accomplished, no doubt, far more than the few morbid and immature novels and miscellaneous essays which he bequeathed as a legacy to the world, and would have left behind him a more enduring name in the field of letters. But in literature as in every other sphere of human activity, men must be judged by actual achievement, not by promise. So Brown's claim to the honor of being the founder of American literature may be dismissed with the Scotch verdict "not proven."

Unlike his rival Brown, Irving as a writer was perfectly healthy and normal, free from all objectionable idiosyncrasies. Though his physical constitution was never robust, his temperament was that of an optimist. He looked habitually on the bright side of life, and his works reflect, in a remarkable manner, his sunny disposition. There is nothing gloomy or pessimistic in his pages. Unlike his contemporary Poe, he is entirely free from the morbid, the weird and the uncanny. Irving, however, did not posses that virile creative imagination which was Poe's most conspicuous characteristic. Irving's plummet could never reach the depths of horror which the imaginative genius of Poe sounded again and again, in his grotesque and weird tales. Irving's constructive faculty and his analytical faculty as well were unquestionably inferior to Poe's. The author of "Knickerbocker" could not have written such a gruesome, analytical tale, for example, as the "Gold Bug," the "Murders in the Rue Morgue," the "Black Cat," or such a weird, supernatural tale as the "Fall of the House of Usher," "William Wilson," or "Ligeia." A story of this character was altogether out of keeping with Irving's taste and feelings, even if it was not beyond the range of his imagination to conceive. On the other hand, Poe, chiefly because of his undeveloped sense of humor, could never have produced such a delightful, pathetic and humorous tale as the inimitable "Rip Van Winkle." Nor would the author of "The Raven" have been content to treat the legends of the Hudson in the simple, whimsical, humorous and charming manner of Irving, without recourse to the grotesque and supernatural. But it is not our purpose here to make a comparative study of Poe and Irving.

Irving's early career contained but slight promise of his subsequent success as a man of letters. He at first intended to enter the profession of law, and was, in fact, admitted to the bar; but law was not congenial to his taste. While in a law office, he began to show some indication of his literary bent by writing squibs for the *Morning Chronicle,* under the pen-name of "Jonathan Oldstyle." But his failing health soon compelled him to abandon his sedentary life in a law office, and he spent two years in foreign travel. Upon his return to New York he undertook, in co-operation with his friend James K. Paulding, the publication of a semi-monthly journal *Salmagundi.* To this periodical Irving contributed a number of breezy, humorous papers, in the Addisonian style, on the foibles and fads of society. This vivacious and entertaining magazine, which was designed, as the editors expressed it, "simply to instruct the young, reform the old, correct the town, and castigate the age," proved to be a short-lived venture and was abruptly suspended after the twentieth number.

With the publication of "Knickerbocker's History of New York," however, Irving leaped at once into fame and was hailed on both sides of the Atlantic as the coming American author. This bold venture proved an immediate success, and paved the way for a cordial reception by the English literati when Irving visited the Old World, for the second time, in 1815. The illusion that the author of "Knickerbocker" created by his art and skill was so complete and realistic that some accepted the history at its face value as the *bona fide* production of a certain Diedrich Knickerbocker. Moreover, some of the old residents of Dutch descent strongly resented the bold and free manner in which the

supposititious historian had handled the revered
and hallowed traditions and legends of their sturdy
ancestors. But the pervading good-natured satire
and broad rollicking humor which brightened the
pages served to convince the observant reader that
the book was fiction, not history, and was evolved
from the fertile imagination of some very clever
writer.

"Knickerbocker's History of New York" was a
happy conception and was largely indebted for its
success to the author's characteristic abundant
sense of humor. It was this quality that redeemed
the burlesque from mere caricature in execution
and stamped it an artistic production. The book
was written in the vein of Swift, but the satire
lacked the sting and bite which the famous Dean of
St. Patrick's generally infused into his work.
Irving's satire is of a mild type, and his pervading
humor robs it of its sting, causing the victim to be
amused, not exasperated, at his own foibles. The
portraits of the old Dutch governors are sketched
with evident pleasure and ease by a hand altogether
untrammeled by literary traditions. The freshness
and buoyancy of the narrative and the whimsical,
charming style combine with the rollicking humor
to make the book quite without a parallel in English literature. It is, however, but just to observe
that the first few chapters which, by the way, are
the product of the collaboration of his brother
Peter with Irving, appear somewhat stilted, pompous and pedantic and make the unhappy impression
that the authors were feeling their way and were
not yet sure of their footing. But the illusion cast
over the reader later, as he progresses, makes him
forget the weakness of grip which the authors show
in the opening chapters. After Peter's departure

for Europe, Irving recast the entire work (which
was designed as a burlesque on Dr. Samuel Mitch-
ell's "History of New York") and no doubt greatly
improved the book.   Each of the old Dutch governors of New York is depicted with such minuteness
of detail and with such a vividness of incident and
with such a mock seriousness of style withal, as
they were in turn confronted with the various problems of state, that the narrative is invested with an
air of reality and might readily be taken, on first
blush, as veritable history.   All in all, the fanciful
idea of this piece of historical burlesque and its
clever execution seem a stroke of genius, and the
result is a masterpiece of humor, unsurpassed in
American or English literature.   Small wonder
that Sir Walter Scott was delighted with the book
and laughed heartily over it as he read it aloud to
his family.   And the world has not yet ceased to
read it with interest and zest and to find in it a
never-failing source of entertainment and pleasure.

Strange to say, after the manifest "hit" Irving
had made in the first product of his invention, he
did not regard the success of "Knickerbocker's History of New York" as marking out a literary career
for himself and pointing his way to fame and fortune.   He looked upon the venture rather as a *jeu
d' esprit* than as a serious literary effort indicating
the bent of his genius.   It was not till the failure
of his firm in England, in 1818, where he and his
brother had engaged in the hardware business, that
he decided to adopt literature as a profession. Then
for the first time only does Irving seem to have reflected upon the possibilities that a literary career
held out to him.   His mind once definitely made up,
he addressed himself to his literary pursuits with
an ardent, unswerving devotion and spurned all

offers, however tempting and remunerative, both at home and abroad. Only in one or two instances, years after, when he was no longer a stranger to fame or fortune, did he deviate from his set purpose and consent to accept a diplomatic post at London and subsequently at Madrid.

At thirty-six Irving settled down to literary work in London, and the first product of his labors was the famous "Sketch-Book." Though resident in the British metropolis, his heart was in America,— on the historic and picturesque Hudson along whose banks, in his earlier years, he had so often roamed and hunted game, in quest of health. Despite the oft-repeated charge of lack of patriotism, Irving is a brilliant illustration of Horace's dictum, *Coelum, non animum, mutant qui trans mare currunt*. The "Sketch-Book" is distinctively American, racy and smacks of the soil. The old legends of the Hudson are here clothed with life and beauty and are now recognized almost as a part of our national history. Irving gave these local traditions of our American Rhine celebrity and currency, and they have now become as familiar as household words.

The treatment of the "Sketch-Book" is somewhat unequal. Some of the sketches are naturally better than others. A popular vote would probably put "Rip Van Winkle" and the "Legend of Sleepy Hollow" easily first, and this verdict would be confirmed by critical judgment. While all are good, these two sketches are felt to be the finest. Their tender pathos, imaginative humor, simplicity and grace have already endeared these three to the hearts of thousands of readers who have lingered, almost spellbound, over their pages; and their charm and beauty will, no doubt, commend them to generations of readers yet unborn. Of the sketches "Rip Van

Winkle," in the popular estimate (perhaps also in
the estimate of the critics), is entitled to first place.
This, even more than the others, Irving seems to
have suffused with the soft hues of his romantic
fancy and to have invested with unusual glamour
and pathos. Who has not been alternately delighted and moved to tears by Mr. Jefferson's
matchless interpretation of this creation, however
much altered, of Irving's genius?

Irving scored a signal success in the "Sketch-
Book." The volume met with a reception, on both
sides of the Atlantic, which far exceeded the
author's most sanguine expectations. Irving himself had some misgivings about the publication of
the book. Speaking, in a letter to a friend, of the
cordial reception given it, he wrote in 1819: "The
manner in which the book has been received, and the
eulogiums that have been passed upon it in the
American papers and periodical works, have completely overwhelmed me. They go far, *far* beyond
my most sanguine expectations, and indeed are expressed with such peculiar warmth and kindness as
to affect me in the tenderest manner. The receipt
of your letter, and the reading of some of the criticisms this morning, have rendered me nervous for
the whole day. I feel almost appalled by such success, and fearful that it cannot be real, or that it is
not fully merited, or that I shall not act up to the
expectations that may be formed. We are whim-
sically constituted beings. I had got out of conceit
of all that I had written, and considered it very
questionable stuff; and now that it is so extrava-
gantly bepraised, I begin to feel afraid that I shall
not do as well again. . . . I hope you will not
attribute all this sensibility to the kind reception I
have met to an author's vanity. I am sure it pro-

ceeds from very different sources. Vanity could not bring the tears to my eyes as they have been brought by the kindnesses of my countrymen. I have felt cast down, blighted, and broken-spirited, and these sudden rays of sunshine agitate me more than they revive me. I hope—I hope I may yet do something more worthy of the appreciation lavished on me."

After a silence of a few years spent in travel on the Continent, for the benefit of the author's health, "Bracebridge Hall" appeared and a little later the "Tales of a Traveller." The former collection of stories is good—the best of them is the "Stout Gentleman,"—but did not add materially to Irving's reputation. The latter book, as the title implies, contains Irving's impressions and experiences of his European travel. The author himself believed that this volume was one of his finest pieces of work,—an opinion in which the critics generally concur. "There was more of an artistic touch about it," said he in a letter to Brevort, "though this is not a thing to be appreciated by the many." Despite the favorable judgment of Irving and the critics as to the excellent art of the "Tales," the public appears not to have appreciated the volume and so manifested but slight enthusiasm over it. Irving felt this tacit criticism keenly.

The "Tales of a Traveller" had failed to measure up to the public expectation chiefly because of its lack of novelty. Irving therefore decided to attempt a new and more ambitious flight in his next bid for the favor of the people. Since the public demanded something novel and more pretentious from his facile pen, he responded to this demand in a series of four books on Spanish themes,—the "Alhambra," "Conquest of Granada," "Legends of the Conquest of Spain" and "The Life of Columbus." These volumes were the outgrowth of the author's three years' residence in Spain. They were an entirely new departure, a rich virgin vein in historical research. The result was highly gratifying to Irving. He now felt that he had, at least in some measure, discharged the debt of gratitude he had incurred for the generous appreciation the public had lavished upon his earlier works. By his investigations into a most romantic chapter of Spanish history in the days of the Moslem invaders and the glorious times of Ferdinand and Isabella, Irving brought to the attention of his readers much valuable information upon a subject hitherto neglected by American writers, presented in his characteristically engaging and graceful style. The American reading public was thereby placed under lasting obligations to him for opening up for their delight and instruction that vast domain of early Spanish history and romance, and pointed with pardonable pride to the permanent contribution one of their own countrymen had made to English literature.

There are two obvious reasons why Irving was happy in the selection of his theme. In the first place, he was himself in ardent sympathy with this romantic chapter in Spanish history, and his magic pen was fully equal to the laborious and delicate task he imposed upon himself of recreating a long-forgotten period when the spirit of adventure was abroad in the land and the old men were dreaming dreams and the young men were seeing visions of future discovery and conquest, with resulting glory and renown. Those were days pregnant with events which were destined to inflame men's minds with "enterprises of great pith and moment." In the second place, the English-speaking public was eager to have this romantic period of Spanish history explored by a writer who united such charming literary style with his gift of the spirit of inquiry. By the magic of his pen and his creative genius Irving has succeeded in bringing back to our delighted imagination those far-away, by-gone days and has made those historic characters and picturesque personages live again. He has conjured up before our rapt vision, as if with a magician's wand, entrancing views of architectural splendor and magnificence and landscapes of rare and gorgeous beauty in sunny Spain. Who has not been charmed by the vivid descriptions in the "Alhambra" and "Granada," of the arid wastes and melancholy ruins contrasted with the magnificence and beauty of city and country in that land of alternating squalor and wealth? No wonder that Coleridge's verdict after reading the "Conquest of Granada" was that it is "a *chef d'oeuvre* of its kind."

Of this Spanish group of volumes, however, "The Life of Columbus" is today regarded as the most important and serious work. Irving himself, so we are informed by his biographer, Mr. Warner, regarded the "Conquest of Granada" as the best, not only of his Spanish themes, but of all his works. The "Columbus" as a biography is not above criticism. According to the tastes of the present generation, the work is too diffuse and elaborate and has, perhaps, too much rhetorical coloring. Probably "antiquated" is the word to describe more accurately its form. But if somewhat antiquated, compared with more modern standards of biography, the "Columbus" yet has much to commend it. Irving bestowed upon it much pains and study and endeavored to make it accurate and trustworthy. The test of historical accuracy the book still meets, in the main, successfully. It is, moreover, clear,

just and discriminating. The portrait of the great
discoverer is certainly clear-cut and definite enough,
even if the color is somewhat more rich than warranted by the dry facts of history. Irving appears
to have had a true and proper conception of Columbus' life and mission and to have sympathized with
the world-dreamer in the keen disappointments that
sorely tried his abiding buoyant faith. The success
of his "Columbus" was a source of profound gratification to our author. Before its publication, as
usual, he was very dubious about its reception by
the public. In a letter to Brevort, Irving tells us
that the biography had really cost him more toil
and trouble than all his other productions. But
he felt amply repaid for his pains when, in consequence of the popularity of his "Columbus" in his
native country, an urgent demand was made by the
publishers for an abridgment of the work.

The reader of Irving's biography cannot but be
strongly impressed with his sensitiveness as to the
esteem of his own countrymen. His exceeding sensitiveness sometimes had a depressing influence,
though more frequently it acted as a stimulus to his
genius. It was his constant desire to produce some
work which would merit the spontaneous admiration of his countrymen. The slightest adverse criticism by the American press, as, for instance, his
alleged Anglomania, cut him to the quick. "I have
lost confidence," wrote he to a friend, in reference
to the prospective reception of his "Columbus," "in
the favorable disposition of my countrymen, and
look forward to cold scrutiny and stern criticism."
Again, in a letter to Brevort, he deprecates the loss
of "that delightful confidence which I once enjoyed
of not the good opinion, but the good will, of my
countrymen. To me it is always ten times more
gratifying to be liked than to be admired; and I

confess to you, though I am a little too proud to confess it to the world, the idea that the kindness of
my countrymen toward me was withering caused
me for a long time the most weary depression of
spirits, and disheartened me from making any
literary exertions."

Irving's cordial reception upon his return to
America, after retiring from the London legation
in 1831, gave him indubitable evidence of his countrymen's high appreciation. The foremost American man of letters at that time, Irving was greeted
with such a spontaneous and enthusiastic acclaim
as to leave no room for doubt as to the sentiments
of his countrymen. If, however, any additional
evidence was needed to convince him of the popular
esteem which he enjoyed in his native land, it came
later in the form of the Madrid mission,—an honor
which was tendered him quite as much in recognition of his noble service to American letters as of
his manifest fitness for that important ministry.
The appointment was hailed with universal approval; and Irving regarded it as the "crowning
honor of his life."

The product of Irving's ten years' residence at
Sunnyside, on the Hudson, (he was on the shady
side of fifty when he settled there), was "A Tour of
the Prairies," "Recollections of Abbotsford and
Newstead Abbey," "Legends of the Conquest of
Spain," "Astoria" and "Captain Bonneville." Besides these may be mentioned a collection of ephemeral essays subsequently published under the
caption of "Wolfert's Roost." These works are of
a miscellaneous character. The "Recollections"
were made up of the author's reminiscences of his
visit to Scott's home and to the historical old abbey
indicated in the title. The "Legends of the Con-

quest of Spain" followed as an aftermath of his famous Spanish themes. "A Tour of the Prairies," "Astoria," and "Captain Bonneville" are of the nature of travels and contain the record of our author's experiences during his explorations in the far West. These books are, in the main, graphic descriptions of the hardy adventurers who were thrown together somewhat promiscuously in the frontier settlements, in the pioneer days. Irving has sketched these odd, picturesque characters of various nationalities with such a clearness of outline and with such an accuracy of detail as to make them stand out from his pages in bold relief. The daring hunter and the intrepid trapper, with the other bold adventurers, in their exciting encounters with wild animals and the treacherous Indians form a motley, fantastic group as they stand silhouetted against the dark background of the trackless prairies and pathless forests of the vast Western frontier.

The duties of the Spanish mission proved so exacting that Irving found but little leisure for writing during his tenure of the honor. On his return to his beloved Sunnyside, however, when the cares of state were permanently laid aside, he applied himself once more with unremitting industry to his literary pursuits. His laborious "Life of Washington" now absorbed his attention. The task proved irksome, and the author thrust aside this undertaking, for a time, in order to write two other biographies less exacting and pretentious. These were his "Life of Goldsmith" and "Mahomet and his Successors." His "Life of Washington" appears to have taxed Irving's strength and literary resources. He himself informs us that it dragged heavily, and we believe he is using no figure of speech, for the work lacks spontaneity and vivacity and is not the most delightful reading. It is little better than a *tour de force*. The biography must have been uncongenial and, for some reason, seems not to have furnished sufficient inspiration to the writer, especially in his declining years when his natural vigor was waning. Perhaps the reason is, that the subject was not far enough removed from the author's own times, and was not therefore surrounded with the glamour and atmosphere of romance which enveloped the personality of Columbus or even the prosaic life of Goldsmith. Still there are some fine passages in the "Washington" and some incisive characterization, and surely the patriotic motive that inspired the conception of the book was eminently worthy. But if Irving had consulted his reputation, he would not have undertaken so voluminous a work at his advanced age, seeing that his powers were hardly equal to the completion of the "Washington" and that his fame could not be greatly enhanced thereby.

Of Irving's "Mahomet and his Successors" it is more difficult to speak a favorable word than of his "Washington." But his "Life of Goldsmith" may be commended without doing violence to one's literary conscience. For this is by far the best of Irving's later productions and has much of the charm and freshness of his earlier work. The subject was doubtless congenial to the biographer. The vagabondish life of the generous-hearted, improvident Goldsmith appealed to Irving's sympathies and kindled once more his waning imagination till it glowed again as if with its earlier accustomed warmth. The result is a biography showing deep insight into the character and worth, and tender sympathy with the foibles and frailties, of one of the most beloved authors of English literature in the eighteenth century. Irving's "Goldsmith" has not been surpassed, if indeed it has been equaled, by any subsequent biographer. You will read it through from cover to cover without finding a dull page in it.

Irving richly deserves the distinction usually accorded him of being the first American author to win for himself a conspicuous and unfading name in the department of letters. His star now for well-nigh half a century has shone with undimmed lustre and shows no sign of being immediately eclipsed. This honor has been achieved not by our author's intellectual force and acumen, nor by his creative imagination and incisive literary touch, but by the free play of his romantic fancy, his pervading sentiment, his unfailing, delightful humor and his charming style. Herein lies the secret of his success. The charm of Irving's style is remarkable, and proves clearly, as Shakespeare's brilliant example does, that the literary art and vital spark are not confined exclusively to academic halls.

Irving appeals to the sensibilities rather than to the intellect, to the heart rather than to the head. His register, to use a musical term, is not great; his range is not wide. There are notes he never sounded, depths and heights he never reached. The tragedy of life, the profoundest problems of human existence, the realm of philosophical speculation—these were to Irving an unexplored country which his creative mind never entered. The subtle analysis of Poe and the perplexing social problems and deep mysteries of Hawthorne had for Irving no special interest or attraction. He did not make his works a medium for communicating to the world mere metaphysical exercises of marvelous originality, or great moral truths. Such studies awaken in us the spirit of inquiry and speculation, disturb our peace of mind and tend to unsettle our convictions. Irving's works, on the other hand, induce to repose and quiet musing; they do not agitate or ruffle our spirits. They reflect their author's own quiet and reposeful nature, as that nature is enlivened by a delightful vein of humor and sentiment. For this reason Irving is not especially stimulating or suggestive. He is the author to be read when one desires particularly amusement and unfeigned delight. For this reason he is a favorite with the general public and young readers, for he possesses, above all things, the power of entertaining and at the same time refines and elevates the taste. This is due quite as much to his style as to his subject-matter. It is little short of marvelous that Irving, who never kept terms at a university or college and whose education was quite defective, should have elaborated a style which, in the words of an eminent critic, "is distinctively his own, and is as copious, felicitous in the choice of words, flowing, spontaneous, flexible, engaging, clear and as little wearisome when read continuously in quantity as any in the English tongue."

Irving did not share the restless energy of the typical American. Unlike most of his countrymen he seems to have found more to interest him in the past than in the present or future. Janus-like, his face was set both toward the east and toward the west. However, Irving's inclination to the east with its Old World traditions, some think, made his love for the west kick the beam. It is true he found in the historic personages and romantic traditions of the past the chief sources of his inspiration. The Old World exercised over him a preponderating influence. Yet Irving was American to his finger-tips. Where can we find a bit of literature more distinct-

ively American than "Knickerbocker's History of
New York," or the "Sketch-Book," or "Captain Bonneville," or "Astoria," or "A Tour of the Prairies"?
Surely, these smack of the soil and have the genuine, unmistakable American flavor. We treasure
them as a part of Irving's valuable legacy to American literature.

IRVING

RIP VAN WINKLE.

Times grew worse and worse with Rip Van Winkle as years of matrimony rolled on; a tart temper never mellows with age, and a sharp tongue is the only edged tool that grows keener with constant use. For a long while he used to console himself, when driven from home, by frequenting a kind of perpetual club of the sages, philosophers, and other idle personages of the village; which held its sessions on a bench before a small inn, designated by a rubicund portrait of His Majesty George the Third. Here they used to sit in the shade through a long lazy summer's day, talking listlessly over village gossip, or telling endless sleepy stories about nothing. But it would have been worth any statesman's money to have heard the profound discussions that sometimes took place, when by chance an old newspaper fell into their hands from some passing traveler. How solemnly they would listen to the contents, as drawled out by Derrick Van Bummel, the school-master, a dapper learned little man, who was not to be daunted by the most gigantic word in the dictionary; and how sagely they would deliberate upon public events some months after they had taken place.

The opinions of this junto were completely controlled by Nicholas Vedder, a patriarch of the village, and landlord of the inn, at the door of which he took his seat from morning till night, just moving sufficiently to avoid the sun and keep in the shade of a large tree; so that the neighbors could tell the hour by his movements as accurately as by a sun-dial. It is true he was rarely heard to speak, but smoked his pipe incessantly. His adherents, however (for every great man has his adherents), perfectly understood him, and knew how to gather his opinions. When anything that was read or related displeased him, he was observed to smoke his pipe vehemently, and to send forth short, frequent and angry puffs; but when pleased, he would inhale the smoke slowly and tranquilly, and emit it in light and placid clouds; and sometimes, taking the pipe from his mouth, and letting the fragrant vapor curl about his nose, would gravely nod his head in token of perfect approbation.

From even this stronghold the unlucky Rip was at length routed by his termagant wife, who would suddenly break in upon the tranquillity of the assemblage and call the members all to naught; nor was that august personage, Nicholas Vedder himself, sacred from the daring tongue of this terrible virago, who charged him outright with encouraging her husband in habits of idleness.

Poor Rip was at last reduced almost to despair; and his only alternative, to escape from the labor of the farm and clamor of his wife, was to take gun in hand and stroll away into the woods. Here he would sometimes seat himself at the foot of a tree, and share the contents of his wallet with Wolf, with whom he sympathized as a fellow-sufferer in persecution. "Poor Wolf," he would say, "thy mistress leads thee a dog's life of it; but never mind, my lad, whilst I live thou shalt never want a friend to stand by thee!" Wolf would wag his tail, look wistfully in his master's face, and if dogs can feel pity I verily believe he reciprocated the sentiment with all his heart.

In a long ramble of the kind on a fine autumnal day, Rip had unconsciously scrambled to one of the highest parts of the Kaatskill Mountains. He was after his favorite sport of squirrel shooting, and the still solitudes had echoed and re-echoed with the reports of his gun. Panting and fatigued, he threw himself, late in the afternoon, on a green knoll, covered with mountain herbage, that crowned the brow

of a precipice. From an opening between the trees
he could overlook all the lower country for many a
mile of rich woodland. He saw at a distance the
lordly Hudson, far, far below him, moving on its silent
but majestic course, with the reflection of a purple
cloud, or the sail of a lagging bark, here and there
sleeping on its glassy bosom, and at last losing itself in
the blue highlands.

On the other side he looked down into a deep mountain glen, wild, lonely, and shagged, the bottom filled
with fragments from the impending cliffs, and scarcely
lighted by the reflected rays of the setting sun. For
some time Rip lay musing on this scene; evening was
gradually advancing, the mountains began to throw
their long blue shadows over the valleys; he saw that
it would be dark long before he could reach the village,
and he heaved a heavy sigh when he thought of encoun-
tering the terrors of Dame Van Winkle.

As he was about to descend, he heard a voice from
a distance, hallooing, "Rip Van Winkle! Rip Van
Winkle!" He looked round, but could see nothing
but a crow winging its solitary flight across the mountain. He thought his fancy must have deceived him,
and turned again to descend, when he heard the same
cry ring through the still evening air: "Rip Van
Winkle! Rip Van Winkle!"—at the same time Wolf
bristled up his back, and giving a low growl, skulked
to his master's side, looking fearfully down into the
glen. Rip now felt a vague apprehension stealing
over him; he looked anxiously in the same direction,
and perceived a strange figure slowly toiling up the
rocks, and bending under the weight of something he
carried on his back. He was surprised to see any
human being in this lonely and unfrequented place;
but supposing it to be some one of the neighborhood
in need of his assistance, he hastened down to yield it.

On nearer approach he was still more surprised at
the singularity of the stranger's appearance. He was
a short, square-built old fellow, with thick bushy hair,

and a grizzled beard. His dress was of the antique
Dutch fashion: a cloth jerkin strapped round the
waist, several pair of breeches, the outer one of ample
volume, decorated with rows of buttons down the
sides, and bunches at the knees. He bore on his
shoulder a stout keg, that seemed full of liquor, and
made signs for Rip to approach and assist him with
the load. Though rather shy and distrustful of this
new acquaintance, Rip complied with his usual alac-
rity; and mutually relieving one another, they clam-
bered up a narrow gully, apparently the dry bed of a
mountain torrent. As they ascended, Rip every now
and then heard long rolling peals like distant thunder,
that seemed to issue out of a deep ravine, or rather
cleft, between lofty rocks, towards which their rugged
path conducted. He paused for a moment, but supposing it to be the muttering of one of those transient
thunder-showers which often take place in mountain
heights, he proceeded. Passing through the ravine,
they came to a hollow, like a small amphitheatre, surrounded by perpendicular precipices, over the brinks
of which impending trees shot their branches, so that
you only caught glimpses of the azure sky and the
bright evening cloud. During the whole time Rip and
his companion had labored on in silence; for though
the former marvelled greatly what could be the object
of carrying a keg of liquor up this wild mountain, yet
there was something strange and incomprehensible
about the unknown, that inspired awe and checked
familiarity.

On entering the amphitheatre, new objects of wonder
presented themselves. On a level spot in the centre
was a company of odd-looking personages playing at
ninepins. They were dressed in a quaint outlandish
fashion; some wore short doublets, others jerkins, with
long knives in their belts, and most of them had enormous breeches of similar style with that of the guide's.
Their visages, too, were peculiar; one had a large
beard, broad face, and small piggish eyes; the face of

another seemed to consist entirely of nose, and was surmounted by a white sugar-loaf hat, set off with a little red cock's tail. They all had beards, of various shapes and colors. There was one who seemed to be the commander. He was a stout old gentleman, with a weather-beaten countenance; he wore a laced doublet, broad belt and hanger, high-crowned hat and feather, red stockings, and high-heeled shoes, with roses in them. The whole group reminded Rip of the figures in an old Flemish painting in the parlor of Dominie Van Shaick, the village parson, which had been brought over from Holland at the time of the settlement.

What seemed particularly odd to Rip was, that though these folks were evidently amusing themselves, yet they maintained the gravest faces, the most mysterious silence, and were, withal, the most melancholy party of pleasure he had ever witnessed. Nothing interrupted the stillness of the scene but the noise of the balls, which, whenever they were rolled, echoed along the mountains like rumbling peals of thunder.

As Rip and his companion approached them, they suddenly desisted from their play, and stared at him with such fixed, statue-like gaze, and such strange, uncouth, lack-lustre countenances, that his heart turned within him, and his knees smote together. His companion now emptied the contents of the keg into large flagons, and made signs to him to wait upon the company. He obeyed with fear and trembling; they quaffed the liquor in profound silence, and then returned to their game.

By degrees Rip's awe and apprehension subsided. He even ventured, when no eye was fixed upon him, to taste the beverage, which he found had much of the flavor of excellent Hollands. He was naturally a thirsty soul, and was soon tempted to repeat the draught. One taste provoked another; and he reiterated his visits to the flagon so often that at length his senses were overpowered, his eyes swam in his head, his head gradually declined, and he fell into a deep sleep.

On waking, he found himself on the green knoll whence he had first seen the old man of the glen. He rubbed his eyes—it was a bright, sunny morning. The birds were hopping and twittering among the bushes, and the eagle was wheeling aloft, and breasting the pure mountain breeze. "Surely," thought Rip, "I have not slept here all night." He recalled the occurrences before he fell asleep. The strange man with a keg of liquor—the mountain ravine— the wild retreat among the rocks—the woe-begone party at nine-pins—the flagon—"Oh! that flagon! that wicked flagon!" thought Rip—"what excuse shall I make to Dame Van Winkle?"

He looked round for his gun, but in place of the clean, well-oiled fowling-piece, he found an old fire-lock lying by him, the barrel incrusted with rust, the lock falling off, and the stock worm-eaten. He now suspected that the grave roisters of the mountain had put a trick upon him, and, having dosed him with liquor, had robbed him of his gun. Wolf, too, had disappeared, but he might have strayed away after a squirrel or partridge. He whistled after him, and shouted his name, but all in vain; the echoes repeated his whistle and shout, but no dog was to be seen.

He determined to revisit the scene of the last evening's gambol, and if he met with any of the party, to demand his dog and gun. As he rose to walk, he found himself stiff in the joints, and wanting in his usual activity. "These mountain beds do not agree with me," thought Rip, "and if this frolic should lay me up with a fit of the rheumatism, I shall have a blessed time with Dame Van Winkle." With some difficulty he got down into the glen; he found the gully up which he and his companion had ascended the preceding evening; but to his astonishment a mountain stream was now foaming down it, leaping from rock to rock, and filling the glen with babbling

murmurs. He, however, made shift to scramble up its
sides, working his toilsome way through thickets of
birch, sassafras and witch-hazel, and sometimes
tripped up or entangled by the wild grapevines that
twisted their coils or tendrils from tree to tree, and
spread a kind of network in his path.

At length he reached to where the ravine had
opened through the cliffs to the amphitheatre; but no
traces of such opening remained. The rocks presented
a high, impenetrable wall, over which the torrent came
tumbling in a sheet of feathery foam, and fell into a
broad, deep basin, black from the shadows of the surrounding forest. Here, then, poor Rip was brought
to a stand. He again called and whistled after his
dog; he was only answered by the cawing of a flock
of idle crows, sporting high in air about a dry tree
that overhung a sunny precipice; and who, secure in
their elevation, seemed to look down and scoff at the
poor man's perplexities. What was to be done? the
morning was passing away, and Rip felt famished for
want of his breakfast. He grieved to give up his dog
and gun; he dreaded to meet his wife; but it would
not do to starve among the mountains. He shook his
head, shouldered the rusty firelock, and, with a heart
full of trouble and anxiety, turned his steps homeward.

As he approached the village he met a number of
people, but none whom he knew, which somewhat surprised him, for he had thought himself acquainted
with every one in the country round. Their dress,
too, was of a different fashion from that to which he
was accustomed. They all stared at him with equal
marks of surprise, and whenever they cast their eyes
upon him, invariably stroked their chins. The constant recurrence of this gesture induced Rip, involun-
tarily, to do the same, when, to his astonishment, he
found his beard had grown a foot long!

He had now entered the skirts of the village. A
troop of strange children ran at his heels, hooting
after him, and pointing at his gray beard. The dogs,

too, not one of which he recognized for an old acquaintance, barked at him as he passed. The very village was altered; it was larger and more populous. There were rows of houses which he had never seen before, and those which had been his familiar haunts had disappeared. Strange names were over the doors —strange faces at the windows,—everything was strange. His mind now misgave him; he began to doubt whether both he and the world around him were not bewitched. Surely this was his native village, which he had left but the day before. There stood the Kaatskill Mountains—there ran the silver Hudson at a distance—there was every hill and dale precisely as it had always been—Rip was sorely perplexed—"That flagon last night," thought he, "has addled my poor head sadly!"

It was with some difficulty that he found the way to his own house, which he approached with silent awe, expecting every moment to hear the shrill voice of Dame Van Winkle. He found the house gone to decay—the roof fallen in, the windows shattered, and the doors off the hinges. A half-starved dog that looked like Wolf was skulking about it. Rip called him by name, but the cur snarled, showed his teeth, and passed on. This was an unkind cut indeed—"My very dog," sighed poor Rip, "has forgotten me!"

He entered the house, which, to tell the truth, Dame Van Winkle had always kept in neat order. It was empty, forlorn, and apparently abandoned. This desolateness overcame all his connubial fears—he called loudly for his wife and children—the lonely chambers rang for a moment with his voice, and then again all was silence.

* * * * * * *

CHAPTER IV

JAMES FENIMORE COOPER

It is now more than a half century since J. Fenimore Cooper joined the silent majority and ceased to wield his facile and prolific pen. He was the most voluminous of American authors, writing well-nigh a hundred volumes in all, and turning out "copy" almost till the day of his death. Even when he died, on the eve of his sixty-second birthday, he had several literary works well planned out in his mind, and left some of them practically finished. At the time of his death his "Towns of Manhattan" was in press, though not actually completed.

After the lapse of fifty-three years, when the antagonism and calumny which embittered his latter days, it may be presumed, have all passed away,—or, if they are still alive, survive only as a memory,—we may review, with some hope of fairness and impartiality, Cooper's life work and form a critical estimate of the service of the American Scott (as he used to be called in the heyday of his fame) to American letters. Such an estimate could hardly have been formed a half century ago by the men of Cooper's own generation, because of the prejudice and bitter feeling entertained against him as a man; for of all deceased American men of letters Cooper was the least esteemed and most harshly criticised at the time of his demise. The storm of unpopularity which burst upon his head came as the inevitable result of his severe strictures upon the manners and customs of his own country-

men, and the numerous lawsuits he instituted
against the offending American press. Despite the
claim of the hostile critics that Cooper threatened
to curtail the freedom of the press, he was awarded
damages in a succession of libel suits. But his victories over the press proved Pyrrhic victories in the
end, since they cost him as an author the sympathy
and esteem of the entire American press, which
ultimately came to regard him as an inveterate
enemy, dubbing him contemptuously the "Great
Persecutor."

Cooper's unpopularity had its inception in a mistake of judgment on his part and the consequent
misrepresentation by the press. He forfeited the
esteem of his countrymen by his own impetuosity
and constitutional inability to remain silent, when
attacked, till a suitable opportunity offered to vindicate his course. As a matter of fact, Cooper's
offensive conduct originated in a commendable
effort on his part to resent certain imputations
upon his own country made during his residence
abroad. The verdict of the press to the contrary,
Cooper was intensely patriotic and could not find it
in his nature to endure in silence any reflections
upon his native land. When abroad he was quick,
if occasion arose, to break a lance in behalf of
America and Americans. When he arrived in England at the height of his fame, the recollection of
the second galling defeat of the British arms on
American soil still lingered in the minds of the
English people, and they did not always exercise
precaution when they vented their prejudices
against America. It was this occasional unfriendly
criticism of Americans that led Cooper to cross the
Channel and take up his residence in France.
While here he was reluctantly drawn into a warm

controversy about the economy of a republican form of government as opposed to monarchy, which originated in the French Chamber of Deputies. A discussion of finance in connection with American politics grew out of this controversy. Cooper, becoming involved in the discussion, addressed an open letter to the American people which provoked several papers to assail his conduct abroad as an American citizen. The effect of this unfortunate incident was to sour and embitter Cooper and hasten his return to America. He even made a rash promise to himself to abandon writing altogether.

Cooper, somehow, seems not to have kept in close touch with American sentiment and ideas during his foreign residence. It is noteworthy that when he returned to America, soured and embittered in consequence of the hostile criticism by his own countrymen, he found himself out of sympathy and harmony with many institutions and ideals characteristically American. Some changes in American manners and customs had taken place during his absence abroad that did not commend themselves to his judgment or meet his approval. When he moved to his old home at Cooperstown, he became embroiled in an ugly dispute with the citizens of that town as to his possession of a piece of land much used as a public resort. At this unhappy juncture he rushed into print. He gave forceful and vigorous expression to the grievances, real and fancied, he had been nursing, and vindicated his course in an ill-advised "Letter to His Countrymen." Besides ventilating freely his grievances, Cooper took occasion in this letter to administer a rebuke to the administration and to criticise the government in general. This wholesale censure and vituperation invited attack from all quarters, and Cooper soon found himself the victim of repeated newspaper assaults, which he only stopped by availing himself of the law against libel. But implacable hostility and unrelenting obloquy followed him to his grave.

Cooper was born in 1789, at Burlington, New Jersey, where the Coopers were residing for a short time, till their vast estate in Central New York was ready for occupancy. His father, who had represented New York State in Congress, had acquired large tracts of land on Otsego Lake and, in opening up this vast region of dismal waste and pathless forest, founded the town still called after his name—Cooperstown. The family moved into that country when James Fenimore was only a year old. Here on the border of a boundless wilderness the lad grew up among the pioneers, and here the prospective writer received his first impressions amid the primitive surroundings of Nature, almost in the primeval forest. After a brief schooling at an academy in Albany and later at Yale, the young collegian marked out for himself a naval career and shipped before the mast in 1806, soon becoming a midshipman. But he afterwards grew tired of the navy, which proved uncongenial to his tastes, and resigned from the service in 1811. Within a year we find him married and settled down to the easy life of a country gentleman on a farm near his paternal estate. Here he lived in apparent contentment, giving all his time and attention to his farm, and showing not the least indication of his latent literary ambition. Indeed, it was not till he was thirty years old that he turned his attention, as if by mere accident, to literature.

Cooper began his literary career under favorable auspices. The beginning, however, seems the result of mere whim and accident. Reading in his home at Angevine a novel descriptive of English society,

he threw the book down in sheer disgust, and remarked to his wife, "I believe I could write a better
story myself!" He was challenged to make good
his boast, and, inspired by the encouraging words
of his wife as the work advanced, he produced at
length the two-volume novel "Precaution," which
was published in New York, November, 1820. This
novel is not a work of any great merit, but it is
interesting as being the first heir of Cooper's invention. "Precaution" is a story of English society, and purports to have been written by an
Englishman. The conception of the story is conventional enough, and reflects the prevailing literary sentiment and fashion of the times. The title
was suggested by the obvious moral of the desira-
bility of precaution in the selection of a husband
or wife. Yet, paradoxical as it may appear, the
chief incidents of the story,—the misunderstand-
ings and perplexing situations in which the leading characters are placed,—all arise from an excess
of precaution, and illustrate forcibly the undesira-
bility of too much precaution. The book did not
awaken much interest either in America or in England, where it was subsequently published. In
some quarters in England it received favorable notice; nor was its American authorship for a moment
suspected. The author had succeeded somewhat
in describing scenes he was unfamiliar with and a
society with which he was practically unacquainted. Cooper's friends, for this reason, saw in
his first novel promise of success under favorable
conditions, and urged him to write another story
describing a society that he knew.

At the urgent instance of his friends, therefore,
Cooper resolved to write another novel, and, in his
own phrase, to inflict a second volume upon the
world to atone for the first. Acting upon the wise

suggestion of his critics, he turned to his own country this time for his inspiration, and chose a theme from an incident in the American Revolution. The resulting novel was "The Spy," which appeared within fourteen months after "Precaution." "The Spy" is important, not only for its intrinsic merit as a literary production, but also because it revealed a new and unexplored field for American fiction. In this country the book met with an unprecedented sale, and was very favorably received on the other side of the Atlantic. Indeed, it is but truth to say that this novel made Cooper's reputation both at home and abroad. "The Spy" speedily found its way to the Continent through a French version made by the translator of the Waverley novels, and was soon accessible in all the principal tongues of modern Europe. It was everywhere hailed with acclamation and delight, except perhaps in England. In that country it did not arouse quite so much enthusiasm, because the English naturally did not find the same unmixed pleasure in the subject-matter of the story as the readers of other nationalities. Yet, in spite of the historical theme, the tale, from the point of view of mere art, arrested the attention of English readers and compelled their admiration.

Cooper scored a great and instantaneous success in "The Spy." To begin with, he was happy in the choice and conception of his theme, and no less happy in its execution. He was no longer, as in his "Precaution," on foreign ground, delineating strange, unfamiliar scenes and characters. He stood on the soil of his own native country, and knew the land made famous by the heroic struggles of the Revolutionary forces. He had a personal acquaintance, too, with not a few of the men who took part in that war. In addition to this, he was conversant with the history and unwritten traditions of the great conflict between the colonies and the mother country, which never failed to quicken his imagination and inspire his pen. The times were also propitious for such an historical romance as "The Spy"; for the recent publication of the unparalleled series of the Waverley novels had given rise to an all-absorbing popular interest in romance which swept like wildfire over the reading world. America at that time had not declared her literary independence of English supremacy, so that Scott had unconsciously created the romantic atmosphere for "The Spy." It is evident, then, that all the attendant circumstances conspired to make Cooper's second venture a success, if it possessed any real merit of its own, which it did.

The unbounded popularity achieved by "The Spy" stimulated Cooper to renewed effort and industry. But he was not yet sure of his literary calling, and determined to make one more trial before reaching a final decision. He thought the success of "The Spy" might, somehow or other, be due to a happy hit, or to a fortunate combination of circumstances, rather than to any exceptional power and skill which its author himself possessed. Accordingly, he set to work again to depict the scenes and characters of frontier life in America he had learned to know in his childhood. This effort crystallized in a third novel, "The Pioneers," which appeared in 1823.

"The Pioneers" is the first, chronologically, of the five noted stories commonly known as the Leather-Stocking Tales. This series, as is well known, contains the author's characterizations of the frontier men he used to see when a boy, and many of the stirring situations are reproduced largely from memory. It is hard to say, therefore, where fiction ceases in these tales and fact begins. "The Pioneers" is usually regarded the poorest of the Leather-Stocking series, though it contains some thrilling scenes and fine descriptions. Yet the book was warmly received, three thousand five hundred copies being sold by noon of the day of its publication. Of course the reputation of "The Spy," which had left a good taste in the mouth of the public, helped the sale of the new novel. But "The Pioneers" was not forced to trade upon the reputation of its predecessor: it had literary excellence of its own. It is entitled, by the verdict of the critics, to rank among the best of Cooper's novels. The marked success of this novel settled the question of a literary career for its author. From this time forth till the day of his death, Cooper wrote with untiring energy and unwavering purpose.

The Leather-Stocking Tales were suspended after the publication of the initial novel, and Cooper meanwhile worked an entirely different vein. The new path blazed out proved almost as successful a venture as any previously attempted by Cooper. He furnished additional evidence of the versatility of his genius by writing a striking, original sea story, "The Pilot." By the production of this entirely original and unconventional type of fiction, Cooper placed the American public under lasting obligation to him. Smollett, it is true, had attempted the delineation of the naval character, but not on a sufficiently broad scale to entitle him to the distinction of the originator of the sea story. It remained for Cooper to win this honor by the signal success of his new departure. His triumph is all the more remarkable since it was achieved in the face of strenuous opposition from his literary advisers who, from the novelty and difficulty of the sea story, saw only failure in that direction. But, contrary to all expectations, "The Pilot" proved an immediate and complete success. Cooper's daring example in this unexplored domain of fiction had the effect of stimulating many would-be rivals; but his sea stories have held their own amid an ever-increasing host of competitors, and show no indication of being soon superseded.

Cooper's early experiences as a naval officer furnished him a rich fund of material to draw upon for the subject-matter and local color of his sea tales, and he turned it to good account. He showed good judgment, in the first place, in the selection of a theme for his first sea story. He gave proof, at the same time, of his ardent patriotism in harking back to the Revolution for his hero in the intrepid and daring adventurer John Paul Jones, who is so thinly disguised in the story that, though not once named, no one fails to recognize him. This wise choice of a hero enlisted at once the sympathy of the American public. When Cooper invested Paul Jones with an atmosphere of romance and lavished upon him the wealth of his artistic touch, he recreated an historical personage of prepossessing interest and produced a sea story which contains some scenes as thrilling and stirring as any to be found in any novel of its kind in our literature.

Cooper's interest in the American Revolution was so dominant as to induce him to resort thither for the subject of his next novel—"Lionel Lincoln, or the Leaguer of Boston." This work cost its author a vast deal of investigation and untold labor. Besides poring over the dusty tomes of historical records, Cooper made a special study of the topography of the country around Boston, in the hope of making his story accurate in every detail. The virtue of historical accuracy "Lionel Lincoln" may possess; but it lacks imagination, and the want of this prime essential in the romance degrades it as an artistic production below the level of mere mediocrity to that of flat failure. A glaring defect of the story is seen in the fact that the characters act from insufficient motive. As a novelist, Cooper is especially vulnerable on this score. His characters are not clearly defined. Those in the story under discussion appear stilted and under considerable restraint in their intercourse with one another. They lack grace and freedom of action, and seem like puppets. The redeeming quality of "Lionel Lincoln" is the conceded excellence of the battle scenes, which contribute much to the reader's interest to atone for the want of life and action in the characters.

The failure of "Lionel Lincoln" was fully offset, however, by the phenomenal success of the novel that followed it—"The Last of the Mohicans." This is regarded by many critics as the best of the famous "Leather-Stocking" series, and perhaps the finest story Cooper ever wrote. Certainly it is true that of all Cooper's novels "The Last of the Mohicans" is the novel, preëminently, in which the interest is sustained throughout, and the tale is replete with excitement, bristling with incident and action. Unlike some of its author's stories, "The Last of the Mohicans" does not contain those dreary wastes of verbiage here and there which tax the reader's attention. On the contrary, this tale holds the reader's rapt attention from beginning to end, without interruption. But the book, to use a somewhat hackneyed phrase, is not faultily faultless. It, too, shows, in some measure, its author's characteristic defect of insufficiency of motive for action and lack of precision in characterization. But these drawbacks do not appreciably detract from the engaging, unflagging interest of the story, and they are not generally noticed except by the critical eye on the close hunt for flaws.

"The Last of the Mohicans," as compared with "The Pioneers," represents Leather-Stocking as greatly advanced in dignity and strength of character. In "The Pioneers" he is portrayed as an irritable, petulant, ignorant old man, moving farther and farther away from civilization, into the interior of the trackless forests, and deploring the inevitable results of the march of progress. In "The Last of the Mohicans," on the other hand, his weaknesses are no longer emphasized, while the strong points of the bold adventurer's character are made to stand out in bold relief. He remains, to be sure, the same fearless, observant scout, but his senses have grown much more acute and his resources are a match for any situation, however perilous. This clever idealization and delineation of the intrepid hunter is a notable feature of "The Last of the Mohicans," and remains a great achievement in American literature. The delineation of the Indian character in Chingachook and Uncas, on the contrary, is not regarded as quite so successful an achievement. Still Cooper's conception of the Indian character, as elaborated in this and other novels of the Leather-Stocking series, has been almost universally adopted, and has entered permanently into the popular imagination.

The publication of "The Last of the Mohicans" raised Cooper's popularity to its high-water mark.

His novels now appeared simultaneously in America and England. His reputation as a writer of fiction was unrivaled in America, and was surpassed in Europe only by that of Scott, the Wizard of the North. The English, however, were not so enthusiastic in their admiration as the French. Yet even in England some critics were unbounded in their praise, and considered Cooper's novels as no whit inferior to the romances of Scott. "Have you read the American novels?" asked Mary Russell Mitford, herself a novelist of no mean repute, of a friend of hers, in 1842. "In my mind," continued she, "they are as good as anything Sir Walter ever wrote. He has opened fresh ground, too (if one may so say of the sea). No one but Smollett has ever attempted to delineate the naval character; and then his novels are so coarse and hard. Now this has the same truth and power with a deep, grand feeling. . . . Imagine the author's boldness in taking Paul Jones for a hero, and his power in making one care for him! I envy the Americans their Mr. Cooper. . . . There is a certain Long Tom who appears to me the finest thing since Parson Adams." Referring particularly to "The Last of the Mohicans," she remarked subsequently, in a letter to Haydon: "I like it better than any of Scott's, except the first three and 'The Heart of Midlothian.' "

Such golden opinions as these, it need hardly be observed, were not generally current and openly expressed in England. It would have been regarded as literary heresy for the English press to speak of Cooper as the peer of Sir Walter Scott. Indeed, the professional critics in Great Britain, on account of certain traditional prejudices, were rather slow to render Cooper his due meed of praise. They did not venture openely to concede his merit until his power was everywhere freely acknowledged on the Continent as well as in America. The reason, presumably, is that Cooper displayed very little regard for English prejudices in the choice of his subjects for literary treatment, often selecting themes that were positively distasteful and offensive to them, as in "The Spy" and "The Pilot." Of American writers Irving was far more acceptable to English readers than Cooper. In fact, Irving was a favorite with them. Comparisons of course are proverbially odious (sometimes also odorous, as Mrs. Malaprop puts it) ; and this is not the place to compare these two gifted American authors. Still, in the realm of romance, comparison between Cooper and Irving would greatly redound, beyond all question, to the credit of the former. This, however, is not intended to the disparagement of Irving, who, in this, as well as in other departments, rendered generous and enduring service to American letters.

Cooper sailed for Europe in 1826 when he was at the height of his fame. During his residence abroad his literary activity was incessant. "The Prairie," "The Red Rover," "The Wept of Wishton-Wish," and "The Water Witch" followed one another in quick succession, and attest his industry. These stories all portray scenes and characters distinctively American, and were in the vein of his former fiction. "The Prairie" is pervaded with a spirit of submission and lacks the bustle and excitement that characterized its predecessor in the Leather-Stocking series. The scenes and characters are enveloped in an atmosphere of grandeur and solitude such as we may imagine filled the primitive forests when the lonely white man pushed his way

through their pathless domains. Natty Bumpo,
or Leather-Stocking, is represented with his same
unfaltering resolution and dauntless courage and
woodland craft withal, forging his way farther and
farther from the stir and din of the settlements and
becoming more and more resigned in his old age to
the advance of civilization which was destined to
destroy utterly the "majestic solitude of nature"
and make it contribute to man's comfort and
luxury.

"The Red Rover" fully maintained its author's
reputation as a writer of sea stories. Taken as a
whole, it is probably the best thing Cooper ever did
of its special kind of fiction. But "The Wept of
Wishton-Wish,"—the very title is perplexing and
altogether infelicitous,—was not a success. In this
tale Cooper attempted to delineate the Puritan
character of New England, which was beyond the
breadth of his sympathy, and the attempt proved
abortive. "The Wept of Wishton-Wish" may therefore be passed over as a story of little merit, which
did not enhance its author's reputation. If all of
Cooper's novels had been like the last two of this
group, he would never have won the distinguishing
soubriquet, "the American Scott."

Cooper's halcyon days were now fast approaching an end. The decade of his life from 1830 to
1840 was a period of vexatious stress and strain,
when his popularity passed under a shadow and
gave place to persistent misrepresentation and relentless calumny. This was not without its influence upon the subsequent productions of his pen.
The political turmoil in Europe engrossed his attention and lent color to his imagination. His feelings are reflected in his next three stories—"The
Bravo," "The Heidenmauer," "The Headsman"—

all of which were indebted to the political conditions in the Old World for their inspiration. They
belong to that class of fiction known as the purpose
novel, of which but few brilliant examples have
ever been written. Cooper's purpose in these
novels was to exalt republican institutions to the
disadvantage of monarchical. The doctrine is
sound enough. But Cooper's novels met with a
cool reception at home as well as abroad. Cooper
himself, becoming embroiled in a political controversy, soon returned to his native land a disgusted
and embittered, but not a wiser, man. He vented
his feelings in a novel written in a satiric vein and
entitled "The Monikin." It fell flat, a sad failure.
Cooper thereupon published a series of ten volumes
of travels—"Sketches of Switzerland" and "Gleanings in Europe." These contain some fine descriptive passages interspersed with the author's sage
reflections upon the respective countries visited.
The travels were followed by two volumes of very
unequal value—"Homeward Bound" and "Home as
Found." These are of the nature of novels, and the
first, as the title implies, has its scenes laid upon
the water, and is a tolerable story. The second is a
decidedly unfortunate book in consequence of its
drastic censure of the American people, and worked
its author irreparable damage. It was this unto-
ward book that brought down a storm of hostile
criticism upon Cooper's head, utterly undermining
his quondam popularity. During Cooper's war
with the American press appeared his excellent
"History of the Navy"—a capital piece of historical
research. This book never received the attention
and credit it richly deserved because of the intense
hatred and odium that Cooper, by his indiscreet
conduct, had incurred in the public estimation. In-

deed, its appearance was but the signal for a renewal of those scathing, envenomed attacks which the press made upon the author.

The bitter controversy and the resulting disfavor, far from silencing Cooper, seemed rather to stimulate his productivity, so that the period from 1840 to 1845 was the most fecund of his creative genius. "The Pathfinder" and "The Deerslayer," representing to a conspicuous degree the very best in Cooper's literary art, are both products of this period. These form the concluding volumes of the "Leather-Stocking" series and, for artistic creation and finish, mark the culmination of Cooper's skill and power, in the opinion of his biographer, Professor Lounsbury. They are certainly up to their author's early achievements and, together with the former stories of the series, form a complete history of the fitful, eventful life of Natty Bumpo—the noblest creation of Cooper's imagination. "It is beautiful, it is grand," said Balzac to a friend in reference to "The Pathfinder." "Its interest is tremendous. He surely owed us this masterpiece after the last two or three rhapsodies he has been giving us. You must read it. I know no one in the world, save Walter Scott, who has risen to that grandeur and serenity of colors." Yet notwithstanding the "unquestionable worth of "The Pathfinder" and "The Deerslayer," the American Press, whenever it noticed them, simply did so to decry and disparage them, so intense were the animosity and malignity of the editors as a class toward Cooper. After the triumph achieved in these last two novels, Cooper reverted to his love for the sea and gave to the world two more sea stories—"The Two Admirals" and "Wing and Wing." Of these the first is by far the better tale, and is really the last of Cooper's numerous novels it is worth while specifically to mention in this imperfect sketch.

Cooper is a strikingly unequal author. He attempted to cover a wide range—from sea to forest. As long as he kept within the realm of his imagination, he succeeded admirably. But when he transcended these bounds and wrote for an ulterior purpose, his inspiration deserted him completely, and the result was a dismal failure. Among his thirty-four distinct works of fiction are included eight fine novels which will amply repay the reader. These are the five Leather-Stocking Tales, the two sea stories, "The Pilot" and "The Red Rover," and the Revolutionary tale, "The Spy." The remaining novels, though they contain some brilliant bits of description scattered through them here and there, are hardly worth the laborious effort of reading them. Cooper as a writer has some glaring defects, such as the prolixity and tedium of his introductions, his want of definite characterization, the weakness of his dialogue, the thinness of his plot, and his insufficiency of motive for action. Moreover, his novels show unmistakable signs of haste and immature workmanship both in matter and manner. His language, too, is not above criticism. He appears to have experienced little concern for the beauty of style, although he doubtless appreciated this grace. These are the faults and blemishes in Cooper which have led to an undue depreciation of his works by the critics. With those of untrained and uncultivated taste, with the great unwashed, he remains still a favorite author.

Cooper's forte, *par excellence*, is his superior descriptive power. He is a master in the realm of description, and has greatly enriched our literature by his copious pages. Cooper occupies a unique place among American men of letters, also, as the discoverer of a new region of romance, which he worked with brilliant success. His romances even rivaled those of Scott, and afforded genuine delight to countless readers of two continents. They cast a spell over such an undisputed master of fiction as Balzac, who paid a glowing tribute to Cooper's creative imagination and power of description, ranking him with Scott. Surely it required genius to produce work of this class and to create such imaginative characters as Natty Bumpo and Long Tom Coffin.

COOPER

THE LAST OF THE MOHICANS

(OPENING CHAPTER).

Mine ear is open and my heart prepared:
The worst is worldly loss thou canst unfold.
Say, is my kingdom lost?
SHAKESPEARE, *King Richard II.*, III. ii. 93.

It was a feature peculiar to the colonial wars of
North America, that the toils and dangers of the wilderness were to be encountered before the adverse hosts
could meet. A wide and apparently an impervious
boundary of forests severed the possessions of the hostile provinces of France and England. The hardy
colonist, and the trained European who fought at his
side, frequently expended months in struggling against
the rapids of the streams, or in effecting the rugged
passes of the mountains, in quest of an opportunity to
exhibit their courage in a more martial conflict. But,
emulating the patience and self-denial of the practiced
native warriors, they learned to overcome every difficulty; and it would seem that, in time, there was no
recess of the woods so dark, nor any secret place so
lonely, that it might claim exemption from the inroads
of those who had pledged their blood to satiate their
vengeance, or to uphold the cold and selfish policy of
the distant monarchs of Europe.

Perhaps no district throughout the wide extent of the
intermediate frontiers can furnish a livelier picture of
the cruelty and fierceness of the savage warfare of those
periods than the country which lies between the head
waters of the Hudson and the adjacent lakes.

The facilities which nature had there offered to the march of the combatants were too obvious to be neglected. The lengthened sheet of the Champlain stretched from the frontiers of Canada, deep within the borders of the neighboring province of New York, forming a natural passage across half the distance that the French were compelled to master in order to strike their enemies. Near its southern termination, it received the contributions of another lake, whose waters were so limpid as to have been exclusively selected by the Jesuit missionaries to perform the typical purification of baptism, and to obtain for it the title of lake "du Saint Sacrement." The less zealous English thought they conferred a sufficient honor on its unsullied fountains, when they bestowed the name of their reigning prince, the second of the house of Hanover. The two united to rob the untutored possessors of its wooded scenery of their native right to perpetuate its original appellation of "Horican."

Winding its way among countless islands, and imbedded in mountains, the "holy lake" extended a dozen leagues still further to the south. With the high plain that there interposed itself to the further passage of the water, commenced a portage of as many miles, which conducted the adventurer to the banks of the Hudson, at a point where, with the usual obstructions of the rapids, or rifts, as they were then termed in the language of the country, the river became navigable to the tide.

While, in the pursuit of their daring plans of annoyance, the restless enterprise of the French even attempted the distant and difficult gorges of the Alleghany, it may easily be imagined that their proverbial acuteness would not overlook the natural advantages of the district we have just described. It became, emphatically, the bloody arena, in which most of the battles for the mastery of the colonies were contested. Forts were erected at the different points that commanded the facilities of the route, and were taken and

retaken, rased and rebuilt, as victory alighted on the
hostile banners. While the husbandman shrank back
from the dangerous passes, within the safer boundaries
of the more ancient settlements, armies larger than
those that had often disposed of the sceptres of the
mother countries were seen to bury themselves in these
forests, whence they rarely returned but in skeleton
bands, that were haggard with care, or dejected by defeat. Though the arts of peace were unknown to this
fatal region, its forests were alive with men; its shades
and glens rang with the sounds of martial music, and
the echoes of its mountains threw back the laugh, or
repeated the wanton cry, of many a gallant and reck-
less youth, as he hurried by them, in the noontide of his
spirits, to slumber in a long night of forgetfulness.

It was in this scene of strife and bloodshed that the
incidents we shall attempt to relate occurred, during
the third year of the war which England and France
last waged for the possession of a country that neither
was destined to retain.

The imbecility of her military leaders abroad, and the
fatal want of energy in her councils at home, had low-
ered the character of Great Britain from the proud
elevation on which it had been placed by the talents
and enterprise of her former warriors and statesmen.
No longer dreaded by her enemies, her servants were
fast losing the confidence of self-respect. In this mor-
tifying abasement, the colonists, though innocent of
her imbecility, and too humble to be the agents of her
blunders, were but the natural participators.

They had recently seen a chosen army from that
country, which, reverencing as a mother, they had
blindly believed invincible—an army led by a chief who
had been selected from a crowd of trained warriors,
for his rare military endowments—disgracefully routed
by a handful of French and Indians, and only saved
from annihilation by the coolness and spirit of a Virginia boy, whose riper fame has since diffused itself,
with the steady influence of moral truth, to the utter-

most confines of Christendom. A wide frontier had
been laid naked by this unexpected disaster, and more
substantial evils were preceded by a thousand fanciful
and imaginary dangers. The alarmed colonists believed that the yells of the savages mingled with every
fitful gust of wind that issued from the interminable
forests of the west. The terrific character of their
merciless enemies increased immeasurably the natural
horrors of warfare. Numberless recent massacres were
still vivid in their recollections; nor was there any ear
in the provinces so deaf as not to have drunk in with
avidity the narrative of some fearful tale of midnight
murder, in which the natives of the forests were the
principal and barbarous actors. As the credulous and
excited traveler related the hazardous chances of the
wilderness, the blood of the timid curdled with terror,
and mothers cast anxious glances even at those children which slumbered within the security of the largest
towns. In short, the magnifying influence of fear began to set at naught the calculations of reason, and to
render those who should have remembered their manhood, the slaves of the basest of passions. Even the
most confident and the stoutest hearts began to think
the issue of the contest was becoming doubtful; and
that abject class was hourly increasing in numbers,
who thought they foresaw all the possessions of the
English crown in America subdued by their Christian
foes, or laid waste by the inroads of their relentless
allies.

When, therefore, intelligence was received at the fort
which covered the southern termination of the portage
between the Hudson and the lakes, that Montcalm had
been seen moving up the Champlain, with an army
"numerous as the leaves on the trees," its truth was
admitted with more of the craven reluctance of fear
than with the stern joy that a warrior should feel, in
finding an enemy within reach of his blow. The news
had been brought, towards the decline of a day in mid-
summer, by an Indian runner, who also bore an urgent

request from Munro, the commander of a work on the
shore of the "holy lake," for a speedy and powerful
reinforcement.   It has already been mentioned that the
distance between these two posts was less than five
leagues.   The rude path, which originally formed their
line of communication, had been widened for the passage of wagons; so that the distance which had been
travelled by the son of the forest in two hours might
easily be effected by a detachment of troops, with their
necessary baggage, between the rising and setting of a
summer sun.   The loyal servants of the British crown
had given to one of these forest fastnesses the name of
William Henry, and to the other that of Fort Edward;
calling each after a favorite prince of the reigning
family.   The veteran Scotchman just named held the
first, with a regiment of regulars and a few provincials;
a force really by far too small to make head against
the formidable power that Montcalm was leading to
the foot of his earthen mounds.   At the latter, however, lay General Webb, who commanded the armies of
the king in the northern provinces, with a body of more
than five thousand men.   By uniting the several detachments of his command, this officer might have arrayed nearly double that number of combatants against
the enterprising Frenchman, who had ventured so far
from his reinforcements, with an army but little superior in numbers.

But under the influence of their degraded fortunes,
both officers and men appeared better disposed to wait
the approach of their formidable antagonists, within
their works, than to resist the progress of their march,
by emulating the successful example of the French at
Fort du Quesne, and striking a blow on their advance.

After the first surprise of the intelligence had a little
abated, a rumor was spread through the entrenched
camp, which stretched along the margin of the Hudson,
forming a chain of outworks to the body of the fort
itself, that a chosen detachment of fifteen hundred men
was to depart, with the dawn, for William Henry, the

post at the northern extremity of the portage. That
which at first was only rumor soon became certainty,
as orders passed from the quarters of the commander-
in-chief to the several corps he had selected for this
service, to prepare for their speedy departure. All
doubt as to the intention of Webb now vanished, and
an hour or two of hurried footsteps and anxious faces
succeeded. The novice in the military art flew from
point to point, retarding his own preparations by the
excess of his violent and somewhat distempered zeal;
while the more practiced veteran made his arrange-
ments with a deliberation that scorned every appearance of haste; though his sober lineaments and anxious
eye sufficiently betrayed that he had no very strong professional relish for the as yet untried and dreaded warfare of the wilderness. At length the sun set in a flood
of glory, behind the distant western hills, and as darkness drew its veil around the secluded spot the sounds
of preparation diminished; the last light finally disappeared from the log cabin of some officer; the trees cast
their deeper shadows over the mounds and the rippling
stream, and a silence soon pervaded the camp, as deep
as that which reigned in the vast forest by which it
was environed.

According to the orders of the preceding night, the
heavy sleep of the army was broken by the rolling of the
warning drums, whose rattling echoes were heard issuing, on the damp morning air, out of every vista of the
woods, just as day began to draw the shaggy outlines
of some tall pines of the vicinity on the opening brightness of a soft and cloudless eastern sky. In an instant
the whole camp was in motion; the meanest soldier
arousing from his lair to witness the departure of his
comrades, and to share in the excitement and incidents
of the hour. The simple array of the chosen band was
soon completed. While the regular and trained hire-
lings of the king marched with haughtiness to the right
of the line, the less pretending colonists took their
humbler position on its left, with a docility that long

practice had rendered easy. The scouts departed; strong guards preceded and followed the lumbering vehicles that bore the baggage; and before the gray light of the morning was mellowed by the rays of the sun, the main body of the combatants wheeled into column, and left the encampment with a show of high military bearing, that served to drown the slumbering apprehensions of many a novice, who was now about to make his first essay in arms. While in view of their admiring comrades, the same proud front and ordered array was observed, until the notes of their fifes growing fainter in distance, the forest at length appeared to swallow up the living mass which had slowly entered its bosom.

The deepest sounds of the retiring and invisible column had ceased to be borne on the breeze to the listeners, and the latest straggler had already disappeared in pursuit; but there still remained the signs of another departure, before a log cabin of unusual size and accommodations, in front of which those sentinels paced their rounds, who were known to guard the person of the English general. At this spot were gathered some half dozen horses, caparisoned in a manner which showed that two, at least, were destined to bear the persons of females, of a rank that it was not usual to meet so far in the wilds of the country. A third wore the trappings and arms of an officer of the staff; while the rest, from the plainness of the housings, and the traveling mails with which they were encumbered, were evidently fitted for the reception of as many menials, who were, seemingly, already awaiting the pleasure of those they served. At a respectful distance from this unusual show were gathered divers groups of curious idlers; some admiring the blood and bone of the high-mettled military charger, and others gazing at the preparations, with the dull wonder of vulgar curiosity. There was one man, however, who, by his countenance and actions, formed a marked exception to those who composed the latter class of spectators, being neither idle, nor seemingly very ignorant.

CHAPTER V

EDGAR ALLAN POE

In the history of American authors there has
probably not been a life of more pathetic interest
than that of Edgar Allan Poe. Indeed, misfortune
seems to have pursued him to his grave; and even
after his death his memory was unmercifully tra-
duced. Griswold's spiteful and vicious attack in
the memoir prefixed to his edition of Poe's works
set the fashion, which, except in rare instances, has
been followed somewhat blindly. But here and
there a few brave writers have dared to offer a word
in defence, and to state the facts, even at the risk
of being voted biased and narrow of view. Some
essayists, however, emboldened by these sporadic
efforts, have recoiled to the other extreme, and by
their unbounded admiration of everything that
came from Poe's pen have done his cause quite as
much harm as those who shamefully defame him.
Needless to say, somewhere between these two extremes lies the region of truth. Wholesome advice
is contained in the maxim *Ne quid nimis;* and this
motto will furnish us a safe guide in literary as well
as in political controversies.

It is wellnigh impossible to give a just and correct estimate of an author either during his life or
immediately after his death. Proximity to a beautiful landscape distorts our view, and prevents our
receiving a correct and adequate impression of its
beauty. We must get the proper perspective and
view the landscape from a point not too near, on

the one hand, or too remote, on the other. Surely, then, after the lapse of half a century we may turn our glass upon Poe, in the hope of obtaining a fairer and more adequate view of the author's genius than was possible on the part of his contemporaries.

Poe's detractors have indicted him on the charge of gross immorality. To be more specific, they have said that he was an habitual drunkard, an ingrate, a scoffer, and a libertine. Now, it is not the purpose of this paper to defend Poe against the charge of occasional drunkenness. Not even his most ardent admirers, unless so utterly biased as to be incapable of appreciating an established fact, would presumably attempt to exonerate him from this accusation. But while it is true that Poe indulged all too freely his convivial passion, it is equally true that he endeavored to abstain, and that he actually did abstain, from such indulgence sometimes for several months in succession. Like many others, however, he had been reared in a household where liberal potations seem to have been encouraged, or, at all events, not forbidden. Poe, unfortunately, inherited from his parents, who were stage people, a lack of self-control; and it was against this inherited weakness and deficiency in will-power that he fought with varying success and failure all his mature years, until at last he yielded and sank down in utter despair.

Little need be said in reply to the other specific charges. The conviction has grown upon us, after a careful study of his life and works, that, although at times he seemed to show but scant appreciation of the kindnesses bestowed upon him by some of his friends, Poe nevertheless was not an ingrate. He had many friends, who, when after his death an attempt was made by his enemies to plant thorns

upon his grave, interposed and themselves planted
roses there. We do not believe Poe was a scoffer.
Nor, on the other hand, do we think that he had any
deep and abiding religious convictions, or that he
ever drew much comfort from his religion. In reference to the last count in the indictment, we feel,
after reading his biography, that few men have ever
proved more devoted and faithful husbands than
did Poe to his beautiful but frail Virginia. Upon
the evidence of Mrs. Clemm, Poe's mother-in-law,
his conjugal relations were entirely free from every
discordant element; and his untiring devotion to
his wife in her last lingering illness was as beautiful as it was pathetic. Moreover, there is not the
slightest suggestion of immorality in any poem or
story which Poe wrote. His works are as chaste as
an icicle. This is far more than can be said of
much of our present-day fiction.

Poe's biographers are not agreed as to some of
the events in his life. Much of the uncertainty
concerning him is to be charged to Poe himself, for
his own autobiographical statements were not
always consistent, and these discrepancies he never
satisfactorily explained. Yet his recent biographers, especially Woodberry and Harrison, by diligent and thorough investigation, have cleared up a
number of points in his life which before were in
dispute.

Poe was born in Boston, January 19, 1809. On
his father's side he traced his ancestry back to an
Italian family of the tenth century that had settled
in Normandy and that later removed, successively,
to England, Wales and Ireland. But Edgar's immediate ancestors on the spear side of the house
had settled in Maryland, while on the spindle side
they were still English. His father was David Poe

and his mother Elizabeth Arnold, both of whom
followed the stage as a profession. They were
filling an engagement at the Federal Street, Theatre, Boston, when Edgar was born. The parents
both died before Edgar was two years old, and the
boy with an elder brother and a younger sister were
left objects of charity in Richmond, Virginia, where
the family had been stranded. Edgar was adopted
by Mr. John Allan, a wealthy tobacconist of Richmond, whose wife took a fancy to the bright child,
and he was reared in comfort and affluence. In
1815 the Allans visited England, taking young
Edgar with them, and they remained there for five
years and put Edgar to school at Stoke Newington.
When the family returned to Richmond, Edgar was
sent to a local academy, where he attained profi-
ciency in languages and exhibited special aptitude
for verse-writing. He also showed considerable
fondness for outdoor exercises and was recognized
as a good athlete.

In February, 1826, Poe matriculated at the University of Virginia, recently founded, and there he
made satisfactory progress in his studies. But he
was there associated, unfortunately, with many
dissipated students and himself lost heavy sums of
money at cards, thereby incurring considerable
debts. These his god-father refused flatly to pay
and, moreover, summarily removed young Poe from
the institution. Edgar then returned to Richmond,
smarting under his disgrace chiefly because he was
thus forced to leave his debts of honor unpaid, and
was placed in Mr. Allan's counting-room. But this
prosaic occupation proved altogether uncongenial
to the prospective poet, as was to be expected; and
so resenting such treatment, he deserted his foster-

father's roof and shook the dust of Richmond from his feet, to make his own way in the cold world.

We next find Poe in Boston, where on May 26, 1827, under an assumed name—E. A. Perry—he enlisted in the United States Army. However, during his sojourn in Boston he published anonymously his first volume of poetry, "Tamerlane and Other Poems." In the autumn he was transferred to Fort Moultrie, South Carolina, and later to Fortress Monroe, Virginia. It was while he was serving at this last-named post that a reconciliation was effected with Mr. Allan, who provided a substitute for his errant foster-son and secured him a cadet appointment at West Point. Young Poe entered the Academy July 1, 1830, but the rigid discipline of that renowned institute was far too exacting for so restless and wayward a youth as Poe, who chafed under its martinet life. He desired to resign, but Mr. Allan would not consent to this; so he wilfully neglected his duties, in order to facilitate his early dismissal, which occurred in January, 1831.

Poe thereupon made his way to New York and published a second volume of verse, entitling it simply "Poems," in which he included "Israfel" and "To Helen." He had previously published (in 1829, while in the army) an acknowledged volume of verse, "Al Aaraaf, Tamerlane and Other Poems," which was an enlargement of his maiden volume. But neither of these ventures had proved a financial success, and their author perhaps experienced some foreboding and disquietude as to his resolution to live by his pen. For even down to the Civil War a purely literary career in America gave assurance of extremely meager support and promised to the man wholly relying upon his pen for his daily bread only the proverbial Grub Street comforts of life. However fine his writings, Poe had no reason, therefore, to expect to live in affluence upon the receipts from his royalty. Furthermore, all hope of aid from his foster-father had been abandoned now that Mr. Allan had married again and had utterly broken with him. Yet Poe had to his credit experience, industry, culture and genius,—qualities which ordinarily go a long way to make for success in this life. On the other hand, and as an offset to these, Poe had developed as well as inherited moral weakness, extreme sensitiveness, an excitable and nervous temperament and surroundings which were not propitious to his temperament. Possessed of these defects, which were as serious as his qualities were brilliant, this talented young Southerner started on what ought to have been a noble career with a happy end. But alas! the performance of a life too frequently proves unequal to the promise.

Poe left New York for Baltimore, where he took up his residence at the home of Mrs. Clemm, his father's widowed sister, whose beautiful, but frail daughter Virginia afterwards, at the early age of fourteen, became his bride. Here he was unable to secure steady work, and amid his disappointments was buoyed up by the encouraging words of the angel in the house, his beloved Virginia. He received a windfall in the shape of a prize of $100.00 which he won in October, 1833, by his story, the "Manuscript Found in a Bottle." His poem, "The Coliseum," was awarded a smaller prize, but this had to be waived by the conditions of the contest which did not permit the same author to carry off both prizes. One of the judges was John P. Kennedy, the romancer, who thereupon became interested in the promising young author, and, by way of befriending him, secured for him a congenial position as assistant to Thomas W. White, proprietor of the newly established *Southern Literary Messenger*. Accordingly, in 1834, Poe assumed practical control of this famous Richmond journal, to the pages of which he contributed some of his cleverest stories and most trenchant critiques. To be sure, his literary criticisms were sometimes scathing and drastic enough, almost to the point of flaying his victim. Yet this severe type of review had a wholesome and tonic effect in an age when provincial eulogy on the one hand, or fulsome flattery on the other, passed for real literary criticism.

In 1837, Poe's bibulous habits cost him his position with the *Southern Literary Messenger,* and he set out for New York to try his fortune in the great metropolis. There he was unable to secure sufficient work to maintain himself; and so Mrs. Clemm, who kept house for him and his wife, supported the impecunious author by taking boarders. Meanwhile Poe wrote and published his longest story, "The Narrative of Arthur Gordon Pym." Failing to secure employment in New York, he moved his small family to Philadelphia, where he was offered a permanent position as editor of *Graham's Magazine,* with the opportunity to do hackwork to supplement his slender salary. Here he managed not only to keep the wolf from the door, but to live in comparative comfort, till 1842, when his besetting vice of intemperance forced the severance of his connection with *Graham's Magazine.* Much of his best work was done during his residence in Philadelphia, and to this period in his career we must assign his "Tales of the Grotesque and Arabesque," published in the collection of 1839; "Ligeia," "The Fall of the House of Usher,"

"The Murders in the Rué Morgue," and "The Gold Bug," the setting of which last story is a reminiscence of his army days at Fort Moultrie.

In 1844, Poe again settled in New York, where fortune had already dealt with him so harshly before. But this time she relented somewhat. He secured an appointment on the staff of some of the newspapers, and in January, 1845, he contributed to *The Evening Mirror* his immortal "Raven," which greatly enhanced his reputation as a poet with the general public and heralded his name abroad throughout the land. After this he was connected with *The Broadway Journal* under the management of Charles F. Briggs, but a quarrel ensuing, Briggs retired and Poe assumed entire control, only to run the periodical in the ground within a year. Poe also signalized the year 1845 by issuing an edition of his collected poems with the "Raven," which had spread his fame far and wide, as leader. In 1846, he removed to Fordham, where a chapter of misfortunes followed, culminating in the death, toward the end of 1847, of his devoted wife, who was the inspiration of his life. Dire want and acute suffering marked his ill-fated days at Fordham.

After the death of his fair young wife Poe appears to have lost heart, and from that time on, his course was one of gradual moral deterioration till the tragic end came. True, he had a few fitful seasons of moral reformation and creative impulse, but these were only temporary,—brief intervals, when by extraordinary exertion of his enfeebled volition he strove to pull himself together again and work with his wonted interest and zest. During these intervals when he was himself and had his evil genius under control, he produced such work as "Eureka," "Ulalume," "Annabel Lee" and "The

Bells," in which he married music to poetry in a manner as marvelous as it was unprecedented. In his brave struggle he sought feminine sympathy, which apparently never failed to stimulate him to his best effort and to brace him up morally. Indeed, it was a mission of this kind that brought him to Richmond in the early autumn of 1849, to arrange for his wedding with an old sweetheart. On his way North to complete his plans for the wedding he stopped over in Baltimore where he fell victim to his fatal moral weakness, and died on a drunken debauch, Sunday morning, October 7,—a pitiable outcast. He was buried in that city in the Westminster churchyard, where some years later a monument was erected over his grave by the children of the local public schools.

Poe's irregularities and intemperate habits and irritable disposition all combined to make him a great many enemies. Moreover, his lack of poise and his whims and fancies led him frequently into error in his literary criticism, as for instance, his savage attack upon Longfellow, to cite only a single case in point. Of course this naturally brought about a reaction which prejudiced many against Poe, and his detractors have sought to malign him and to underrate his works. The New England school of critics specially strove to decry his influence and to bring his writings into disrepute, chiefly because the leaders of that school could not dissociate literature from morality. They rejected Poe's artistic principles because his life failed to measure up to the Puritan standard of morality.

So much for Poe, the man. It is now time to consider Poe, the author.

Poe's genius may be considered in a threefold aspect. He may be regarded as a critic, as a poet, and as a romancer. In each of these realms Poe attained to eminence; but it is mainly in the last two aspects that we wish especially to consider him now. We need hardly say that we do not intend by this to imply any disparagement of his critical genius. On the contrary, Poe, in our judgment, is rightly entitled to the distinction of being the first American man of letters to write criticism deserving the name. Before his advent into journalism criticism had been but little better than fulsome flattery. After his appearance journalistic criticism entered upon a new era. His reviews, though frequently drastic, and sometimes it must be admitted inspired by personal prejudice, had, nevertheless, a wholesome and stimulating effect upon American authorship. His "Marginalia" awakened a sense of injustice and resentment in the breasts of the more virile, and struck sheer terror to the hearts of the weaklings. Mr. Stedman justly calls his sketches "a prose Dunciad, waspish and unfair, yet not without touches of magnanimity." It has been truly observed that whenever Poe, unbiased by personal motives, pronounced favorably upon the talents of an author, such as Bayard Taylor, Mrs, Browning, or Tennyson, his judgments have been sustained by the verdict of the present generation. But his prejudice made him merciless and unrelenting to the New England poets, as a class. According to his view nothing good or beautiful could come out of the Nazareth of Boston. It need hardly be remarked that the present generation has, in many instances, reversed Poe's critical dicta.

But enough of Poe as a critic. Let us now take up his poetry. In his masterly essay on Thomas Gray, Matthew Arnold says of that writer that his whole history as a poet is contained in a remark,

made by an appreciative friend, to the effect that
"he never spoke out in poetry." The same remark is
equally applicable to Poe; for it is a common feeling, shared alike by the present generation and by
his contemporaries, that he never really gave complete utterance to the poetry which kindled his imagination and stirred his soul.

Poe was not a prolific writer. All the poetry he
ever published could be pressed between the covers
of a very slender book. But volume is not the only,
or even the main, criterion in determining the
standing of a poet. Indeed, it is rather an insignificant factor. In the determination of a poet's standing, spontaneity and passion, not volume, are the
criteria. "Poetry," says Poe, in the preface to his
juvenile productions "has been with me a passion,
not a purpose." Still, we heartily wish that he had
written more of purpose, though no less of passion.

It must be conceded that Poe's range of subject—
his register, to borrow a musical term—was quite
narrow. In his youth, as a critic has observed, he
struck the key-notes of a few themes; and the output
of his mature years was but a variation on these.
The death, in his youth, of a lady to whom he was
devoted made a profound impression upon his sus-
ceptible heart, and filled his soul with a poignant
feeling of sadness and of longing for one far removed from human companionship and beyond recall.
This henceforth was to be the inspiration of his
genius and the burden of his song. Says Mr.
Edmund Grosse, the eminent English critic, himself
no mean poet: "If Poe had not harped so persist-
ently on his one theme of remorseful passion for the
irrevocable dead, if he had employed his extraordinary, his unparalleled gifts of melodius invention,

with equal skill, in illustrating a variety of themes, he must have been with the greatest poets."

Poe's best-known poems, those upon which his fame as a poet rests, are "The Raven," first of all, "The Bells," "For Annie," "Ulalume," "The City in the Sea," "The Haunted Palace," and "The Conqueror Worm." Of these "The Raven," written in 1845, is by far the most widely known, and deservedly the most popular. With its publication Poe, like Byron with the publication of "Childe Harold," leaped immediately into fame. His manuscript articles which, up to this time, editors had kept in dark pigeon-holes were now brought to the light of day, and were greatly in request; and enterprising magazines were eager to announce, as a special attraction, a new poem by the author of "The Raven." The instant success of this production provoked a new edition of Poe's writings, which appeared toward the end of the year 1845, under the title, "The Raven and Other Poems." This volume contained wellnigh all the verse Poe had ever written. The early poems had undergone alterations more or less slight, in accordance with the author's fashion of recasting and republishing his early work as if it were appearing for the first time.

In view of the popularity of "The Raven" and of its importance as being Poe's greatest poem, it will not be out of place to linger over it for a while and notice it somewhat in detail. In his "Philosophy of Composition," Poe gives a detailed account of his method of composing "The Raven" and of its *motif;* and the story has such a *vraisemblance* and such a positiveness about it as almost to compel belief. Moreover, the author's peculiar views, which he set forth elsewhere, in respect of the poetic principle are involved in the account; and he uses "The

Raven" to illustrate his theory as to the aim and scope of poetry.

Poe believed, with Coleridge, that the pleasure arising from the contemplation of beauty is keener, more chaste, and more elevating to the soul than that which springs from the contemplation of truth by the mere intellect, or even than that which springs from any passion of the heart. He maintained, further, that it is through this sentiment of beauty that man acquires his clearest conceptions of eternal nature, and is consequently brought into closest touch with the divine. This subtle power exists in the beauty of nature, which inspires man with a belief in something beyond nature, fairer and more beautiful still, to be discerned only by the imagination. It is the province of art to fashion this ideal beauty for the gratification of man's spiritual emotion. This is the end and aim of all the fine arts, but more especially of the crowning arts of music and poetry. The incitements of passion, the precepts of duty, and even the lessons of truth are included; but they must be subordinated to the main point of the contemplation of beauty. It follows, therefore, that beauty is the sole legitimate theme of poetry; and so Poe defined poetry as "the rhythmical creation of beauty."

However, Poe in his definition did not take the term beauty in its widest and broadest sense, which would include all truth, emotion, and ethics. On the contrary, he restricted the term to what he was pleased to call supernal beauty, that is, the domain of sadness and regret. He regarded a beautiful woman as the very quintessence of beauty, and the death of such a woman as the most poetical theme in the world. This is the *motif* and inspiration of "The Raven." On the general principle that vice can never be beautiful, of course nothing base or degrading could legitimately fall within the province of poetry.

As a minor consideration Poe insisted that, from the very nature of our mental constitution, it is necessary that a poem be brief and aim at a single artistic effect, since the undivided attention cannot be held for several consecutive hours by one subject. This canon, however, was inspired by Schlegel's dictum of the unity or totality of interest. Such a long poem as the "Iliad," the "Odyssey," or "Paradise Lost," according to Poe's theory, depends for its interest and effect upon the various briefer incidents or poems which go to make it up. When we read a poem of great length the attention naturally relaxes at intervals; and, since the interest is not sustained throughout, the poem fails to produce a single artistic effect. Furthermore, Poe maintained that, in order for a poem to produce a characteristic effect, it should possess a distinct rhythm or metre, together with a certain grotesqueness of conception and quaintness of language. Now, all these conditions, Poe claimed, were met in "The Raven" in particular, and in his other poems in general. For in the former we find as the *motif* of the poem the death of a beautiful woman, Lenore; the unique refrain "Nevermore;" a certain grotesqueness of conception in the setting; and an air of quaintness about the language.

Like Lanier, another Southern singer whose career offers almost as many pathetic incidents, Poe was endowed by nature with a keen appreciation of rhythm and music. He was preëminently a melodist; and, what is more, the melody of his verse has not been equalled in the history of American literature, and is not surpassed by any British poet. But, as has been already stated, his register was not wide. Within a limited range he could and did achieve remarkable results, as in the refrain of "The Bells" or "The Raven." The musical effect of the ballad of either of these poems was, up to the time of their publication, unequalled, and it has not been surpassed since. Poe, with a few choice words, like Paganini with his simple violin, produced a spell which was truly marvellous. It is said of the great musician that such was his control of his instrument, and such his perfection of technique, that in every part of musical Europe even with his very first notes he held vast audiences spell-bound. It may be said of Poe that such was his intuitive sense of beauty, and such the melody of his verse, that he arrested the reluctant attention of the reading public of the two English-speaking nations, and by his haunting music cast a glamour over their poets which none of them, after repeated efforts, has ever since succeeded in reproducing. Mr. Gosse tells us that Poe has proved himself to be the Piper of Hamelin to all later English poets, of whom there is hardly one whose verse music does not show traces of his influence. Surely, it is no small distinction thus to have stamped the impress of one's own genius for melodious verse upon the succeeding generation of English poets, and that, too, of the Victorian era.

Poe is sometimes called a poet of one poem; and the criticism is not altogether unjust. For to the world at large he is generally known as the author of "The Raven." We think Mr. Stedman comes nearer the truth, however, when in an epigrammatic sentence he says: "Poe was not a single-poem poet, but a poet of a single mood." The theme is the same in almost all his poems, namely, ruin. This is the

burden of his song; this is the one poetic subject
that always kindled his imagination. To be sure,
the treatment varies, as might be expected; but the
inspiration of his poetry is almost invariably drawn
from this one source. "Israfel" furnishes an exception, but it is an exception which proves the rule.

This is Poe's greatest limitation; and a serious
limitation it certainly is. It undermines the foundation of his claim to being regarded a great poet,
in the sense that English poets like Milton, Dryden,
Byron, Wordsworth, Tennyson, and many others
that might be named are entitled to rank as great
poets. Poe, in our judgment, is an artist in verse;
a great artist, indeed, but hardly a great poet. It is
true that he possesses "originality in the treatment
of themes, perennial charm, exquisite finish in execution, and distinction of individual manner"—elements of poetical greatness as set forth by an eminent English essayist and critic—but he lacks, it
seems to us, one of the qualifications needed to entitle him to rank with the great poets. His fatal
defect is his narrowness of range. "The Raven" may
wing its ceaseless flight through anthologies, and be
admired by generations yet unborn; but this alone
does not make its author a great poet any more than
the "Elegy Written in a Country Churchyard" entitles Gray to rank with the world's great poets.
However, although this Southern poet may fail of
the distinction of being entitled to rest in the Valhalla of the world's great poets, yet in our opinion,
he justly deserves to rank with the greatest American poets, if, indeed, he is not the very greatest
among them.

But it is time for us to consider our author in the
aspect of romance. Dearly as he loved it, poetry
was never a serious purpose with Poe, as he himself

informed the reading public in his youthful preface.
It was upon his prose romance and his critical work
that he relied to establish his fame. Upon these he
was willing to stake his claim to immortality. It
ought to be remarked here, however, that it was
more especially in the province of romance that he
exhibited, in the highest degree, his intellectual
force—his vigorous imagination and his acute analytical powers. He has handed down his name to
the present generation as the founder of the school
of writers, now so popular, who practise the short
story. He also deserves the distinction of being the
founder of the modern detective story and the modern sea story. Dr. A. Conan Doyle, whether he
acknowledges it or not, must be classed as a disciple
of Poe; for his "Adventures of Sherlock Holmes" is
but the method of Poe carried to its logical conclusion.

Poe's power developed early. Indeed, his genius
may be called precocious. Some of his early stories
were among his best, and were hardly surpassed in
his mature years. His earliest effort, "A MS. Found
in a Bottle," exhibits practically the same distinctive qualities as appear in the flower of his work.
The difference is one of degree, not of kind. That
was a suggestive comment made by Kennedy, to
whom young Poe submitted his maiden manuscript:
"The young fellow is highly imaginative, and a little given to the terrific." And the criticism is just;
for there is no story written by Poe which is not
more or less grotesque, and which does not give unmistakable evidence of the author's rare gift of
imagination.

His stories naturally divide themselves into two
classes: first, the analytical tales, dealing with the
grotesque and the terrible; and, secondly, the spec-

ulative tales, dealing with the weird and the supernatural. Examples of the former class are "The Black Cat," "The Gold Bug," "The Tell-Tale Heart," and "The Murders in the Rue Morgue;" examples of the latter are "The Fall of the House of Usher," "Ligeia," "A Tale of the Ragged Mountains," and "William Wilson." The latter class constitutes the author's earlier work in fiction. In the tales of this class Poe gradually worked up to a *dénouement* through a complicated series of facts and incidents. In the tales of the former group, starting with the *dénouement,* he gradually unravelled the plot by his ratiocinative method until he worked his way, incident by incident, back to the very beginning. The end aimed at is different, as well as the starting-point. In the imaginative group it is the emotional element which is emphasized; whereas in the ratiocinative group the solution of the mystery is all important, and the attention is accordingly focused upon the incidents leading up to this mystery. In both classes of tales Poe showed his inventive genius, his rare imagination, and his subtle artistic power in the selection and in the grouping of the facts—this last especially in the ratiocinative tales.

The following paragraph is interesting as setting forth in the author's own words the aim which he sought and the method which he followed in the construction of his tales:

A skillful literary artist has constructed a tale. If wise, he has not fashioned his thoughts to accommodate his incidents; but having conceived, with deliberate care, a certain unique or single *effect* to be wrought out, he then invents such incidents—he then combines such events as may best aid in establishing this preconceived effect. If his very initial sentence tend not to the out-bringing of this effect, then he has failed in his

first step. In the whole composition there should be
no word written, of which the tendency, direct or in-
direct, is not to the one preëstablished design. And
by such means, with such care and skill, a picture is at
length painted which leaves in the mind of him who
contemplates it, with a kindred art, a sense of the
fullest satisfaction. The idea of the tale has been presented unblemished, because undisturbed; and this is
an end unattainable by the novel.

In all Poe's stories, subtly conceived and cleverly
and exquisitely executed as some of them incon-
testably are, there is no one character that has
taken hold of the affections or that really lives.
Poe never painted a single live character. Though
a consummate artist, he yet lacked that subtle
power of characterization which Thackeray exhibited, in so eminent a degree, in the creation of his
immortal Becky Sharp, and Dickens in the creation
of his equally famous Sam Weller. These characters are as well known as if they had been real flesh
and blood, and will doubtless continue to live in the
affections of the people as long as English literature lives. But we search in vain in Poe's fiction
for any counterpart to the tactful, impudent Becky
Sharp or the resourceful Sam Weller. We find
nothing in Poe that even remotely approaches
either of these famous characters. His men and
women are as cold as marble, and about as destitute of feeling. They do not appeal to the sympathies; they do not touch the heart. They are clever
sketches, faultlessly drawn; but they are, after all,
simply "ingenious studies in black and white."
Pygmalion so loved Galatea, the beautiful creation
of his chisel, that the gods inspired the cold marble
with life, to satisfy the prayerful yearning of the
artist's heart. But Poe never had any deep rever-

ence or tender feeling for any of the cold, soulless creations of his genius. It is said that some novelists have wept when they have killed the heroes of their own invention. Poe was not of these. He did not hesitate to alter and make over again any of his uninspired, lifeless characters, or even to reduce Deity itself—as in "Eureka"—to a mere mathematical formula. Poe's men and women were conceived in the head, not in the heart, and born of the intellect; consequently they had no warmth of feeling, no soul. This fatal defect in characterization is due, in large measure, to Poe's woeful lack of human sympathy and his utter lack of humor. In no other part of his writings did he make such a signal, glaring failure as in his humorous tales.

Moreover, Poe did not know how to combine people and situations in ordinary life. He could paint one character only at a time. He never learned the art of painting from life, and never succeeded in portraying characters in their interplay upon one another. Indeed, when he painted he took his models not from real life, but from his own imagination. He was the victim of his own overdeveloped fancy. Here is the weak spot in Poe's artistic equipment. His imagination was abnormally developed, and he lacked the will-power to control and direct it. It was this abnormal imagination that gave color and direction to all he ever achieved, not only in fiction, but also in actual life. It was the promptings of his imagination that he followed when, in his effort to throw men and women upon the canvas, he projected morbid persons like himself, not robust, healthy characters. He could, it is true, invent single situations that resembled those of actual life; but he could not follow these up in a natural sequence. In short, he was

a romancer, not a novelist. We believe, with Mr.
Stedman, that Poe could never have written a
novel.

Yet, despite the limitations of his tales, Poe was
an entertaining, a charming romancer withal. Of
his sixty tales or prose narratives it will be found,
when they are sifted, that only about a third deserve
to live. But these will live; and they have already
won for their author, abroad as well as at home, a
fame which, perhaps, no other American has excelled. By his intellectual characteristics he seems
to have appealed to the French reading public with
special force. Indeed, the French were the first
foreigners to discover his star, which they hailed
with characteristic delight—a star whose light,
after more than half a century, shows no sign of
waning brilliance. It appears from the biography
appended to the definitive edition of Poe that between 1890 and 1895 there were made at least ten
translations of his works into various foreign languages. What could have brought about such a remarkable result? In a word, it must be Poe's
unique genius—his intense originality, which has
hardly been paralleled in literary history, and his
indefinable, inimitable charm of manner, which appeals not simply to men of one particular clime or
country, but to all men everywhere.

POE

THE RAVEN

Once upon a midnight dreary, while I pondered, weak
and weary,
Over many a quaint and curious volume of forgotten
lore—
While I nodded, nearly napping, suddenly there came
a tapping,
As of some one gently rapping, rapping at my chamber door.
" 'T is some visitor," I muttered, "tapping at my chamber door:
  Only this and nothing more."

Ah, distinctly I remember it was in the bleak December,
And each separate dying ember wrought its ghost upon
the floor.
Eagerly I wished the morrow;—vainly I had sought
to borrow
From my books surcease of sorrow—sorrow for the
lost Lenore,
For the rare and radiant maiden whom the angels
name Lenore:
  Nameless here for evermore.

And the silken sad uncertain rustling of each purple
curtain
Thrilled me—filled me with fantastic terrors never felt
before;
So that now, to still the beating of my heart, I stood
repeating
" 'T is some visitor entreating entrance at my chamber
door,
Some late visitor entreating entrance at my chamber
door:
  This it is and nothing more."

Presently my soul grew stronger; hesitating then no
    longer,
"Sir," said I, "or Madam, truly your forgiveness I
    implore;
But the fact is I was napping, and so gently you came
    rapping,
And so faintly you came tapping, tapping at my cham-
    ber door,
That I scarce was sure I heard you"—here I opened
    wide the door:—
        Darkness there and nothing more.

Deep into that darkness peering, long I stood there
    wondering, fearing,
Doubting, dreaming dreams no mortals ever dared to
    dream before;
But the silence was unbroken, and the stillness gave
    no token,
And the only word there spoken was the whispered
    word, "Lenore?"
This I whispered, and an echo murmured back the
    word, "Lenore:"
        Merely this and nothing more.

Back into the chamber turning, all my soul within me
    burning,
Soon again I heard a tapping somewhat louder than
    before.
"Surely," said I, "surely that is something at my
    window lattice;
Let me see, then, what thereat is, and this mystery
    explore;
Let my heart be still a moment and this mystery
    explore:
        'T is the wind and nothing more."

Open here I flung the shutter, when, with many a flirt
and flutter,
In there stepped a stately Raven of the saintly days of
yore.
Not the least obeisance made he; not a minute stopped
or stayed he;
But, with mien of lord or lady, perched above my
chamber door,
Perched upon a bust of Pallas just above my chamber
door:
    Perched, and sat, and nothing more.

Then this ebony bird beguiling my sad fancy into
smiling
By the grave and stern decorum of the countenance it
wore,—
"Though thy crest be shorn and shaven, thou," I said,
"art sure no craven,
Ghastly grim and ancient Raven wandering from the
Nightly shore:
Tell me what thy lordly name is on the Night's Plu-
tonian shore!"
    Quoth the Raven, "Nevermore."

Much I marvelled this ungainly fowl to hear discourse
so plainly,
Though its answer little meaning—little relevancy
bore;
For we cannot help agreeing that no living human
being
Ever yet was blessed with seeing bird above his chamber door,
Bird or beast upon the sculptured bust above his chamber door,
    With such name as "Nevermore."

But the Raven, sitting lonely on the placid bust, spoke
  only
That one word, as if his soul in that one word he did
  outpour,
Nothing further then he uttered, not a feather then he
  fluttered,
Till I scarcely more than muttered,—"Other friends
  have flown before;
On the morrow *he* will leave me, as my Hopes have
  flown before."
    Then the bird said, "Nevermore."

Startled at the stillness broken by reply so aptly
  spoken,
"Doubtless," said I, "what it utters is its only stock
  and store,
Caught from some unhappy master whom unmerciful
  Disaster
Followed fast and followed faster till his songs one
  burden bore:
Till the dirges of his Hope that melancholy burden
  bore
    Of 'Never—nevermore.' "

But the Raven still beguiling all my fancy into smiling,
Straight I wheeled a cushioned seat in front of bird
  and bust and door;
Then, upon the velvet sinking, I betook myself to
  linking
Fancy unto fancy, thinking what this ominous bird of
  yore,
What this grim, ungainly, ghastly, gaunt, and ominous
  bird of yore
    Meant in croaking "Nevermore."

This I sat engaged in guessing, but no syllable expressing
To the fowl whose fiery eyes now burned into my
  bosom's core;

This and more I sat divining, with my head at ease re-
clining
On the cushion's velvet lining that the lamp-light
gloated o'er,
But whose velvet violet lining with the lamp-light gloat-
ing o'er
  She shall press, ah, nevermore!

Then, methought, the air grew denser, perfumed from
an unseen censer
Swung by seraphim whose foot-falls tinkled on the
tufted floor.
"Wretch," I cried, "thy God hath lent thee—by these
angels he hath sent thee
Respite—respite and nepenthe from thy memories of
Lenore!
Quaff, oh quaff this kind nepenthe, and forget this lost
Lenore!"
  Quoth the Raven, "Nevermore."

"Prophet!" said I, "thing of evil! prophet still, if bird
or devil!
Whether Tempter sent, or whether tempest tossed thee
here ashore,
Desolate yet all undaunted, on this desert land en-
chanted—
On this home by Horror haunted—tell me truly, I im-
plore:
Is there—is there balm in Gilead?—tell me—tell me,
I implore!"
  Quoth the Raven, "Nevermore."

"Prophet!" said I, "thing of evil—prophet still, if bird
or devil!
By that Heaven that bends above us, by that God we
both adore,
Tell this soul with sorrow laden if, within the distant
Aidenn,

It shall clasp a sainted maiden whom the angels name
Lenore:
Clasp a rare and radiant maiden whom the angels name
Lenore!"
Quoth the Raven, "Nevermore."

"Be that word our sign of parting, bird or fiend!" I
shrieked, upstarting:
"Get thee back into the tempest and the Night's Plu-
tonian shore!
Leave no black plume as a token of that lie thy soul
hath spoken!
Leave my loneliness unbroken! quit the bust above my
door!
Take thy beak from out my heart, and take thy form
from off my door!"
Quoth the Raven, "Nevermore."

And the Raven, never flitting, still is sitting, still is
sitting
On the pallid bust of Pallas just above my chamber
door;
And his eyes have all the seeming of a demon's that
is dreaming,
And the lamp-light o'er him streaming throws his
shadow on the floor:
And my soul from out that shadow that lies floating
on the floor
Shall be lifted—nevermore!

LENORE

Ah, broken is the golden bowl! the spirit flown forever!
Let the bell toll!—a saintly soul floats on the Stygian
river;
And, Guy De Vere, hast *thou* no tear?—weep now or
nevermore!

See, on yon drear and rigid bier low lies thy love,
    Lenore!
Come, let the burial rite be read—the funeral song be
    sung:
An anthem for the queenliest dead that ever died so
    young,
A dirge for her the doubly dead in that she died so
    young.

"Wretches, ye loved her for her wealth and hated her
    for her pride,
And when she fell in feeble health, ye blessed her—that
    she died!
How shall the ritual, then, be read? the requiem how
    be sung
By you—by yours, the evil eye,—by yours, the slander-
    ous tongue
That did to death the innocence that died, and died
    so young?"

Peccavimus; but rave not thus! and let a Sabbath song
Go up to God so solemnly the dead may feel no wrong.
The sweet Lenore hath gone before, with Hope that
    flew beside,
Leaving thee wild for the dear child that should have
    been thy bride:
For her, the fair and debonair, that now so lowly lies,
The life upon her yellow hair but not within her eyes;
The life still there, upon her hair—the death upon her
    eyes.

"Avaunt! avaunt! from fiends below, the indignant
    ghost is riven—
From Hell unto a high estate far up within the
    Heaven—
From grief and groan, to a golden throne, beside the
    King of Heaven!

Let no bell toll, then,—lest her soul, amid its hallowed
   mirth,
Should catch the note as it doth float up from the
   damned Earth!
And I!—to-night my heart is light!—no dirge will I
   upraise,
But waft the angel on her flight with a Pæan of old
   days."

ULALUME

The skies they were ashen and sober;
   The leaves they were crisped and sere,
   The leaves they were withering and sere;
It was night in the lonesome October
   Of my most immemorial year;
It was hard by the dim lake of Auber,
   In the misty mid region of Weir:
It was down by the dank tarn of Auber,
   In the ghoul-haunted woodland of Weir.

Here once, through an alley Titanic
   Of cypress, I roamed with my Soul—
   Of cypress, with Psyche, my Soul.
These were days when my heart was volcanic
   As the scoriac rivers that roll,
   As the lavas that restlessly roll
Their sulphurous currents down Yaanek
   In the ultimate climes of the pole,
That groan as they roll down Mount Yaanek
   In the realms of the boreal pole.

Our talk had been serious and sober,
   But our thoughts they were palsied and sere,
   Our memories were treacherous and sere,
For we knew not the month was October,
   And we marked not the night of the year,
   (Ah, night of all nights in the year!)

We noted not the dim lake of Auber
    (Though once we had journeyed down here),
Remembered not the dank tarn of Auber
    Nor the ghoul-haunted woodland of Weir.

And now, as the night was senescent
    And star-dials pointed to morn,
    As the star-dials hinted of morn,
At the end of our path a liquescent
    And nebulous lustre was born,
Out of which a miraculous crescent
    Arose, with a duplicate horn,
Astarte's bediamonded crescent
    Distinct with its duplicate horn.

And I said—"She is warmer than Dian:
    She rolls through an ether of sighs,
    She revels in a region of sighs:
She has seen that the tears are not dry on
    These cheeks, where the worm never dies,
And has come past the stars of the Lion
    To point us the path to the skies,
    To the Lethean peace of the skies:
Come up, in despite of the Lion,
    To shine on us with her bright eyes:
Come up through the lair of the Lion,
    With love in her luminous eyes."

But Psyche, uplifting her finger,
    Said—"Sadly this star I mistrust,
    Her pallor I strangely mistrust:
Oh, hasten!—oh, let us not linger!
    Oh, fly!—let us fly!—for we must."
In terror she spoke, letting sink her
    Wings until they trailed in the dust;
In agony sobbed, letting sink her
    Plumes till they trailed in the dust,
    Till they sorrowfully trailed in the dust.

I replied—"This is nothing but dreaming:
    Let us on by this tremulous light!
    Let us bathe in this crystalline light!
Its sibyllic splendor is beaming
    With hope and in beauty to-night:
    See, it flickers up the sky through the night!
Ah, we safely may trust to its gleaming,
    And be sure it will lead us aright:
We safely may trust to a gleaming
    That cannot but guide us aright,
    Since it flickers up to Heaven through the night."

Thus I pacified Psyche and kissed her,
    And tempted her out of her gloom,
    And conquered her scruples and gloom;
And we passed to the end of the vista,
    But were stopped by the door of a tomb,
    By the door of a legended tomb;
And I said—"What is written, sweet sister,
    On the door of this legended tomb?"
    She replied—"Ulalume—Ulalume—
    'T is the vault of thy lost Ulalume!"

Then my heart it grew ashen and sober
    As the leaves that were crisped and sere,
    As the leaves that were withering and sere,
And I cried—"It was surely October
    On this very night of last year
    That I journeyed—I journeyed down here,
    That I brought a dread burden down here:
    On this night of all nights in the year,
    Ah, what demon has tempted me here?
Well I know, now, this dim lake of Auber,
    This misty mid region of Weir:
Well I know, now, this dank tarn of Auber,
    This ghoul-haunted woodland of Weir."

ANNABEL LEE

It was many and many a year ago,
    In a kingdom by the sea,
That a maiden there lived whom you may know
    By the name of ANNABEL LEE;
And this maiden she lived with no other thought
    Than to love and be loved by me.

I was a child and she was a child,
    In this kingdom by the sea,
But we loved with a love that was more than love,
    I and my ANNABEL LEE;
With a love that the winged seraphs of heaven
    Coveted her and me.

And this was the reason that, long ago,
    In this kingdom by the sea,
A wind blew out of a cloud, chilling
    My beautiful ANNABEL LEE;
So that her highborn kinsman came
    And bore her away from me,
To shut her up in a sepulchre
    In this kingdom by the sea.

The angels, not half so happy in heaven,
    Went envying her and me;
Yes! that was the reason (as all men know,
    In this kingdom by the sea)
That the wind came out of the cloud by night,
    Chilling and killing my ANNABEL LEE.

But our love it was stronger by far than the love
    Of those who were older than we,
    Of many far wiser than we;
And neither the angels in heaven above,
    Nor the demons down under the sea,
Can ever dissever my soul from the soul
    Of the beautiful ANNABEL LEE:

For the moon never beams, without bringing me dreams
   Of the beautiful ANNABEL LEE;
And the stars never rise, but I feel the bright eyes
   Of the beautiful ANNABEL LEE;
And so, all the night-tide, I lie down by the side
Of my darling—my darling—my life and my bride,
     In her sepulchre there by the sea,
     In her tomb by the sounding sea.

ISRAFEL

   In Heaven a spirit doth dwell
     Whose heart-strings are a lute;
   None sing so wildly well
   As the angel Israfel,
   And the giddy stars (so legends tell)
   Ceasing their hymns, attend the spell
     Of his voice, all mute.

   Tottering above
     In her highest noon,
     The enamored moon
   Blushes with love,
     While, to listen, the red levin
     (With the rapid Pleiads, even,
     Which were seven)
     Pauses in Heaven.

   And they say (the starry choir
     And the other listening things)
   That Israfeli's fire
   Is owing to that lyre
     By which he sits and sings,
   The trembling living wire
     Of those unusual strings.

But the skies that angel trod,
Where deep thoughts are a duty,
Where Love's a grown-up God,
  Where the Houri glances are
Imbued with all the beauty
  Which we worship in a star.

Therefore thou art not wrong,
  Israfeli, who despisest
An unimpassioned song;
To thee the laurels belong,
  Best bard, because the wisest:
Merrily live, and long!

The ecstasies above
  With thy burning measures suit:
Thy grief, thy joy, thy hate, thy love,
  With the fervor of thy lute:
  Well may the stars be mute!

Yes, Heaven is thine; but this
  Is a world of sweets and sours;
  Our flowers are merely—flowers,
And the shadow of thy perfect bliss
  Is the sunshine of ours.

If I could dwell
  Where Israfel
  Hath dwelt, and he where I,
He might not sing so wildly well
  A mortal melody,
While a bolder note than this might swell
  From my lyre within the sky.

TO HELEN

HELEN, thy beauty is to me
  Like those Nicæan barks of yore,
That gently, o'er a perfumed sea,
  The weary, wayworn wanderer bore
  To his own native shore.

On desperate seas long wont to roam,
  Thy hyacinth hair, thy classic face,
Thy Naiad airs, have brought me home
  To the glory that was Greece
And the grandeur that was Rome.

Lo! in yon brilliant window-niche
  How statue-like I see thee stand,
  The agate lamp within thy hand!
Ah, Psyche, from the regions which
  Are Holy Land!

TO ONE IN PARADISE

THOU wast all that to me, love,
  For which my soul did pine:
A green isle in the sea, love,
  A fountain and a shrine
All wreathed with fairy fruits and flowers,
  And all the flowers were mine.

Ah, dream too bright to last!
  Ah, starry Hope, that didst arise
But to be overcast!
  A voice from out the Future cries,
"On! on!"—but o'er the Past
  (Dim gulf!) my spirit hovering lies
Mute, motionless, aghast.

For, alas! alas! with me
  The light of Life is o'er!
No more—no more— no more—
(Such language holds the solemn sea
  To the sands upon the shore)
Shall bloom the thunder-blasted tree,
  Or the stricken eagle soar.

And all my days are trances,
  And all my nightly dreams
Are where thy gray eye glances,
  And where thy footstep gleams—
In what ethereal dances,
  By what eternal streams.

CHAPTER VI

WILLIAM HICKLING PRESCOTT

Critics are generally agreed now to give Prescott the first place among our early American historians. Few of his predecessors in the realm of American history are readable. They are, almost to a man, of the dry-as-dust type of historian, and their musty, dust-covered tomes enjoy an unbroken sleep on the top shelves of our libraries. Who, it may very pertinently be asked, now thinks of reading such desiccated annals as those of Governor Hutchinson or Abiel Holmes? Yet these chronicles are trustworthy and accurately relate the events of our early history. But they are insufferably tedious and wearisome to the reader's spirit. Not so Prescott. He does not tire or fatigue us; on the contrary, he holds our interest and attention almost like a romancer. The reader is simply fascinated with his graphic and romantic page.

But Prescott is conspicuous among our early historians quite as much for his historic value as for his chaste, classical style. It is true, that the brilliant literary qualities which adorn the pages of his history so as, occasionally, to challenge comparison with Macaulay's rhetorical paragraphs have raised a question, in the minds of some, as to our author's conscientious adherence to fact. One is inclined to doubt whether such glowing pictures as embellish Prescott's history are not the product of an imagination untrammeled and more or less divorced from fact. To such a degree has the historian invested the dry and uninviting annals with the warmth and glow of his poetic imagination and made the events of those romantic days again unfold themselves before our eyes under the touch of his brilliant pen. Yet subsequent investigators in this field have assured us that Prescott had a scrupulous regard for fact combined with his gift of a vivid imagination. By this happy union of his mental qualities he was enabled to make his pages exceedingly attractive, without distorting the facts of history. However, it may be presumed that Prescott did not paint with an absolute fidelity to fact, such as is exacted by the present-day standard of writing history. He colored his picture a little, perhaps, using the license of historical writing then in vogue. But he did not allow his love of rhetorical adornment materially to warp the truth. He was compelled in writing his narratives to rely upon documents highly colored and sometimes really misleading. He lacked those aids to arriving at the facts which archæological research has brought to light since his day. Perhaps, too, he lacked to some extent that rare analytical faculty for weighing evidence with tedious minuteness and for making nice distinctions which historians ever and anon are forced to put into requisition.

Prescott marks an epoch in American historical writing. His predecessors' works constitute a veritable valley of dry bones. But Prescott broke with the traditions which the bald chroniclers had followed, when he began to write his "Ferdinand and Isabella," and himself followed the lead of Washington Irving, who blazed out the path of romance in American letters. Moreover, Prescott left the beaten track in the selection of a subject for investigation and chose a period for his historical writing which is by nature romantic and which, therefore, readily lends itself to imaginative treatment. The age of Ferdinand and Isabella is a period of history which appeals strongly to the imagination and the theme itself is naturally inspiring and invites attention. Though a foreign subject, it is more picturesque and attractive than any purely American theme which the author might have selected for his narrative powers. Besides, Prescott was especially fitted for this kind of work. It was his ambition from youth to lead a literary life, and he resolved to fashion that life after the model of Gibbon, the great English historian of the "Decline and Fall."

Prescott was born of a distinguished family in the quaint old New England town of Salem, in 1796. He was graduated at Harvard, where his father before him was graduated. Young Prescott inherited an ample fortune, so that he was relieved of the necessity of working for his bread. This is an important fact in his career. For only a man of considerable wealth could have carried out Prescott's ambition of writing an epoch-making history, which entailed so great a draft on his purse not only for collecting the necessary documents and data, but also for maintaining himself while he was engaged in writing his historical works. Prescott early conceived the idea of writing history and spared no pains or expense to equip himself thoroughly for his chosen field of labor. Unfortunately, while at college he sustained the irreparable loss of one eye, which proved a most serious handicap to him the remainder of his life, for the injury soon extended to the other eye, and he was rendered almost totally blind. Yet, despite this deplorable drawback, he resolutely followed out his life purpose; and by the services of readers and secretaries whom he employed he was enabled to read through a vast collection of historical literature bearing on the period selected. By means of a "noctograph"—a blind man's writing machine—he even wrote himself, thus facilitating the progress of his work.

After determining definitely upon the period of his historical investigation, Prescott not only collected all the authorities touching his theme, to be had in this country, but he even employed secretaries to make copies of all relevant historical documents to be found in the various European libraries. In this manner he acquired and brought together such a vast mass of historical data on his chosen theme as no other American historian before him had ever done on any subject. This material he studied most assiduously, pondering over it by day and by night, until he thoroughly mastered his subject.

The first fruit of Prescott's facile and graphic pen was his "History of the Reign of Ferdinand and Isabella, the Catholic," published in three volumes, in 1837. This was the finished product of ten years of incessant toil and study. The author was happy in the choice of his theme and equally happy in its treatment. The subject, Spain in her palmiest days, was suggested to the author by the influence and power of that now decadent empire upon the New World. It was an unexplored domain to American historians and for this reason was invested with all the interest of novelty.

The history assuredly does not seem to be the work of a man practically blind. Nor does the author's blindness appear to have had any effect upon his clearness of intellectual vision, or upon his concise expression of thought. On the con-

trary, Prescott's loss of sight seems to have contributed to make his faculty of observation all the
keener and more accurate, just as the loss of one of
the five senses is said to cause the remaining four
to be more highly developed.   He evidently possessed an inner light which was not in the least impaired by the loss of his physical sight.   This
history showed Prescott also to be in the possession
of a marvelous power of assimilation of facts as
well as of a strikingly imaginative cast of mind.
It is not surprising, therefore, that this maiden effort of a patient and careful historian took rank at
once with the best histories of the kind in the English tongue.   The work was everywhere regarded a
brilliant achievement and shed lustre upon American scholarship and research.

His "Ferdinand and Isabella" was no sooner
issued from the press than Prescott set himself a
similar task no less bold and arduous.   This was
his scholarly "History of the Conquest of Mexico,"
which appeared in 1843.   This theme grew quite
naturally out of the Ferdinand and Isabella age
already treated.   Just as the first work covered the
period of Spanish history from 1469 to the time of
Columbus, so this second work was designed to continue the story from the age of the famous discoverer down to the year 1519, which Cortez signalized by his conquest of Mexico.   The period of Spanish history embraced in the life of Columbus,
Washington Irving had already treated very fully
in his "Columbus."   Indeed, Irving was now indus-
triously collecting material for a history of the conquest of Mexico, which he contemplated writing,
when he learned of Prescott's intention of treating
the same subject.   Irving thereupon gracefully
retired from the field in favor of Prescott, who, with

all due appreciation of the former's magnanimity, prosecuted his plan with the utmost diligence and care. The result was a piece of historical work which the scholarly world greeted with loud acclaims of praise.

Prescott's last complete work was his "History of the Conquest of Peru," published in 1847. This continued the early Spanish-American annals down to the year 1530. Immediately after the completion of this treatise Prescott undertook his "History of the Reign of Philip the Second," which he never finished. It is a well-known story how the elder historian, when he learned that young Motley had begun work on his kindred theme, the Rise of the Dutch Republic against Philip the Second in 1572, generously resigned his subject in favor of his junior, although he had already published three volumes of the history. Truly, as Ogden, Prescott's recent biographer, observes, this was a fine example of passing on the torch of learning.

The "Philip the Second" was designed to cover the period from 1555 to 1598. The ground was afterward covered by Motley, but from a different point of view, in his "Rise of the Dutch Republic." This naturally forms an interesting episode in the field of historical investigation which our author had staked off for himself before his sudden and untimely end. It will be seen on examination that Prescott thus covered in his historical work that dramatic and inspiring period of Spanish history, from 1469 to 1598. Those were the days when Spain enjoyed her greatest splendor and prestige as a nation; and Prescott has merited our gratitude for giving us a very graphic and picturesque description both of the domestic affairs of that great monarchy and of its relations to the New World,

during that era of her ascendency. Thus viewed in
its entirety, the work of our author is seen to possess, therefore, a unity and a completeness which,
to the casual reader, is not readily apparent.

Prescott was an indefatigable worker. He allowed himself but little respite from labor from the
time he began his "Ferdinand and Isabella" down to
the day of his sudden death in 1859. As soon as
one stupendous task was finished, another was begun without intermission. After the completion
of his "History of the Conquest of Peru," however,
he did make a brief visit to Europe before beginning
his "Philip the Second." Perhaps it was his habit
of unbroken toil and study that hastened his end.
If he had husbanded his strength and allowed the
bow to unbend oftener, it is not improbable that he
might have lived to enjoy a green old age. But
such was his untiring industry and contempt of
ease that he was loth to relax his studies even upon
the warning note nature sounded for him in the
slight stroke of paralysis he sustained the year before his death. For during those days, despite his
constant suffering from his inveterate enemy rheumatism, he taxed his diminishing strength with the
labor of preparing a new edition of Robertson's
"Charles the Fifth" and a brief biography of
Charles Brockden Brown. Even a few weeks before
his demise he collected a number of miscellanies,
his annual contributions to the *North American Review,* and published them in book form.

It is now time for us to weigh Prescott critically,
if we may, and to make an effort to determine his
place in American literature. Is he really entitled
to be counted among the makers of our literature?
The answer to this question ought, in our judgment,

to be in the affirmative; the reasons will be found in the following paragraphs.

Prescott enjoys the distinction of being the first American historian to write with a charm and grace of style to repay the reader's attention. Unlike his predecessors, he is, in no sense, a mere chronicler who gives the barest record of facts. He is infinitely removed from those annalists who seem studiously to avoid all rhetorical embellishment for fear it may enhance the value of their work as literature. Prescott harked back to the traditions of history writing as practiced by such historians as Gibbon and Macaulay, whom he took as his models. Moreover, he brought to his congenial task a pen that did not scrupulously eschew the attractiveness of a polished literary style; but, on the contrary, he deemed it worth while to impart a certain charm to the expression of the facts of history. Besides, he saw his subject with a poetic imagination and so presented it in his pages. He taxed his powers to portray the departed glory and magnificence of that gorgeous Spanish civilization of the sixteenth century, and we may believe that that ancient grandeur and splendor of Spain are adequately reflected in the narratives he bequeathed us for the enrichment of our literature. He totally rejected the theory now prevalent that the historian must utterly repress the imagination and must spurn all the devices of rhetoric and the graces of style, presenting in his record the simple, unadorned facts.

Prescott's writing is of the class known as "grand." Yet it is not the ordinary "fine writing," which is wearisome and even tawdry. It possesses some quality that redeems it from the charge of being grandiose. Prescott's style and manner are very much like Macaulay's, though less dramatic

and less rhetorical.   Prescott appears to have been
an ardent admirer of the great English stylist and
was consciously or unconsciously under his influence in forming his own literary style.   One notices
in Prescott, as in Macaulay, though to a less extent
in the former, a similar attempt at contrast and
parallel and other tricks of rhetoric resorted to by
stylists, to heighten the effect.   It is to be said to
the credit of the American historian that he does
not sin as egregiously in this respect as the illustrious English historian does.

However, this manner of writing is not the
fashion to-day, and the twentieth century reader is
therefore, disposed to tire somewhat of Prescott's
gorgeous imagery and romantic descriptions, just as
he tires of Macaulay's pictured page with its ever-
recurring contrast, balance and period.   But
fashion is a fickle and capricious goddess, and her
votaries are never compelled to follow one decree
for long.   Who knows when the manner of historical writing practiced by Macaulay and Prescott
may again come into vogue and be in favor?   Then
our present-day ideals in literary style may be considered antiquated and *passé*.

Yet it is very evident that Prescott lacked a certain reserve.   His imagination strikes one as being
rather exuberant, and his flights of fancy in his descriptive passages seem here and there not to be
entirely under control.   The author lacks in a
measure that restraint which inspires absolute confidence in his narrative.   His rivals Motley, Parkman and Bancroft show themselves somewhat superior in this particular.   It is perhaps this lack of
restraint, this exuberance of fancy, that explains in
large measure Prescott's partial loss of favor with
present-day historians.   This is the penalty he has

had to pay for the bold manner in which he painted
his vivid portraits.   As an artist he could not paint
a miniature.   He required a large canvas and relied
for his effect, not upon sharpness of definition or
distinctness of outline, but upon his brilliant coloring.   The psychological explanation of this defect
of our author is to be found, perhaps, in his physical
infirmity of loss of sight.   Anent the effect of this
affliction upon the historian's style, his biographer
Ticknor remarks that Prescott's personality went
into his books because of his loss of sight, in consequence of which he was forced to ponder long and
then to address his readers with the voice, as it
were, and not with the pen.

"His infirmity," continues Ticknor, whom it is
worth while to quote here as throwing light on Prescott's method of composition,—"His infirmity was
a controlling influence, and is to be counted among
the secrets of a manner which has been found at
once so simple and so charming.   He was compelled
to prepare everything, down to the smallest details,
in his memory, and to correct and fashion it all
while it was still held there in silent suspense; after
which he wrote it down, by means of his noctograph,
in the freest and boldest manner, without any opportunity really to change the phraseology as he went
along, and with little power to alter or modify it afterwards.   This, I doubt not, was the principal
cause of the strength, as well as of the grace, ease
and attractiveness of his style.   It gave a life, a
freshness, a freedom, both to his thoughts and to his
mode of expressing them.   .   .   .   He was able
to carry what was equal to sixty pages of printed
matter in his memory for many days, correcting and
finishing its stlye as he walked or rode or drove for

his daily exercise. In 1839, therefore, after going carefully over the whole ground, he said, 'My conclusion is, that the reader may take my style for better or for worse, as it now is.' And to this conclusion he wisely adhered. His manner became, perhaps, a little freer and easier, from continued practice, and from the confidence that success necessarily brings with it, but in essential elements and characteristics it was never changed.''

As for Prescott's historical method, it need hardly be remarked, as has been previously stated, that it is unlike the approved method of research now in vogue. In the first half of the last century it was not the custom for the investigator in the realm of history to go back to the original sources as it is the custom to-day. But Prescott deserves credit for the painstaking and untiring efforts he put forth in order to get at the original documents. However, he did not discriminate as carefully as he ought to have done, the critics tell us, and he did not write history with the absolute accuracy and exactness demanded by the present standard. But his method is the fault of his times, rather than his individual fault. It was the method of the foremost historians of his age, such as Gibbon and Milman. According to that method, the historian clothed his subject with a romantic interest and presented it with an adornment of rhetoric and a charm of style which are tabooed by twentieth century historians as out of harmony with the true spirit of history. The truth is, the ideals of the historian a century ago were, to an appreciable degree, pictorial and literary, not scientific and psychological, as they are to-day. Because of the change that has taken place in the last century in the aim and object of writing history, therefore, and as a logical result of the shifting of ideals, Prescott's fame as an historian is in a temporary eclipse at present.

Still, another word is to be said. Not only is Prescott open to criticism on the score of excessive rhetorical embellishment in which he compromised somewhat scientific accuracy, but he also shows a lack of that power of analysis which is demanded to-day of a writer of history. He fails to meet successfully the test of a philosophical explanation of the causes of events, and in this failure he falls below the highest type of historian. But at this juncture one feels tempted to demur and to raise the question whether there are not several different schools of history. Now, Prescott belongs to the classical school. This being so, it is evidently not quite fair to judge him by the exacting standards of scientific research. The scientific method, no doubt, is better adapted to ascertaining the actual facts of history and, for this reason, is to be preferred to the antiquated methods in use a century ago. Yet the methods of the classical school are not to be lightly condemned and brushed aside as having no claim on our respect and attention. For the historians of that school, under the inspiration of their ideals, produced works of merit which are both an honor to the methods they followed and a noble and enduring monument, as mere literature, to English and American scholarship. Is it not more just, then, to judge Prescott by the standards of the classical school of history and to compare him with the writers of his class—Parkman, Motley and Bancroft?

Compared with the leading American historians of the romantic school, Prescott, it must be conceded, fully holds his own. For his reputation has not yet been eclipsed by any of these, and his star shines with its accustomed lustre in that brilliant constellation of our American historians. But he challenges comparison not only with the best American historians of his age. He even suggests comparison with the great classical historians of England and France—Gibbon and Michelet. Prescott still has hosts of admiring readers on both sides of the Atlantic. Through his pages the reader still beholds with unfeigned pleasure the imperial palaces of Spanish monarchs of a forgotten age and, under the spell of his guidance, roams over enchanted ground where men and women of that romantic period lived, moved and had their being. The critics tell us that of all our American historians Prescott is the one most acceptable to the British reading public to-day. It is a matter of record that when his works first appeared, the English people seemed to vie with the Americans in doing the author honor.

But waiving Prescott's renown as a historical investigator which the critics admit is sufficient to rank him among the first of his class, and considering his work in the light of literature simply, one is forced to the conclusion that the writer enjoys high and enviable esteem. Yet the style and the subject are so indissolubly united in this man of letters that one can not consider him as a man of letters merely without considering him, at the same time, as a historian. Whatever the disparagers of his method may say, it is a significant fact that no English or American author has yet ventured to rewrite the period of Spanish-American history which Prescott has portrayed with so much romantic interest and grace of style. Surely it is no small achievement to have written the lives of Ferdinand and Isabella and of Philip the Second, and to have told the story of the conquest of Mexico and the conquest of Peru in such a manner as to have made the field peculiarly one's own and to have discouraged others from attempting to cover the same ground. This fact ought to compensate, in large measure, for Prescott's waning prestige as a historical investigator, and ought to furnish ample evidence, if evidence is needed, of the substantial trustworthiness and fidelity of his attractive narrative. This, too, may be regarded as proof positive that there is nothing superficial, nothing sensational in his work; otherwise the field would have been a crying invitation to some modern investigator for a fresh treatment of the subject. It is this virtue of essential accuracy as an historian which combines with his positive excellence as a prose artist that places Prescott among the literary leaders of America and establishes his position as one of the makers of our national literature.

PRESCOTT

CONQUEST OF PERU (INTRODUCTION)

Of the numerous nations which occupied the great
American continent at the time of its discovery by the
Europeans, the two most advanced in power and refine-
ment were undoubtedly those of Mexico and Peru. But,
though resembling one another in extent of civilization,
they differed widely as to the nature of it; and the
philosophical student of his species may feel a natural
curiosity to trace the different steps by which these two
nations strove to emerge from the state of barbarism,
and place themselves on a higher point in the scale of
humanity. In a former work I have endeavored to
exhibit the institutions and character of the ancient
Mexicans, and the story of their conquest by the Spaniards. The present will be devoted to the Peruvians;
and, if their history shall be found to present less
strange anomalies and striking contrasts than that of
the Aztecs, it may interest us quite as much by the
pleasing picture it offers of a well-regulated government and sober habits of industry under the patriarchal sway of the Incas.

The empire of Peru, at the period of the Spanish invasion, stretched along the Pacific from about the second degree north to the thirty-seventh degree of south
latitude; a line, also, which describes the western
boundaries of the modern republics of Ecuador, Peru,
Bolivia and Chili. Its breadth can not so easily be
determined; for, though bounded everywhere by the
great ocean on the west, towards the east it spreads out,
in many parts, considerably beyond the mountains, to
the confines of barbarous states, whose exact position
is undetermined, or whose names are effaced from the

map of history. It is certain, however, that its breadth was altogether disproportioned to its length.

The topographical aspect of the country is very remarkable. A strip of land, rarely exceeding twenty leagues in width, runs along the coast, and is hemmed in through its whole extent by a colossal range of mountains, which, advancing from the Straits of Magellan, reaches its highest elevation, indeed, the highest on the American continent—about the seventeenth degree south, and after crossing the line, gradually subsides into hills of inconsiderable magnitude, as it enters the Isthmus of Panama. This is the famous Cordillera of the Andes, or "copper mountains," as termed by the natives, though they might with more reason have been called "mountains of gold." Arranged sometimes in a single line, though more frequently in two or three lines running parallel or obliquely to each other, they seem to the voyager on the ocean but one continuous chain; while the huge volcanoes, which to the inhabitants of the table-land look like solitary and independent masses, appear to him only like so many peaks of the same vast and magnificent range. So immense is the scale on which Nature works in these regions, that it is only when viewed from a great distance, that the spectator can, in any degree, comprehend the relation of the several parts to the stupendous whole. Few of the works of Nature, indeed, are calculated to produce impressions of higher sublimity than the aspect of this coast, as it is gradually unfolded to the eye of the mariner sailing on the distant waters of the Pacific; where mountain is seen to rise above mountain, and Chimborazo, with its glorious canopy of snow, glittering far above the clouds, crowns the whole as with a celestial diadem.

The face of the country would appear to be peculiarly unfavorable to the purposes both of agriculture and of internal communication. The sandy strip along the coast, where rain rarely falls, is fed only by a few scanty streams that furnish a remarkable contrast to the vast volumes of water which roll down the eastern sides of the Cordilleras into the Atlantic. The precipitous steeps of the sierra, with its splintered sides of porphyry and granite, and its higher regions wrapped in snows that never melt under the fierce sun of the equator, unless it be from the desolating action of its own volcanic fires, might seem equally unpropitious to the labors of the husbandman. And all communication between the parts of the long-extended territory might be thought to be precluded by the savage character of the region, broken up by precipices, furious torrents, and impassable *quebradas,*—those hideous rents in the mountain chain, whose depths the eye of the terrified traveller, as he winds along his aerial pathway, vainly endeavors to fathom. Yet the industry, we might almost say, the genius, of the Indian was sufficient to overcome all these impediments of Nature.

By a judicious system of canals and subterraneous aqueducts, the waste places on the coast were refreshed by copious streams, that clothed them in fertility and beauty. Terraces were raised on the steep sides of the Cordillera; and, as the different elevations had the effect of difference of latitude, they exhibited in regular gradation every variety of vegetable form, from the stimulated growth of the tropics, to the temperate products of a northern clime; while flocks of llamas—the Peruvian sheep—wandered with their shepherds over the broad, snow-covered wastes on the crests of the sierra, which rose beyond the limits of cultivation. An industrious population settled along the lofty regions of the plateaus, and towns and hamlets, clustering amidst orchards and wide-spreading gardens, seemed suspended in the air far above the ordinary elevation of the clouds. Intercourse was maintained between these numerous settlements by means of the great roads which traversed the mountain passes, and opened an easy communication between the capital and the remotest extremities of the empire.

The source of this civilization is traced to the valley of Cuzco, the central region of Peru, as the name implies. The origin of the Peruvian empire, like the origin of all nations, except the very few which, like our own, have had the good fortune to date from a civilized period and people, is lost in the mists of fable, which, in fact, have settled as darkly round its history as round that of any nation, ancient or modern, in the Old World. According to the tradition most familiar to the European scholar, the time was, when the ancient races of the continent were all plunged in deplorable barbarism; when they worshipped nearly every object in nature indiscriminately; made war their pastime, and feasted on the flesh of their slaughtered captives. The Sun, the great luminary and parent of mankind, taking compassion on their degraded condition, sent two of his children, Manco Capac and Mama Oello Huanco, to gather the natives into communities, and teach them the arts of civilized life. The celestial pair, brother and sister, husband and wife, advanced along the high plains in the neighborhood of Lake Titicaca, to about the sixteenth degree south. They bore with them a golden wedge, and were directed to take up their residence on the spot where the sacred emblem should without effort sink into the ground. They proceeded accordingly but a short distance, as far as the valley Cuzco, the spot indicated by the performance of the miracle, since there the wedge speedily sank into the earth and disappeared forever. Here the children of the Sun established their residence, and soon entered upon their beneficent mission among the rude inhabitants of the country; Manco Capac teaching the men the arts of agriculture, and Mama Oello initiating her own sex in the mysteries of weaving and spinning. The simple people lent a willing ear to the messengers of Heaven, and, gathering together in considerable numbers, laid the foundation of the city of Cuzco. The same wise and benevolent maxims, which regulated the conduct of the first Incas, descended to their successors, and under their mild scepter a community gradually extended itself along the broad surface of the table-land, which asserted its superiority over the surrounding tribes. Such is the pleasing picture of the origin of the Peruvian monarchy, as portrayed by Garcilasco de la Vega, the descendant of the Incas, and through him made familiar to the European reader.

But this tradition is one of several current among the Peruvian Indians, and probably not the one most generally received. Another legend speaks of certain white and bearded men, who, advancing from the shores of Lake Titicaca, established an ascendency over the natives, and imparted to them the blessings of civilization. It may remind us of the tradition existing among the Aztecs in respect to Quetzalcoatl, the good deity, who with a similar garb and aspect came up the great plateau from the east on a like benevolent mission to the natives. The analogy is the more remarkable, as there is no trace of any communication with, or even knowledge of, each other to be found in the two nations.

The date usually assigned for these extraordinary events was about four hundred years before the coming of the Spaniards, or early in the twelfth century. But however pleasing to the imagination, and however popular, the legend of Manco Capac, it requires but little reflection to show its improbability, even when divested of supernatural accompaniments. On the shores of Lake Titicaca extensive ruins exist at the present day, which the Peruvians themselves acknowledge to be of older date than the pretended advent of the Incas, and to have furnished them with the models of their architecture. The date of their appearance, indeed, is manifestly irreconcilable with their subsequent history. No account assigns the Inca dynasty more than thirteen princes before the Conquest. But this number is altogether too small to have spread over four hundred years, and would not carry back the foundations of the monarchy, on any probable computation beyond two centuries and a half,—an antiquity not incredible in itself, and which, it may be remarked, does not precede by more than half a century the alleged foundation of the capital of Mexico. The fiction of Manco Capac and his sister-wife was devised, no doubt, at a later period, to gratify the vanity of the Peruvian monarchs, and to give additional sanction to their authority by deriving it from a celestial origin.

CHAPTER VII

NATHANIEL HAWTHORNE

Nathaniel Hawthorne was born of excellent family in Salem, Massachusetts, on July 4, 1804. His ancestors for several generations had been sea captains, and one of his uncles had been a privateer in the Revolution. A remote ancestor was a lawyer and a grim judge in some of the witch trials in the seventeenth century. The family was noted for its Puritan characteristics.

Nathaniel's father died when the boy was but four years old, leaving him to be cared for by his mother, a woman of rare beauty and exceptional intellect. But his mother later, for some reason, retired from society and became a complete recluse. So his maternal uncle directed the family matters and superintended young Hawthorne's education. After a year or two spent on his uncle's estate in the wilds of Maine, near Sebago Lake, the boy returned to Salem, where he was prepared for college. He entered Bowdoin College in 1821, and here he had among his mates Horatio Bridge, Longfellow and the youth afterwards known to fame as President Pierce. But Hawthorne's college career was in no respect remarkable. He was fond of the classics, but he showed no exceptional scholarship. He was a desultory reader and liked outdoor sports. He possessed a fine physique and a robust constitution. But he was rather dreamy, extremely sensitive and diffident and did not mingle freely with his college mates.

After his graduation, in 1825, Hawthorne returned to Salem, where, with his mother and two sisters, he led a very secluded life for the next twelve years. He read and wrote much during this period, but he usually destroyed what he wrote. However, he did publish anonymously a sophomoric romance entitled "Fanshawe," and occasionally he contributed an article under an assumed name to some of the periodicals, notably *The Knickerbocker* of New York. But no one took any interest in the stories he published, or read them. Still he continued to write, though at times he felt keenly the lack of appreciation, on the part of the reading public, of his literary efforts. Finally, a young lady living near him identified him as the author of "The Gentle Boy," a sketch which had appeared in *The Token,* published by S. G. Goodrich. A few years later Hawthorne became engaged to the sister of this young lady; and after a brief experiment of the new Brook Farm Community, he married his fiancée, Miss Sophia Peabody, and took up his residence at the Old Manse, at Concord.

Hawthorne's friends now secured for him an appointment as surveyor in the Salem custom-house, and partly from his salary and partly from the receipts from his writings he published, he was enabled to provide for the material wants of his family. In the introduction to "The Scarlet Letter" he gives us a brief sketch of his official life. In 1849 he lost his position. Yet he continued his literary work with all the greater industry and ardor. Before 1849 he had already published four volumes of short stories, under the title "Twice-told Tales" and "Mosses from an Old Manse," in addition to some historical and biographical sketches entitled "Grandfather's Chair" and "Snow Image, and

Other Stories." "The Scarlet Letter" appeared in 1850, and then, successively, the "House of the Seven Gables," "The Blithedale Romance," "The Wonder Book," and "Tanglewood Tales," all within the next three years.

Hawthorne was a staunch Democrat, and when his college mate, Franklin Pierce, was a candidate for the Presidency he of course supported him ardently, even writing a campaign biography of the candidate. In return for his services, President Pierce appointed Hawthorne consul at Liverpool, England, in 1853. Accordingly, Hawthorne removed to England, where he spent several years. Before his term of office expired he resigned his consulship and crossed the Channel, on a prolonged visit to France and Italy. Returning to England in 1859, he wrote his romance, the "Marble Faun," and the following year sailed for his native land.

On his arrival in America, Hawthorne settled at The Wayside, a small estate he owned at Concord. Here he resumed his pen and began work on a new romance; but his disquietude from the Civil War and his failing health compelled him to put aside the undertaking for the nonce. Later he published a volume of sketches of his English experiences, under the title "Our Old Home." Once more he took up the romance and published two instalments of it in *The Atlantic*. This was the last production of his pen which he ever saw in print. For he died suddenly in the spring of 1864, while traveling in New Hampshire, in search of health, his old friend Franklin Pierce being with him when the end came. His "Septimus, a Romance," "American Note-Books," "English Note-Books," "French and Italian Note-Books" and "Doctor Grimshaw's Secret" all appeared after his death.

So much for Hawthorne's career. Now as to a review of his writings.

In one of his "Twice-told Tales" (The Ambitious Guest) Hawthorne speaks of the hero of his story as possessing a high and abstracted ambition. Says the author, referring to the eponymous hero:

Yearning desire had been transformed to hope, and hope, long cherished, had become like certainty that, obscurely as he journed now, a glory was to beam on all his pathway, though not perhaps while he was treading it. But when posterity should gaze back into the gloom of what was now the present, they would trace the brightness of his footsteps, brightening as meaner glories faded, and confess that a gifted one had passed from his cradle to his tomb with none to recognize him.

This passage is usually understood as autobiographical, and as containing a prediction of the appreciation and distinction which the author's works were some day destined to enjoy. If this interpretation is correct, and the passage is an illusion to the writer himself, it gives an interesting glimpse into Hawthorne's feelings and aspirations during that long, uneventful period of twelve years' isolation and seclusion which, after his graduation from Bowdoin College, he spent in the quaint old town of Salem. Dwelling apart in his self-imposed isolation, "the world forgetting and the world forgot," he perhaps felt a lack of human sympathy and public appreciation of his literary work. But disheartened he was not. He had faith in himself and in his work, and believed that if for some reason or other his contemporaries failed to accord him the appreciation which was his due, succeeding generations at least would vote him his well-deserved meed of praise.

But Hawthorne had misjudged the American public. He was not "to pass from his cradle to his tomb with none to recognize him"; nor was he destined to die unhonored and unappreciated. His twelve years of retirement at Salem had made him well-nigh morbid, though by nature he was social and friendly. From the quiet old Massachusetts town he saw the world through the eyes of a recluse, and to his blurred and perverted vision the world appeared gloomy and uninviting. But it was not so dismal and gloomy as it appeared; the gloom was subjective. A brighter day was soon to dawn, which should dispel the mist and gloom. That day came with the publication of the "Twice-told Tales." The long period of seclusion which Hawthorne spent at Salem was now at an end, but it had served a useful purpose. It was the uneventful period of incubation in which unawares the young author was developing his latent possibilities, and acquiring additional resources. It was the wilderness period in which he was silently gathering strength to be used as a reserve force to meet the demands which were soon to be made upon his genius and art. It was a time of meditation as well as a time of growth and development. But to young Hawthorne, eager for literary honors, the time seemed tedious and almost unending. Referring to it some years later in a letter to a friend, he says of these dreary days of waiting: "I am disposed to thank God for the gloom and chill of my early life, in the hope that my share of adversity came then, when I bore it alone." And again in his "English Note-Books":

My early life was perhaps a good preparation for the declining half of life; it having been such a blank that any thereafter would compare favorably with it. For

a long, long while, I have occasionally been visited with
a singular dream; and I have an impression I have
dreamed it ever since I have been in England. It is,
that I am still at college, or sometimes even at school—
and there is a sense that I have been there unconscionably long, and have quite failed to make such progress
as my contemporaries have done; and I seem to meet
some of them with a feeling of shame and depression
that broods over me as I think of it, even when awake.
This dream, recurring all through these twenty or thirty
years, must be one of the effects of that heavy seclusion
in which I shut myself up for twelve years after leaving
college, when everybody moved onward and left me behind. How strange that it should come now, when I
may call myself famous and prosperous!—when I am
happy too.

In his firm resolution to adopt the profession of
letters at whatever cost, Hawthorne furnished signal proof of his rare courage and deep, abiding conviction. For in the forties of the last century that
profession was far from lucrative; and very few
men dared to court the privation and invite the *res
angusti domi* which an exclusively literary career in
those days invariably involved. Our people did not
read books, and especially fiction, then as they do
now. Prior to the Civil War no work of fiction,
however popular it might be, ever reached such phe-
nomenally large sales as some of our recent American novels have attained. Consequently it was rare
that a man devoted himself exclusively to literary
pursuits. Hawthorne from New England and Poe
from the South are the only two noteworthy instances, in those times, of men who had the
exceptional courage and love for letters to follow
exclusively a literary career. Of course there were
many who wrote for publication, but they did not

depend upon their literary work for a livelihood. They engaged in literary pursuits as an avocation rather than as a vocation. As for that matter, however, not even Hawthorne was entirely dependent upon the income from his pen for a living; for he held a federal appointment in Salem, his native town, and was subsequently appointed by his old college-mate, President Pierce, to a lucrative post abroad.

But Hawthorne, as already intimated, had resolutely made up his mind to devote himself to the profession of letters, to become an author; and though at first, before fortune began to smile upon him, disappointment only was his lot, yet he did not become discouraged, or feel that he had mistaken his calling. He persevered in the unremunerative line of work he had marked out for himself, till at length he arrested the attention of a reluctant and unsympathetic reading public and achieved a brilliant success. In his preface to the "Twice-told Tales" he admits that "for many years he was the obscurest man of letters in America," and in a sad tone verging on despair he asks the question, "Was there ever such delay in obtaining recognition?" But recognition had at last come, and with it ample compensation and reward for those long, dreary months and years of waiting.

Hawthorne's early career as a man of letters does not offer anything particularly attractive. It was no flowery path he trod. He tells us of the difficulties he encountered in having his tales published. Publisher after publisher, in chilling succession, declined his manuscript; and he had all the disappointments to face which usually fall to the lot of an unknown writer aspiring after literary fame. In the preface to the second edition of the "Twice-told

Tales," published in 1851, he says that "he had no incitement to literary effort in a reasonable prospect of reputation or profit; nothing but the pleasure itself of composition, an enjoyment not at all amiss in its way, and perhaps essential to the merit of the work in hand, but which in the long run will hardly keep the chill out of the writer's heart, or the numbness out of his fingers." But disappointment, no matter how bitter, did not sour him or make a cynic of him. Such was his equable temperament, and such his sunny disposition, that adversity did not greatly depress him nor prosperity unduly elate him. Yet he was not an optimist. The fact is, as Henry James says, Hawthorne cannot strictly be called either an optimist or a pessimist. His philosophy of life, if he may be said to have had one, was somewhere between these two extremes. We cannot concur in the judgment of the French critic, M. Emile Montégut, who speaks of Hawthorne as a *romancier pessimiste*.

But it is time to speak of our author's works. Hawthorne made his first bid for fame, as has been said, in his "Twice-told Tales." This book is a charming collection of stories. We should have to search English literature far and wide in order to find a collection of tales that surpasses these in spontaneity, finish, and technical execution. As the author himself said of them:

They are not the talk of a secluded man with his own mind and heart (had it been so, they could hardly have failed to be more deeply and permanently valuable), but his attempts to open an intercourse with the world.

This collection was soon followed by another, similar in plan and character, which for convenience of treatment may be mentioned here. This of course is "Mosses from an Old Manse." In his preface to these stories Hawthorne says somewhat apologetically:

These fitful sketches, with so little of external life about them, yet claiming no profundity of purpose—so reserved even while they sometimes seem so frank— often but half in earnest, and never, even when most so, expressing satisfactorily the thoughts which they profess to image—such trifles, I truly feel, afford no solid basis for a literary reputation.

These tales possess a rare charm and beauty, suffused with a soft glow of imagination, which combines with their freshness and piquancy to make them all the more engaging and fascinating. Here and there we find a touch of weirdness and grotesqueness after the manner of Poe. Witness, for example, "The Minister's Black Veil," "The Birthmark," "Roger Malvin's Burial," and "Rappicini's Daughter." It is not meant by this to suggest any trace of borrowing. Hawthorne and Poe were entirely independent, and each original.

Hawthorne's stories will be found upon examination to divide themselves into three classes, each of a different type. In the first class are included the stories of fantasy and allegory, as for example, "The Great Carbuncle," "The Seven Vagabonds," and "The Threefold Destiny." These enjoy the distinction of being the author's most original stories; and of this class those two masterpieces "Malvin's Burial" and "Rappicini's Daughter" are unquestionably the best. These, together with "Young Goodman Brown," which is almost as fine, are among the best of their kind in American literature, and are perhaps unsurpassed in the entire range of

English literature. The second class, which falls
but little below the first in interest and artistic finish, is of a somewhat historical character, being
made up mostly of tales of New England history.
Among this group may be mentioned "The Gray
Champion," "The Maypole of Merry Mount," and
those beautiful legends of "The Province House."
The third class is composed of brief sketches of
local scenes, objects, and customs, such as, "A Rill
from the Town Pump," "The Village Uncle," "The
Toll-gatherer's Daughter," and so forth. These,
while possessing rare grace and beauty, are not
quite so clever or imaginative, and do not exhibit
the same degree of skill in conception and execution,
as the other two groups. One feels that if by any un-
toward accident all of Hawthorne's works were
blotted out of existence except these tales, they
alone would be sufficient to reveal to the world their
author's genius and that distinctive quality of romantic imagination which the critics call Haw-
thornesque. These stories all exhibit a considerable
degree of spontaneity, piquancy, and naturalness of
fancy, and, withal, that high moral tone which is a
marked characteristic of Hawthorne's writings. It
is this last-named quality, especially, by which
Hawthorne betrays his Puritan ancestry. He inherited from his Puritan ancestors a conscience
exceedingly sensitive to sin. But along with this
inherited gift he possessed a vivid imagination,
which relieved by its light, airy touch the heavy
moral responsibility his Puritan heritage would inevitably have imposed upon his genius. Consequently the conscience, which is so clearly manifest
in Hawthorne's numerous stories dealing with the
sense of sin and its effects upon the life of man, is
prevented by his robust imagination from serving

as a clog upon his genius to weigh down and oppress his spirit; and thus the depressing effect of the sense of moral obliquity is forestalled, or thwarted. And what might have been a dull, heavy story, written simply to point a moral, is transformed by the romantic imagination into a light, graceful fancy of exceptional beauty and cleverness. Hawthorne's romantic imagination therefore saved him from his grim Puritan conscience, of which he might otherwise have become a haunted victim.

In the "Scarlet Letter" Hawthorne made his first attempt at a long story; and he scored a success as lasting and far-reaching as it was brilliant. Like Byron upon the publication of "Childe Harold," Hawthorne awoke to find himself famous. The fascinating romance heralded the author's fame abroad and served to give it an enduring foundation at home. The book still continues to be read, and is counted among the finest examples of American fiction. The treatment of the theme furnishes a conspicuous illustration of the genius of Hawthorne. The theme itself is naturally a vulgar and repulsive subject—the sin of adultery. But not withstanding this fact, there is nothing repellent or even indelicate in the book, nothing which would require it to be placed on the *index expurgatorius*, or to be forbidden to boys and girls. So far is the story from containing any offensive passages that there is perhaps not a purer piece of fiction to be found in all English literature. The author displayed his sound moral judgment and innate good taste in selecting out of the possible aspects of his theme that aspect which lends itself most readily to wholesome literary treatment. He therefore passes over in silence the prurient subject of the commission of the sin, as that could subserve no spiritual purpose. Your modern realist would have been disposed to give this considerable prominence. But Hawthorne, with his innate good taste, selected for his narrative the interesting theme of the consequences of the sinful act upon the natures of the actors. Closely allied with this theme, though subordinate, is the method adopted by society for the punishment of the woman, together with the effect of the silent guilt upon the hypocritical minister who is tortured by a guilty conscience, and yet, from fear of the pending disgrace and shame, lacks the courage to confess his crime. The author develops this idea very elaborately by numerous artistic devices which add much to the interest of the story. The most notable of these is the scarlet letter, which he handles with consummate skill and effect. This in the hands of an inferior artist would have proved a serious handicap, if indeed it would not have deteriorated into sheer bathos. In Hawthorne's hands, however, this symbol contributes vastly to the dramatic interest of the story by suggesting impressions almost too delicate to be expressed in words.

The "Scarlet Letter" is not a bright or cheerful novel, despite the fact that the interest never lags and is sustained throughout from cover to cover. On the contrary, it is dark, gloomy, and somber. Henry James says of it: "It is densely dark, with a single spot of vivid color in it; and it will probably long remain the most consistently gloomy of English novels of the first order." But though somber and sad, it is yet a fine piece of imaginative work, and is generally conceded to be its author's masterpiece. Nothing produced in American literature prior to 1860 surpassed it; and, indeed, but few novels published before or after that date have equaled it. Though usually denominated a romance, the book is in no sense an ordinary love story. The chief characters are Hester Prynne and Arthur Dimmesdale, and, except in the latter part of the story, the interest settles around Dimmesdale. Little Pearl, the unique child of their illicit union, is the most original character of the book. She is a distinctively new creation, and occupies a place peculiarly her own in English fiction. Hawthorne shows a high degree of dramatic skill in the pungent, racy interplay of Pearl and her mother. Chillingworth, the injured husband, is made a somewhat unnatural minor character, and however ingeniously conceived, he is yet felt to be a mere accessory figure. Nor does he enlist our sympathies in his behalf, as would naturally be expected of an outraged husband. Far from enlisting our sympathies, by his intriguing and malignant arts in preying, vampire-like, upon the miserable, conscience-tortured minister, Chillingworth becomes downright offensive to us, and we almost detest him. We sympathize rather with the sinning, suffering minister than with the perfidious, injured husband. The wretched minister carries the secret guilt of his own fall from purity in his breast, and the consciousness of this sin gnaws at his very vitals. Yet to the outside world he is forced to live above reproach, and thus he adds, almost perforce, the heinous sin of hypocrisy to his already guilt-burdened, sin-sick soul.

The "Scarlet Letter" is a true product of colonial New England. The book smacks of the soil, and was, so to say, written by one to the manner born. The story could hardly have been written by an author born outside of Puritan Massachusetts. It has the earmarks all through it which betray the locality of its origin. Not that it has any very decided or unmistakable local coloring, and yet it has considerable local coloring; nor that it abounds in provincial locutions, or is written in the Yankee dialect, like Lowell's famous "Biglow Papers." On the contrary, the language of Hawthorne's romance is strikingly pure and chaste; in a word, it is classic. But the conception as well as the entire setting of the book is Puritan; and from lid to lid it is impregnated with Puritan ideas and breathes the Puritan spirit. Dimmesdale, the leading character of the story, is preëminently a Puritan creation. The *motif* of the book is the old Puritan idea of the consciousness of life with its burdening responsibilities and conscience-tortured victim. This is not intended in the nature of stricture or disparagement of the work. Possessed of the Puritan conscience, which he inherited from his ancestors, Hawthorne conceived the plan of bodying forth a certain moral idea; and he very fittingly gave this idea a Puritan setting and reproduced with masterly art this old-fashioned manner of looking upon the world, with the contemporary types of character now fast fading, if not entirely vanished. As a work of art, however, the book, while on the whole excellent, is not absolutely faultless. It invites criticism in a few particulars. The most serious defect of the book is that the illusion produced is not complete or compelling. In reading the story one feels a sense of unreality about it, a certain degree of exaggeration. The author overstepped the bounds of art in his excessive use of symbolism, as when by a ghastly mystery he makes the symbol of the scarlet letter reveal itself upon the minister's bosom and then emblazon itself in glowing, flashing characters in the

heavens. Moreover, the personages of the romance
are not as individual, real, and lifelike as they might
be. Nor do they act and move upon the page as rapidly and as vividly as could be desired. Yet the
story is entertaining and at times exceedingly dramatic; but the interest lies rather in the situation
than in the action of the characters.

The "House of Seven Gables," Hawthorne's second American novel, is somewhat like the "Scarlet
Letter" in *motif* and setting. The "House of Seven
Gables" is more elaborate, has more dramatic situations, more threads of suggestion, in a word, more
detail, than its predecessor; but it is not so complete. Because of its elaboration, this novel is regarded by some critics as Hawthorne's finest. The
story is a picture of colonial New England. It has
an antique odor about it, an air of bygone days. It
represents a transitional stage in which the old
gives place to the new, the shabby and antiquated to
the fresh and modern. The picture has a soft, mel-
low setting, like a venerable, weather-beaten mansion, in the cool, dense shade of a quiet, drowsy
summer evening.

The characters of the novel are all figures, shadows, not real men and women, though they exhibit a
certain degree of life and action. The most salient
character is a scowling, lemon-faced old spinster,
dismal, simple, tender-hearted, and poverty-stricken
withal, yet unconscionably proud of her pedigree.
In sharp contrast with her is a bright, happy, ingenuous country girl of sixteen summers, a poor
niece who has come to the old Pyncheon mansion to
visit her old maid aunt and brighten her gloomy
home. In this home is the old spinster's eccentric
brother, of feeble intellect and shattered health, who
has spent twenty years in prison for the murder of

his uncle—a crime of which he was really innocent. Occupying a room in the old house is a young man who is eager to take up the latest views of philosophy and life, a faddist who has dabbled a little in every profession and made a success of none. In addition to these characters is another, a relative of the old spinster's, a judge and rich banker, highly esteemed by the community, but at heart a grasping, ambitious, selfish man, little short of a hypocrite. These, with a few accessory figures, constitute the *dramatis personae* of this interesting romance.

Of the characters of the "House of Seven Gables" that of the scowling old spinster, Miss Hephzibah Pyncheon, is unquestionably the most clearly portrayed, the most distinctly drawn. Her sad life, with its disappointments, poverty, and consequent humiliation, enlists our sympathies; and we feel that in the sketch of her character the romancer has given us an excellent piece of description. Young Phœbe Pyncheon, with her bright, sunny disposition is a ray of sunshine in the dank, musty old mansion. She carries with her the beauty, freshness, and charm of a May morning, and is by far the most attractive personage in the entire book. As for Judge Pyncheon, whose portrait is the most studied and elaborate of the whole group, we feel that he is a blatant Pharisee, a bland hypocrite, masquerading in the ermine of the bench. It may be observed, however, by the way of parenthesis, that his tragic end, with its weird, eerie setting, is the most powerfully conceived and cleverly executed scene in the book. In the skilful blending of conflicting emotions, as exhibited in this scene, Hawthorne has produced an effect which is almost without a parallel in American literature. Clifford Pyncheon, the victim of circumstance, and the faddist, young Holgrove, are the least distinctly drawn of all the personages in the novel. They are mere types; they do not stand out upon the page. But Holgrove, who is a mere son of the earth, a *novus homo,* without antecedents or family traditions, serves the artistic end of a foil to Miss Hephzibah, who can never forget her illustrious lineage and ever piques herself upon it.

The moral of the "House of Seven Gables" is that families that isolate themselves and cut themselves off from association with the people, and refuse to recognize the broad principle of the brotherhood of man, are destined to be eventually overwhelmed in ruin and disaster. The first member of the Pyncheon house representing the landed gentry had committed a gross, ignoble crime against the first Maule, a poor laborer; but though the punishment is long delayed, two hundred years, the crime is finally avenged in the extinction of the Pyncheon house. The pride and Pharisaism of that family are at last brought down and dissolved by love, the universal solvent for all difficulties, real or fancied, and for all grievances, real or imaginary. So Holgrove and Phœbe, the latest descendants of the two families which were at enmity, agree to forget the past and forestall retribution by sinking their inherited animosities in the bonds of wedlock.

Hawthorne's third American novel, the "Blithedale Romance," possesses a certain historic interest. The story grew out of the Brook Farm episode, in which the novelist himself figured as a character. But it is not an accurate account of the manners or of the people who established that once famous community. While it is true that the picture has a historic background, it is not true that the characters are strictly historic personages. As a matter

of fact, the men and women are the creation of the
novelist's fancy, heirs of his own invention. Miles
Coverdale, however, is generally interpreted as the
counterpart of Hawthorne; and some critics think
that Zenobia is modeled after Margaret Fuller. But
these are mere surmises. Certainly Coverdale has
much in common with his creator, whether intended
as a portrait of Hawthorne or not. He is portrayed
as a contemplative, observing man, with an imagination ever active, who finds his happiness not so
much in actual achievement as in conceiving plans
and adventures. In a word, as some one has characterized him, he is half a poet, half a critic, and all
a spectator. Who the prototype of Hollingsworth
was, critics have not ventured to determine. In his
earnestness of purpose, strength of conviction, and
zeal for reform, he offers a sharp contrast to the
somewhat irresolute, unconcerned Coverdale. Zenobia is the heroine of the romance, and her character
is sketched with more definiteness of outline than
any other in the story. Unlike most of Hawthorne's
characters, she is not a mere picture: she stands out
from the page, and, as an eminent critic has remarked of her, she is the nearest approach Hawthorne
has made to the complete creation of a person. She
is the most sharply outlined of all his female characters, and lacks but little of being a woman of real
flesh and blood, such as Rubens painted. But, not
to mention all the characters, suffice it to say that
those named, together with the gentle, artless Priscilla, comprise the leading characters around whom
the interest of the story centers.

One might suppose that the author would have
woven a thread of satire into the warp of his
romance, but it is singularly free from satire. The
social experiment of the Brook Farm was certainly

not beyond the legitimate bound of criticism, and
we can hardly think that Hawthorne, by his failure
to criticise the scheme, intended to indicate thereby
his unqualified indorsement of the theory underlying the establishment of the once famous community. Indeed, the entire purport of the "Blithedale
Romance" seems to be in condemnation of the plan.
The moral of the book, if it may be said to have a
moral, is to show that by adopting principles alien
to those recognized by society as generally constituted, and by setting up abnormal standards based
on abstractions of individual intellects, we are
likely to sacrifice those drawn to us by strong affinity or generous impulse. The sacrifice of Zenobia
by the resolute Hollingsworth must be intended to
teach this lesson. The book contains many interesting situations, teems with incident, and like all
of Hawthorne's romances, possesses a rare charm;
but, after all, it does not strike the reader as a
strong novel. It makes the impression of being
feebly conceived, and is, in our judgment, the weak-
est of Hawthorne's American novels.

After the achievement of three triumphs in his
American novels, Hawthorne, during his residence
abroad, ventured upon a new field in the production
of the "Marble Faun," which was first published in
England under the title of "Transformation." The
setting of this charming romance is Italian, and the
scene is Rome. The book contains many fine passages of descriptive writing, as accurate as beautiful; and its pages are eagerly perused by every
English-speaking traveler who contemplates a visit
to the Eternal City; for the "Marble Faun" (the
title is a misnomer and singularly infelicitous)
gives a very faithful description of many of the
historic monuments and streets of Rome, and repro-

duces the *locale* of the romance with an accuracy and fidelity entirely foreign to the author's American novels. The city on the banks of the Tiber, therefore, is the background upon which the romancer with admirable art has painted the four leading characters of his story, Miriam and Donatello, Hilda and Kenyon.

Miriam and Donatello, between whom a kind of Platonic love develops, do not possess much in common. Miriam is a strong feminine character, who combines a wide acquaintance with life with her exceptional intelligence and power, and exercises a strange fascination over her lover. Donatello, on the other hand, is a gentle, disingenuous Italian youth of little experience, who is endowed with a peculiar fawn-like nature. Over him Miriam casts a powerful spell, which he is unable to break. In keeping with his impulsive nature, Donatello, under the influence of this mysterious spell, murders a man whom he fancied to be an enemy of Miriam; and by the common secret of the murder the two lovers are knit together in a close friendship which insulates them morally from society. Kenyon, the sculptor, and the gentle, innocent Hilda, by their romance, hold the reader's attention almost as completely and unintermittedly as Miriam and the fawn-man Donatello. The guileless Hilda is by accident made a reluctant witness of the murderous secret of Donatello and Miriam, whom she loved devotedly. Hilda was a New England girl of Puritan ancestry, and so sensitive was her Puritan conscience that, although she was in no sense a participant in the murder and was absolutely innocent, she yet felt that wrong-doing had become a part of her experience in consequence of the fact that she merely happened to be a witness of Donatello's crime. Her conscience became so burdened with her imagined guilt that, strenuous Puritan as she was, she entered St. Peter's and made a full confession to the priest. The burden was then removed, and she became again free as before. This chapter is the finest touch of inspiration in the book, and this conception of Hilda's character is a mark of genius. The sin which Donatello committed brought him to himself, enabled him to find himself, and revealed to his consciousness a new world of moral obligation of which he had never even dreamed before. In short, his nature was transformed, and from being a mere fawn destitute of all sense of moral obligation, he became a man with man's distinctive characteristic of a moral faculty. Remorse and passion were the means adopted to awaken and develop in him his dormant moral nature.

The "Marble Faun" is probably Hawthorne's most popular romance. As a piece of imaginative work it is admirable, and deserves to be widely read; yet as a work of art it has some serious weaknesses. To begin with, the story is weak from the point of view of narration. The narrative art requires a story to move continuously forward, and any incident that fails to contribute to this end must be eliminated. The progress of the "Marble Faun" is too frequently interrupted by the introduction of incidents that are mere side issues, and the story seems to wander and lose itself in the numerous digressions and vague fancies into which the author lapses. The tale as an artistic product lacks directness and coherence. Again, the element of the unreal is not kept under control, as in the allusions to Donatello's fawn nature. His delineation vacillates between the fanciful and the

real, and places him in a region between myth and
fact. His character therefore produces a sense of
unreality in the mind of the reader. Moreover, the
action of the story wavers between the realm of
physical fact, where the streets of Rome are described with the familiarity and accuracy of a native resident, and the airy realm of imagination,
where everything is vague and indeterminate, without local habitation or name. This defect did not
presumably escape the observation of the author
himself, for in a letter he speaks of the story as his
"moonshiny romance," which is not an inapt description. But after all has been said the "Marble
Faun" remains a charming romance, and contains
some of the finest pieces of imaginative writing in
American literature.

Hawthorne occupies a prominent place in the
American republic of letters. He was preëminently
a romancer. He can hardly be called a novelist,
certainly not in the strict meaning of that term.
Like his gifted contemporary, Poe, he did not, perhaps he could not, write a first-class novel. In
their genius and art these two men of letters have
some points of contact and some of departure. They
both combined a vivid, strong imagination with an
exquisite artistic sense. It seems, however, that
Poe had a more exuberant and robust imagination.
Indeed, this faculty in him was abnormally developed. We see indications of it in the intricate plots
of his tales. His genius was speculative, ratiocinative, and analytical. Hawthorne, on the other
hand, inclined to simplicity and directness; and his
mind was less constructive, and not at all analytical. His stories therefore all have simple plots,
with few accessory devices. The creations of Poe's
invention are like marble statues, beautiful and pol-

ished, but cold and without feeling. They are
studies in black and white, without color or expression. The creations of Hawthorne's genius are perhaps not so polished, but they posseess color and
warmth and have more inspiration and life. His
canvas is always suffused with the warm, rosy glow
of imagination, while Poe's, though finished and
perfect in technical execution, is as cold as an icicle
and without the slightest trace of color.

Hawthorne was something of a moralist. His
romances all have a moral purpose, as have also
most of his short stories. But the moral is not obtrusive, and does not detract from the interest of
the story. The moral purpose is kept below the
surface, so as not to arouse the reader's suspicion.
Still it is present, and if the reader will dive below
the surface, he may with no great effort discover it.
However, this kind of moral is not offensive to good
taste, concealed as it is by the author's spontaneous
and glowing imagination. The conscience was
Hawthorne's theme, but he clothed it in the soft,
airy woof of his creative fancy; and far from being
didactic, dull, or jejune, he rendered it all the more
interesting and engaging.

Hawthorne's romances do not appear to have
been written to portray characters. Indeed, the
romancer is weak in characterization. Like Poe,
Hawthorne never created a character which is destined to live, such as Becky Sharp or Wilkins Mi-
cawber, those inspired creations of Thackeray and
Dickens, respectively. Hawthorne's characters are
more in the nature of types than individuals. For
the most part, they lack definition and sharpness of
outline. They are somewhat vague and shadowy;
nor do they live and move before the reader's eye,
like real men and women. Themselves creations of

a glowing fancy, fashioned out of moonshine, they do not invite inspection in broad daylight, but need to be viewed through the shadowy twilight of romance to be appreciated fully. They therefore appear at their best, not in the dazzling glare of the noonday sunlight, but in the pale, eerie moonlight in which they stand half revealed and half obscured. This is probably what the author himself had in mind when in reference to his own work he used the suggestive phrase, "the moonlight of romance." It was this characteristic of his work, also, that induced critics to apply to him the title of psychological dreamer. But this is simply a defect of his mental equipment, and shows the poetic nature of his genius, his idealistic affinities.

Hawthorne's genius differs vastly from that of Thackeray or Dickens, names which stand at the very top of English writers of fiction. Consummate masters of the art of prose fiction, they could, by the interaction of the personages they portrayed upon their pages, put before the reader a veritable prose drama, with all its intricate parts leading up to the development and *dénouement* of the plot. But Hawthorne, though endowed with a rare creative imagination, lacked this inimitable power, this distinguishing mark of genius, which only the master novelists possess. He could paint dramatic situations, interesting, yea thrilling, scenes; but he lacked that essential and distinguishing gift by which the novelist makes his characters live, move, and act their respective parts till they bring about the final consummation of the plot.

Hawthorne's longer stories, his romances, will be found upon close analysis to be much the same as his short tales. The early tales are of course very much shorter, but contain all the essentials of his romances. The difference is quantitative, rather than qualitative. The romances are simply a series of dramatic situations approximating the length of a novel, but wanting the essential attribute of the novel, namely, the development of a plot. They are merely drawn out; they do not unfold or grow from within out. Hawthorne's stories, therefore, are not novels in the restricted acceptation of that term; they are romances. Moreover, it is noteworthy that the series of dramatic situations constituting his longer stories or romances are designed by the author to impress upon the reader the leading idea of the story, the theme. The situations, therefore, are ideal situations, all having this one end in view. For example, the leading thought of the "Scarlet Letter" is the effect of the sin of adultery, which is set forth in three or four dramatic situations of great power. So in the "House of Seven Gables," and in the other two romances, the principal idea of the respective stories is elaborated by a series of dramatic situations invented for the purpose. This repetition of the leading idea of his romance is the method the author adopted for producing the haunting effect so characteristic of his stories.

However, we are forced to admit in conclusion that Hawthorne has enjoyed a remarkable vogue. He has been read, and is even yet read, almost as much as any other American writer of fiction. He may be eclipsed for a brief period by some new star that shoots like a meteor across the literary heavens, but he is not extinguished. When the meteor has spent its force and disappeared, his star is still seen shining with its accustomed luster, and shows no sign of a waning brilliance. Why is it, then, that amid the vast flood of present-day fiction which

threatens to deluge the reading public Hawthorne
continues to hold his own? The answer is, Because
he put himself into his works, made them reflect
his own vision of life, with his moral seriousness
and devotion to life's noblest aspirations, and irra-
diated those works with the warm glow of his exuberant imagination. His charming art, his exquisite beauty, his originality, his delicate humor, his
purity of thought, his chasteness of language, and
his lofty moral tone—these all combine to give his
work an enduring quality which will insure its
popularity so long as imaginative writing is read
and appreciated.

HAWTHORNE

THE OLD APPLE DEALER

The lover of the moral picturesque may sometimes find what he seeks in a character which is nevertheless of too negative a description to be seized upon and represented to the imaginative vision by word painting. As an instance, I remember an old man who carries on a little trade of gingerbread and apples at the depot of one of our railroads. While awaiting the departure of the cars, my observation, itting to and fro among the livelier characteristics of the scene, has often settled insensibly upon this almost hueless object. Thus, unconsciously to myself and unsuspected by him, I have studied the old apple dealer until he has become a naturalized citizen of my inner world. How little would he imagine—poor, neglected, friendless, unappreciated, and with little that demands appreciation—that the mental eye of an utter stranger has so often reverted to his figure! Many a noble form, many a beautiful face, has flitted before me and vanished like a shadow. It is a strange witchcraft whereby this faded and featureless old apple dealer has gained a settlement in my memory.

He is a small man, with gray hair and gray stubble beard, and is invariably clad in a shabby surtout of snuff color, closely buttoned, and half concealing a pair of gray pantaloons; the whole dress, though clean and entire, being evidently flimsy with much wear. His face, thin, withered, furrowed, and with features which even age has failed to render impressive, has a frost-bitten aspect. It is a moral frost which no physical warmth or comfortableness could counteract. The summer sunshine may fling its white heat upon him, or the good fire of the depot room may

make him the focus of its blaze on a winter's day; but
all in vain; for still the old man looks as if he were in
a frosty atmosphere, with scarcely warmth enough to
keep life in the region about his heart. It is a patient,
long-suffering, quiet, hopeless, shivering aspect.
He is not desperate,—that, though its etymology implies no more, would be too positive an expression,—
but merely devoid of hope. As all his past life, probably, offers no spots of brightness to his memory, so
he takes his present poverty and discomfort as entirely a matter of course: he thinks it the definition
of existence, so far as himself is concerned, to be poor,
cold, and uncomfortable. It may be added, that time
has not thrown dignity as a mantle over the old man's
figure: there is nothing venerable about him: you pity
him without a scruple.

He sits on a bench in the depot room; and before
him, on the floor, are deposited two baskets of a capacity to contain his whole stock in trade. Across from
one basket to the other extends a board, on which is
displayed a plate of cakes and gingerbread, some rus-
set and red-cheeked apples, and a box containing
variegated sticks of candy, together with that delec-
table condiment known by children as Gibraltar rock,
neatly done up in white paper. There is likewise a
half-peck measure of cracked walnuts and two or
three tin half pints or gills filled with the nut kernels,
ready for purchasers. Such are the small commodi-
ties with which our old friend comes daily before the
world, ministering to its petty needs and little freaks
of appetite, and seeking thence the solid subsistence
—so far as he may subsist—of his life.

A slight observer would speak of the old man's quie-
tude; but, on closer scrutiny, you discover that there
is a continual unrest within him, which somewhat re-
sembles the fluttering action of the nerves in a corpse
from which life has recently departed. Though he
never exhibits any violent action, and, indeed, might
appear to be sitting quite still, yet you perceive, when

his minuter peculiarities begin to be detected, that he
is always making some little movement or other. He
looks anxiously at his plate of cakes or pyramid of
apples and slightly alters their arrangement, with an
evident idea that a great deal depends on their being
disposed exactly thus and so. Then for a moment he
gazes out of the window; then he shivers quietly and
folds his arms across his breast, as if to draw himself
closer within himself, and thus keep a flicker of warmth
in his lonesome heart. Now he turns again to his mer-
chandise of cakes, apples, and candy, and discovers
that this cake or that apple, or yonder stick of red
and white candy, has somehow got out of its proper
position. And is there not a walnut kernel too many
or too few in one of those small tin measures? Again
the whole arrangement appears to be settled to his
mind; but, in the course of a minute or two, there
will assuredly be something to set right. At times,
by an indescribable shadow upon his features, too
quiet, however, to be noticed until you are familiar
with his ordinary aspect, the expression of frost-bitten,
patient despondency becomes very touching. It seems
as if just at that instant the suspicion occurred to him
that, in his chill decline of life, earning scanty bread
by selling cakes, apples, and candy, he is a very miserable old fellow.

But, if he think so, it is a mistake. He can never
suffer the extreme of misery, because the tone of his
whole being is too much subdued for him to feel anything acutely.

Occasionally one of the passengers, to while away a
tedious interval, approaches the old man, inspects the
articles upon his board, and even peeps curiously into
the two baskets. Another, striding to and fro along
the room, throws a look at the apples and gingerbread
at every turn. A third, it may be of a more sensitive
and delicate texture of being, glances shyly thither-
ward, cautious not to excite expectations of a purchaser while yet undetermined whether to buy. But

there appears to be no need of such a scrupulous regard to our old friend's feelings. True, he is conscious of the remote possibility to sell a cake or an apple; but innumerable disappointments have rendered him so far a philosopher, that, even if the purchased article should be returned, he will consider it altogether in the ordinary train of events. He speaks to none, and makes no sign of offering his wares to the public: not that he is deterred by pride, but by the certain conviction that such demonstrations would not increase his custom. Besides, this activity in business would require an energy that never could have been a characteristic of his almost passive disposition even in youth. Whenever an actual customer appears the old man looks up with a patient eye: if the price and the article are approved, he is ready to make change; otherwise his eyelids droop again sadly enough, but with no heavier despondency than before. He shivers, perhaps folds his lean arms around his lean body, and resumes the lifelong, frozen patience in which consists his strength. Once in a while a school-boy comes hastily up, places a cent or two upon the board, and takes up a cake, or stick of candy, or a measure of walnuts, or an apple as red cheeked as himself. There are no words as to price, that being as well known to the buyer as to the seller. The old apple dealer never speaks an unnecessary word: not that he is sullen and morose; but there is none of the cheeriness and briskness in him that stirs up people to talk.

Not seldom he is greeted by some old neighbor, a man well to do in the world, who makes a civil, patronizing observation about the weather; and then, by way of performing a charitable deed, begins to chaffer for an apple. Our friend presumes not on any past acquaintance; he makes the briefest possible response to all general remarks, and shrinks quietly into himself again. After every diminution of his stock he takes care to produce from the basket another cake, another stick of candy, another apple, or another meas-

ure of walnuts, to supply the place of the article sold.
Two or three attempts—or, perchance, half a dozen
—are requisite before the board can be rearranged
to his satisfaction. If he have received a silver coin,
he waits till the purchaser is out of sight, then he ex-
amines it closely, and tries to bend it with his finger
and thumb: finally he puts it into his waistcoat pocket
with seemingly a gentle sigh. This sigh, so faint as
to be hardly perceptible, and not expressive of any
definite emotion, is the accompaniment and conclusion
of all his actions. It is the symbol of the chillness
and torpid melancholy of his old age, which only make
themselves felt sensibly when his repose is slightly
disturbed.

Our man of gingerbread and apples is not a specimen of the "needy man who has seen better days."
Doubtless there have been better and brighter days in
the far-off time of his youth; but none with so much
sunshine of prosperity in them that the chill, the depression, the narrowness of means, in his declining
years, can have come upon him by surprise. His life
has all been of a piece. His subdued and nerveless
boyhood prefigured his abortive prime, which likewise
contained within itself the prophecy and image of his
lean and torpid age. He was perhaps a mechanic, who
never came to be a master in his craft, or a petty
tradesman, rubbing onward between passably to do
and poverty. Possibly he may look back to some
brilliant epoch of his career when there were a hundred or two of dollars to his credit in the Savings
Bank. Such must have been the extent of his better
fortune—his little measure of this world's triumphs
—all that he has known of success. A meek, down-
cast, humble, uncomplaining creature, he probably has
never felt himself entitled to more than so much of
the gifts of Providence. Is it not still something that
he has never held out his hand for charity, nor has yet
been driven to that sad home and household of Earth's
forlorn and broken-spirited children, the almshouse?

He cherishes no quarrel, therefore, with his destiny, nor with the Author of it. All is as it should be.

If, indeed, he have been bereaved of a son, a bold, energetic, vigorous young man, on whom the father's feeble nature leaned as on a staff of strength, in that case he may have felt a bitterness that could not otherwise have been generated in his heart. But methinks the joy of possessing such a son and the agony of losing him would have developed the old man's moral and intellectual nature to a much greater degree than we now find it. Intense grief appears to be as much out of keeping with his life as fervid happiness.

To confess the truth, it is not the easiest matter in the world to define and individualize a character like this which we are now handling. The portrait must be so generally negative that the most delicate pencil is likely to spoil it by introducing some too positive tint. Every touch must be kept down, or else you destroy the subdued tone which is absolutely essential to the whole effect. Perhaps more may be done by contrast than by direct description. For this purpose I make use of another cake and candy merchant, who likewise infests the railroad depot. This latter worthy is a very smart and well-dressed boy of ten years old or thereabouts, who skips briskly hither and thither, addressing the passengers in a pert voice, yet with somewhat of good breeding in his tone and pronunciation. Now he has caught my eye, and skips across the room with a pretty pertness which I should like to correct with a box on the ear. "Any cake, sir? any candy?"

No, none for me, my lad. I did but glance at your brisk figure in order to catch a reflected light and throw it upon your old rival yonder.

Again, in order to invest my conception of the old man with a more decided sense of reality, I look at him in the very moment of intensest bustle, on the arrival of the cars. The shriek of the engine as it rushes into the car-house is the utterance of the steam fiend, whom man has subdued by magic spells and compels to serve as a beast of burden. He has skimmed rivers in his headlong rush, dashed through forests, plunged into the hearts of mountains, and glanced from the city to the desert-place, and again to a far-off city, with a meteoric progress, seen and out of sight, while his reverberating roar still fills the ear. The travellers swarm forth from the cars. All are full of the momentum which they have caught from their mode of conveyance. It seems as if the whole world, both morally and physically, were detached from its old standfasts and set in rapid motion. And, in the midst of this terrible activity, there sits the old man of gingerbread; so subdued, so hopeless, so without a stake in life, and yet not positively miserable,—there he sits, the forlorn old creature, one chill and sombre day after another, gathering scanty coppers for his cakes, apples, and candy,—there sits the old apple dealer, in his threadbare suit of snuff color and gray and his grizzly stubble beard. See! he folds his lean arms around his lean figure with that quiet sigh and that scarcely perceptible shiver which are the tokens of his inward state. I have him now. He and the steam fiend are each other's antipodes; the latter's the type of all that go ahead, and the old man the representative of that melancholy class who, by some sad witchcraft, are doomed never to share in the world's exulting progress. Thus the contrast between mankind and this desolate brother becomes picturesque, and even sublime.

And now farewell, old friend! Little do you suspect that a student of human life has made your character the theme of more than one solitary and thoughtful hour. Many would say that you have hardly individuality enough to be the object of your own self-love. How, then, can a stranger's eye detect anything in your mind and heart to study and to wonder at? Yet, could I read but a tithe of what is written there, it would be a volume of deeper and more comprehensive import than all that the wisest mortals have given to the world; for the soundless depths of the human soul and of eternity have an opening through your breast. God be praised, were it only for your sake, that the present shapes of human existence are not cast in iron nor hewn in everlasting adamant, but moulded of the vapors that vanish away while the essence flits upward to the Infinite. There is a spiritual essence in this gray and lean old shape that shall flit upward too. Yes; doubtless there is a region where the lifelong shiver will pass away from his being, and that quiet sigh, which it has taken him so many years to breathe, will be brought to a close for good and all.

CHAPTER VIII

RALPH WALDO EMERSON

The historic old town of Concord is the literary Mecca of New England. Few places in America are richer in historic association, or have more interesting literary traditions clustering about them, than this quaint, typical New England town. Every true American must feel his breast swell with patriotism as he visits Lexington and Concord and observes on all sides the many reminders of our hard-fought battles for American Independence. At the bridge hard by the town are two monuments marking the spot:—

"Where once the embattled farmers stood,
And fired the shot heard round the world."

But the literary traditions and associations of the place are quite as interesting as the historic. What a group of names famous in the history of American literature occurs to our minds at the very mention of Concord! How the pulse is quickened and the imagination kindled as soon as we set foot on the ground once daily trod by men and women whose names loom large in our literary annals! Of these, however, none has greater drawing power than Emerson whose haunts and last resting place in Sleepy Hollow are almost as much frequented as Mount Vernon.

A man may choose the place of his residence, but he has no choice as to his birthplace. Nature was kind to the seer of Concord, in permitting him to be born in Boston (near the place he esteemed above all others), where the sweet light of this world greeted his eyes on a May morning, 1803, now a century agone. His father, Reverend William Emerson, was pastor of a church in Boston at the time of the child's birth. Emerson's ancestors for several generations back were of the clerical order. It is not surprising therefore that Ralph Waldo should have inherited a disposition almost angelic, which he is reputed to have possessed. He is said to have been so naturally good that he hardly knew temptation and was acquainted with the effect of evil in others only by observation. We are told that he had no personal experience of the tendency to evil in human nature, that he was so far from being virtuous that he was pure and good spontaneously, like beings that cannot sin. If then it be true, as reported, that Emerson was that rare phenomenon, a man of pure human innocence who always turned a deaf ear to the siren voice of sin so fascinating to ordinary mortals, small wonder that he made a profound impression on his disciples and was regarded as almost outside the pale of moral law.

His father dying when young Emerson was but eight years old, his aunt, Mary Moody Emerson, and her friend, Sarah Bedford, both women of singular earnestness and fine classical scholarship, prepared the boy for college. At the tender age of fourteen he entered Harvard. There he applied himself diligently of course, but did not distinguish himself above his fellows. He showed a fondness for the classics, but disliked mathematics. Montaigne and the poets he read with keen zest. He did not confine himself to the curriculum in his intellectual training. He acted on the principle enunciated later in his life: "What we do not call education is more gracious than what we do call so." It is significant that the office of class poet fell to his lot on the occasion of his graduation.

After his graduation Emerson began to teach school for a livelihood (an occupation which countless young men and women fall back upon to tide over an impecunious period of indecision). After two years' experience at teaching he decided to prepare himself in obedience to a call to the ministry. After studying under the direction of Dr. William Ellery Channing, Emerson was ready to enter the Unitarian pulpit, when only twenty years old. But at this juncture, failing health compelled him to seek a milder climate; and so he spent the following winter or two in South Carolina and Florida. He preached several times during his sojourn in the South and, upon his return home in 1826, he was "approbated to preach." After several trial sermons preached at various points in his native State, he received a call to the pastorate of the Second Church, in Boston.

Emerson had scarcely become settled as a minister in Boston before a dark shadow was thrown across his path by the early death of his wife, in 1832, after three all too brief years of married life. A few months after this sad event, perplexed by theological doubts concerning the Lord's Supper, he resigned his pastorate and determined to strike out in a new field where he would be untrammeled by religious traditions and free to think and act as his conscience dictated.

He thereupon visited Europe. Here he met a number of distinguished men of letters, including Coleridge, Wordsworth, Landor, De Quincey, and

Carlyle. Of these his acquaintance with Carlyle ripened into a friendship which was fostered by a correspondence till death. In the winter of 1833-4 Emerson returned to America with his mind brimful of impressions and his heart of inspiration. He settled in Concord, taking up his residence in the "Old Manse." This quaint, old-fashioned gambrel-roof house (still standing) was built years ago for Emerson's grandfather, the shepherd of the Concord flock; and in one of its rooms Emerson wrote "Nature," and it is interesting to note in passing that Hawthorne later wrote his famous "Mosses from an Old Manse" in this same room.

Immediately on his return to his native heath Emerson decided to appear in a new rôle, that of a Lyceum lecturer. This rôle was destined to be his vocation for the next forty-six years. In his early *repertoire* he included such subjects as "Water," "The Relation of Man to the Globe," "Michael Angelo," "Milton," "Luther," "George Fox," and "Edmund Burke." In these lectures are contained the germs of many of the thoughts which the seer afterwards expanded into separate productions, both prose and verse.

If it be true, according to Holmes' dictum, that men consciously or unconsciously describe themselves in the characters they draw, Emerson must have found sympathy and congeniality in the great men he made the subjects of his early lectures. It is no tax on our faith to believe our bard had a spirit akin to that of the great Puritan poet of England in the stress he placed upon the purity of life and nobility of character. It is evident he was like him in certain external circumstances of life, as, for instance, his early experience as a schoolmaster, the abandonment of the clerical office from conscientious scruples and the sad bereavement of his early married life. This fact, though only a coincidence, may have exerted some influence on Emerson and stimulated his development in the direction whence Milton drew his inspiration.

"It is the prerogative of this great man," says Emerson in his lecture on Milton, "to stand at this hour foremost of all men in literary history, and so (shall we not say?) of all men in the power to inspire. Virtue goes out of him into others." . . . "He is identified in the mind with all select and holy images, with the supreme interests of the human race."—"Better than any other he has discharged the office of every great man, namely, to raise the idea of man in the minds of his contemporaries and of posterity—to draw after nature life of man, exhibiting such a composition of grace, of strength, and of virtue as poet had not described nor hero lived. Human nature in these ages is indebted to him for its best portrait. Many philosophers in England, France and Germany have formally dedicated their study to this problem; and we think it impossible to recall one in those centuries who communicates the same vibration of hope, of self-reverence, of piety, of delight in beauty, which the name of Milton awakens."

From Concord Emerson made frequent excursions on his lecturing tours. He departed from his beaten path of lectures when he delivered, in 1835, in Boston, a course on English literature, and during the following year on the history of philosophy. Later he delivered a course on human culture. Some of his popular lectures he subsequently recast and published under the title of "Essays and Addresses." He kept his time occupied during these years with Lyceum work, and his services as a public speaker were much in request on special occasions.

In 1836, Emerson published anonymously a slender volume of essays, entitled "Nature." This was the first sheaf of his intellectual harvest, the first fruits of his authorship. Though he withheld his name from the title-page, he could not conceal his identity, despite the fact that the style of the book was quite unlike that of his public lectures. However, this little literary waif did not meet with a cordial reception from the reading public. The contents of the volume were vague and indefinite, mystical and obscure. The thought soared into cloud-land and proved incomprehensible to most of the critics. The uninitiated could not understand the book and so did not read it; and, however much the esoterists might revel in it, they were not numerous enough to make the venture a financial success. Consequently the sales amounted only to 500 copies in twelve years.

"Nature" is a kind of prose poem, like most of Emerson's essays, and is divided into eight chapters containing the author's impressions of the various aspects of his subject. After a delirious outbreak in which he loses himself in the contemplation of his theme, he discovers himself and addresses himself to the proposition of considering nature in the aspect of ministry to the senses. This chapter he denominates *Commodity* or natural conveniences. The second chapter shows how "a nobler want of man is served by Nature, namely, the love of Beauty." Here we find some of Emerson's philosophical ideas advanced which he subsequently clothed in poetic form in his poem "Rhodora." "Beauty," says he, "in its largest and profoundest sense, is one expression for the universe; God is the all fair. Truth and goodness and beauty are but different faces of the same all. But beauty in nature is not ultimate. It is the herald of inward and eternal beauty, and is not alone a solid and satisfactory good. It must therefore stand as a part and not as yet the highest expression of the final cause of nature."

The author next considers *Language,* showing how words are called into being first from nature and later become transformed and exhausted. In the fourth chapter he discusses *Discipline* as illustrating the influences of nature in training the intellect, the moral sense and the will. Then follow two chapters on *Idealism* and *Spirit,* respectively, which prove a stumbling block and rock of offense to the unimaginative reader. Such a reader sees here only the misty vagaries of a morbid imagination. The book closes with a discussion of *Prospects,* which soars far above the level of prose into the region of poetry, detailing "some traditions of man and nature which a certain poet sang." This is the quintessence of transcendentalism of which Emerson was the chief exponent.

If Emerson's philosophy as expounded in "Nature" signified foolishness to the man of average intelligence, not so his superb oration on "The American Scholar" delivered before that learned body at Harvard, on August 31, 1837. This scholarly and inspiring address, we are told, was listened to with rapt attention by an audience that was wellnigh spellbound by the speaker's eloquence. Lowell, referring to it, says that its delivery "was an event without any parallel in literary annals, a scene to be always treasured in the memory for its picturesqueness and its inspiration. What crowded and breathless aisles, what windows clustering with eager heads, what enthusiasm of approval, what grim silence of foregone dissent." Holmes speaks of it, in his Life of Emerson, as our intellectual Declaration of Independence; and his language is not mere rhetorical exaggeration. The essay is a masterly plea for a broad and liberal culture which shall embrace the full development of all the faculties. The general verdict of the auditors was that that address could never be forgotten, which burst upon their ears like a clarion note calling to a broader, fuller and nobler life.

The following year Emerson delivered an address before the Divinity College in Cambridge which proved a rude shock to the orthodox thinkers of the world and threw them into a paroxysm of excitement. This address was in sharp contrast to the memorable address of the year before. Yet the unorthodox address was the logical outcome of the spirit of intellectual independence which breathes through every sentence of "The American Scholar." The publication of this essay proclaiming Emerson's emancipation from dogma was the signal for a veritable swarm of hostile critics of the orthodox school to gather about his head and fill the air with their angry buzz.

In 1841 Emerson gave to the world the first volume of his collected "Essays." The table of contents is stimulating and suggestive: History, Self-Reliance, Compensation, Spiritual Laws, Love, Friendship, Prudence, Heroism, The Over Soul, Circles, Intellect, Art and the Young American (included in the later editions). These essays established Emerson's reputation as the prince of American essayists. This prose vein he developed and made distinctively his own. It is noteworthy that he confined his expression in prose exclusively to this species of composition. He is recognized therefore in American letters as an essayist *par excellence*. The reason why he chose this special form for the expression of his thought is not far to seek. A moment's reflection will explain why a lecturer should adopt the essay style.

This first series of essays is characteristic of their author's manner and method. If, according to Buffon's dictum, the style is the man, these essays reflect Emerson as in a mirror. We observe his subtle wit, his bold, imaginative spirit, his magnetic charm and his power to inspire. The thought is driven home with peculiar force by the author's wealth of happy illustration and is clothed, withal, in crisp, trenchant, vigorous English. The essays abound in short pithy sayings setting forth the sage's philosophy of life. Yet here and there we stumble upon sentences that are wellnigh unintelligible, mere words without sense. Those not initiated into the mysteries of transcendentalism can deduce no meaning from such passages and generally regard them as utter nonsense. An example in point is the conclusion of the essay on history where in a paragraph Emerson exclaims: "I am ashamed to see what a shallow village tale our so-called history is. How many times we must say Rome and Paris and Constantinople! What does Rome know of rat and lizard? What are Olympiads and Consulates to these neighboring systems of being? Nay, what food or experience of succor have they for the Esquimaux seal-hunter, for the Kanaka in his canoe, for the fisherman, the stevedore, the porter?" Now, this passage may be perfectly intelligible to the student versed in transcendentalism. But to the average reader it is a veritable enigma.

Moreover there is a degree of sameness about the several essays that is quite noticeable. The subjects, to be sure, differ. But on close analysis the thought will be seen to be very much the same in all. Each essay serves to present another point of view, another angle from which to look at the truth which is repeated again and again. An eminent divine used to say, after having preached innumerable sermons, that, after all, he had only one sermon, only one truth. Certainly this seems true of Emerson's essays. The message he brings is much the same in all. He had a revelation of the import of creation and this constituted his message to the world. This he presented in a variety of ways and under different figures, but the message was still the same.

Critics have pointed out reminiscences of various philosophers in these "Essays." In one place they recognize the influence of Plato, who was Emerson's favorite among the ancient philosophers. In another place they attribute the original thought to Swedenborg, or to Schelling, or to the God-intoxicated Spinoza. In the essay, "Over Soul," Emerson verges on pantheism in his rhapsodies. But whether this idea is borrowed or is evolved from his own inner consciousness, it would be difficult to determine. The author himself informs us that he read sedulously not only the above-mentioned philosophers, but many others. What is more natural than that his own writings should take tone and color from the works he fed on just as the chameleon takes its color from the object it feeds upon? If questioned himself about this matter, Emerson would probably have replied, "Every book is a quotation; every man is a quotation from all his ancestors.—When we are praising Plato, it seems we are praising quotations from Solon and Sophron and Philolaus."

In 1844, appeared the second series of "Essays." These are very much of the same general character as the first series and embrace such titles as the Poet, Character, Manners, Experience, Gifts, Nature, Politics, and Nominalist and Realist. Two years later Emerson published his first volume of poems. These, however, were not all new. Many of them had already seen the light in "The Dial," and their appearance in book form did not excite much enthusiasm. Besides, the sentiment was strikingly akin to that expressed in the "Essays."

In 1847, Emerson made his second visit to Europe, gathering fresh inspiration and renewing his acquaintance with the literary lights met on his first trip abroad. While in England his admirers and friends prevailed on him to deliver a series of lectures, which were received with considerable demonstration of approval. These lectures were subsequently published under the title of "Representative Men." The men selected as the subjects of the essays, it is interesting to note, were men of thought and action, such as Plato, Swedenborg, Montaigne, Shakespeare, Napoleon and Goethe. In the choice of these men for portrayal Emerson clearly indicated to the world his own affinities and repulsions and revealed his own character perhaps all unconsciously and unintentionally. Of the six representative men Plato seems to approximate most closely his ideal man. Yet he does not hold up even Plato for our unqualified admiration.

Another book, "English Traits," though not published till 1856, was also indebted for its inspiration to this European tour. This volume and "Representative Men" mark something of a departure

from our author's customary method as a literary
artist. "English Traits" is an attempt at portrayal
of character. But no individual Englishman is selected and held up as representative of his nation.
Emerson's plan was rather to delineate the national
characteristics of the English people, and in this
respect he succeeded admirably. For the book is
decidedly original, like all of its author's productions, and contains many clever, piquant observations upon the characteristic ways and manners of
our British cousins across the sea. The strength of
the book, however, lies in its broad generalizations
and in its epigrammatic characterizations, as an
eminent critic has felicitously expressed it. It is
evident to the reader that Emerson was favorably
impressed by the sturdy, stolid character of the
typical Englishman, his indomitable pluck and
vigor, his deep-rooted conservatism, his love of
routine, and, withal, his refreshing self-compla-
cency and contentment.

When the *Atlantic Monthly* was founded, Emerson was solicited to become a contributor. From
this time forth much of his best work, verse as well
as prose, found its way into the columns of this
famous magazine. Here first appeared his poems
"The Romany Girl," "Days," "Brahma," "Waldein-
samkeit," "The Titmouse," "Saadi," and "Termi-
nus," not to mention any of his prose contributions.

In 1860 Emerson published a new collection of
essays, entitled the "Conduct of Life." This volume contained his ripe reflections upon such themes
as power, fate, culture, worship, wealth, behavior,
beauty and illusions. These essays are in a similar
philosophical vein to those previously published
from his pen, and so do not call for a detailed consideration here. Six years after this Emerson col-

lected a slender volume of his fugitive poems, giving them more permanent form under the title, "May-Day and Other Pieces." The booklet contained some of its author's finest poems, but little that was really new. Its reception by the public was not attended with any special demonstration or gush. Nor did Emerson care for this. He did not write for the approval of the public or of the critics. He acted altogether independently of the opinion of his contemporaries. Not that he was altogether insensible to criticism, for he was not. But conscience was his guiding principle.

It is not to be inferred that Emerson's literary productions were not cordially received. Far from this, they were accorded a hearty welcome, especially by the hosts of his ardent admirers on both sides of the Atlantic. This was but the natural consequence from the admiration and reverence in which he was held by all who knew him. His reputation as a philosopher and as an author was not confined to the shores of his native country. He counted his disciples in Europe by the score. He shed lustre upon the republic of American letters, and though he was not a voluminous author, the quality of his writings has extended his fame throughout the world.

After the publication of another collection of essays which he called "Society and Solitude", Emerson left America for a third visit to Europe. Upon his return he published a poetic anthology and resumed his work as a lecturer. But approaching old age admonished his to relax his arduous literary labors. Two volumes in his collected work, "Lectures and Biographical Sketches" and "Miscellanies," represent the last gleanings of his intellectual harvest. Some of the essays, however, which

make up these last two volumes were the product
of his earlier years when his mental vigor showed
no indication of abatement.   The contents of these
volumes embrace a variety of topics, but do not enhance their author's reputation especially.

As we have seen, Emerson was not a prolific
writer.   About a dozen volumes of prose and verse
represent the entire output of his literary labors.
It need hardly be remarked that the bulk of his
work is prose.   Yet his collected poems make a
good stout volume.   He did not produce any
lengthy prose work.   The essay is his favorite form.

After this general survey it is fitting to consider
the question of Emerson's place in American literature.

Emerson's poetry has been variously estimated
by the critics, and has proved an unfailing source
of contention.   It seems to have divided the critics
into two distinct classes.   One class holds that
Emerson was pre-eminently a poet by nature and
instinct, and that even when he lapsed into prose,
his thought was essentially poetic.   The other
class, with equally firm conviction, maintains that
Emerson was a mere versifier, only a poetaster, not
a poet.   In proof of this thesis they cite, with some
pretence of right, the innumerable palpable defects
of versification that blur and mar many of Emerson's pages.

It is true that the mechanical blemishes of his
verse do tend to discount Emerson's poetic gift.
But the question in dispute is a subjective one
which, in the very nature of things, cannot be satisfactorily settled.   Each critic may record his opinion and that is the end of the matter as far as he is
personally concerned; but the question is far from
solution.   Suffice it to say in respect of the present

question, however, that the majority of critics are overwhelmingly in favor of voting Emerson a genuine poet.

First as to Emerson's prose. Emerson confined himself, as is well known, almost exclusively to the essay. He did not enter the vast domain of fiction which at present engaged the attention of most authors. He did not even venture upon the portrayal of character, except in a limited extent in his "English Traits." Emerson did not possess the faculty of definition (if that is the proper word) which is a pre-requisite to the novelist for describing with sharpness of outline the various characters of his story, so that they stand out from his page as clear-cut and distinct from each other as in real life. Nor did Emerson exhibit that type of creative mind which invents characters, and which sketches scenes bristling with action. In short, Emerson could not construct a plot and fill it in with men and women of his own creation.

Emerson's genius was of a distinctly philosophical type. This determined the product of his literary efforts. Not in works of fiction, but in history, in biography and in philosophy did he seek instruction and inspiration. Mere fiction did not appeal to him. His favorite authors were Plato, Plutarch, Montaigne, Goethe, Bacon, Swedenborg, Socrates, Aristotle, Milton and Shakespeare. These were the authors who stimulated his imagination and kindled his genius. These he quotes again and again as emphasizing the proper conception of life and as illustrating the principle of pure living and high thinking. Emerson had an exalted conception of life and human destiny. He realized that he had a message for the world, and he was as much in earnest in the delivery of his message as was his friend Carlyle. Like the sage of Chelsea, Emerson was a moralist and took his mission very seriously, and made a lasting impression upon the world. Though in revolt against the accepted traditions of the Church, he dared to announce to the world his declaration of intellectual independence with absolute unconcern as to authority, names or institutions. Nor was he altogether like one crying in the wilderness. He had a large following. The world admires a man who has the moral courage to express his convictions, regardless of the penalty.

As a philosopher, Emerson's place is difficult to determine. He was not a psychologist. Yet he wrote and delivered lectures on the natural history of the intellect. He was a seer, a man of intuition. He lived and wrote as if by divine instinct. He arrived at truth, not by any mental process of reasoning, but by intuition. Unlike most men, he did not reason out anything. The ratiocinative faculty was not developed in him. If it had been, he would have been more logical and consistent, and less of an enigma to his disciples. This is the reason why his writings appear wanting in logical connection. You may read his essays backward as well as forward with much the same effect. The arrangement is not always logical and the sequence of thought is frequently interrupted. Nor do the titles invariably furnish a true index to the contents. Hence not a few readers find Emerson rambling and incoherent, and sometimes, obscure and unintelligible. The obscurity is perhaps due to his idealism, his mysticism; for he is an idealist, a spiritualist, not a materialist. His mysticism, too, sometimes leads him perilously near the ridiculous and the absurd.

But these lapses, it ought to be added, are only occasional.

Emerson's philosophy offers as its chief and distinctive achievement his analysis and interpretation of nature. This is the purport of his maiden volume and it is the theme of all his subsequent volumes. Nature in its broadest sense he conceives as comprehending everything in the universe except man's soul, and it is the symbol even of this. In nature God has expressed in concrete form his infinite ideas, has incarnated himself, so to say, for man's development. Man represents the highest principle in nature, and the whole effect of nature upon him is disciplinary. Therefore, nature itself cannot be said to have any natural existence apart from man, and things do not exist in space, but are only reflected as from man's soul. The soul conceives the world as one vast canvas, as it were, painted by the master artist upon eternity and embodying his eternal ideas. When nature rises into mind—and its tendency is ever in that direction—individuality begins. Nature gradually evolves itself into spiritual man as the final cause of existence, and is itself but the projection of a Being in the form of man, that is, God. Such, in a nutshell, is Emerson's philosophy.

But Emerson was also a poet. In his verse as in his prose, however, he was still a philosopher. Like Lucretius, Emerson was a philosopher and poet both at one and the same time. But in the poet he is the philosopher transformed. In his philosophical poems expressing the great elementary ideas he is at his best, and is, in a sense, unapproachable. Here he deals in general symbols and abstract ideas, and impresses upon the reader his majestic conception of the infinite. These poems, it is true, contain more or less of mysticism; but, for all that, they are masterly productions of their kind.   In the judgment of some of the most eminent critics these poems are the finest Emerson wrote and reach the very high-water mark of poetic composition. Of this class of poems suffice it to mention "The Sphinx," "Brahma," "Uriel," and "Guy." Yet other critics fail to discover any striking merit in these poems and derive no pleasure from their reading.   They find them unsatisfying as poetry because of their hidden meaning, their mysticism. These poems are assuredly not radiant with light, whatever other excellences they may have to commend them.   For this reason, mainly, they do not appeal to the popular taste.   They are too philosophical to please the average reader, who likes simplicity.   Probably most people prefer Emerson's love poems, such as "To Rhea," "Give All to Love," and "Initial, Daemonic and Celestial Love." Though these may not be models of simplicity and clearness, their meaning is not deep or far to seek. But whether one prefers the love poems or the philosophical poems, is, after all, a matter of taste.

However, Emerson's poetic output is not exhausted by these two kinds of poems. He produced another kind of poetry whose "beauty is its own excuse for being."   Such are "The Humble-Bee," "Rhodora," "Painting and Sculpture," "Forbearance," "Good-Bye," and the famous Concord "Hymn."   The beauty of these poems appeals to all men, the uninitiated as well as the initiated, and every one can appreciate them.   If all his other poems were lost, these would be sufficient of themselves to preserve the bard's reputation as an original poet with a rare gift of expression.

Yet it must be admitted that, excellent as much of Emerson's poetry is, it has some serious defects. Emerson did not possess a faultless ear, as is very evident from a cursory examination of his verse. He paid too little attention to the mechanical structure of his lines, to metre.   Some of his verses show a cloven foot and go limping along in a fashion that offends delicate tastes.   This result is the logical outcome of the "fatal facility" of his favorite metre. Like Byron, Emerson depended upon the inspiration of the moment to mold his thought in final shape, apparently disdaining to supplement the product of his genius with art.   The labor of the file would have easily removed all the metrical blemishes, and that without sacrificing the spontaneity of the verse.   But Emerson was unwilling to revise or to resort to art, to polish and perfect his lines. He concerned himself with the thought, not with the form, acting on the maxim of Cato, *Rem tene, verba sequentur.*

Aside from the mechanical imperfections, Emerson's verse is open to criticism on the same score as his prose.   His poetry no less than his prose is marred by occasional obscurity and lack of coherence.   The poet is sometimes carried off his feet in his rhapsodies and soars into cloudland.   Hence, as has been noted, some of Emerson's poems are enveloped in mysticism and for this reason are difficult to understand.   They smack too strongly of the transcendental school, and too often lapse into doggerel.   Poe who was endowed with a keen artistic touch and was himself no mean judge of verse found much of the Concord bard's verse mere jingling rhymes, devoid of melody, beauty and sentiment.   But Poe could not away with any of the transcendental poets.

Yet after criticism has said her last word, and analysis can go no farther, there still remains a beauty, a charm, about Emerson which is perceived more clearly than it can be expressed. His wealth of imagery and illustration which seems almost Oriental, his breadth and vigor of thought, his delicacy of treatment, his terseness of speech and his moral earnestness withal combine to make him a favorite author even despite his mysticism and transcendentalism. He dwells in a bracing atmosphere on the very mountain top of thought and, as a seer, catches visions of the infinite which he reveals to us for our upbuilding and inspiration. We recognize in him one of the most original and vitalizing forces in our literature.

EMERSON

CONCORD HYMN

By the rude bridge that arched the flood,
  Their flag to April's breeze unfurled,
Here once the embattled farmers stood,
  And fired the shot heard round the world.

The foe long since in silence slept;
  Alike the conqueror silent sleeps;
And Time the ruined bridge has swept
  Down the dark stream which seaward creeps.

On this green bank, by this soft stream,
  We set to-day a votive stone;
That memory may their deed redeem,
  When, like our sires, our sons are gone.

Spirit, that made those heroes dare
  To die, and leave their children free,
Bid Time and Nature gently spare
  The shaft we raise to them and thee.

EACH AND ALL

Little thinks, in the field, you red-cloaked clown
Of thee from the hill-top looking down;
The heifer that lows in the upland farm,
Far-heard, lows not thine ear to charm;
The sexton, tolling his bell at noon,
Deems not that great Napoleon
Stops his horse, and lists with delight,
Whilst his files sweep round yon Alpine height;

Nor knowest thou what argument
Thy life to thy neighbor's creed has lent.
All are needed by each one;
Nothing is fair or good alone.

I thought the sparrow's note from heaven,
Singing at dawn on the alder bough;
I brought him home, in his nest, at even;
He sings the song, but it cheers not now,
For I did not bring home the river and sky;—
He sang to my ear,—they sang to my eye.
The delicate shells lay on the shore;
The bubbles of the latest wave
Fresh pearls to their enamel gave,
And the bellowing of the savage sea
Greeted their safe escape to me.
I wiped away the weeds and foam,
I fetched my sea-born treasures home;
But the poor, unsightly, noisome things
Had left their beauty on the shore
With the sun and the sand and the wild uproar.
The lover watched his graceful maid,
As 'mid the virgin train she strayed,
Nor knew her beauty's best attire
Was woven still by the snow-white choir.
At last she came to his hermitage,
Like the bird from the woodlands to the cage;—
The gay enchantment was undone,
A gentle wife, but fairy none.

Then I said, "I covet truth;
Beauty is unripe childhood's cheat;
I leave it behind with the games of youth:"—
As I spoke, beneath my feet
The ground-pine curled its pretty wreath,
Running over the club-moss burrs;
I inhaled the violet's breath;
Around me stood the oaks and firs;
Pine-cones and acorns lay on the ground;

Over me soared the eternal sky,
Full of light and of deity;
Again I saw, again I heard,
The rolling river, the morning bird;—
Beauty through my senses stole;
I yielded myself to the perfect whole.

THE RHODORA

ON BEING ASKED, WHENCE IS THE FLOWER?

In May, when sea-winds pierced our solitudes,
I found the fresh Rhodora in the woods,
Spreading its leafless blooms in a damp nook,
To please the desert and the sluggish brook.
The purple petals, fallen in the pool,
Made the black water with their beauty gay;
Here might the red-bird come his plumes to cool,
And court the flower that cheapens his array.

Rhodora! if the sages ask thee why
This charm is wasted on the earth and sky,
Tell them, dear, that if eyes were made for seeing,
Then Beauty is its own excuse for being:
Why thou wert there, O rival of the rose!
I never thought to ask, I never knew:
But, in my simple ignorance, suppose
The self-same Power that brought me there brought you.

THE PROBLEM

I like a church: I like a cowl,
I love a prophet of the soul;
And on my heart monastic aisles
Fall like sweet strains, or pensive smiles:
Yet not for all his faith can see
Would I that cowled churchman be.

Why should the vest on him allure,
Which I could not on me endure?

Not from a vain or shallow thought
His awful Jove young Phidias brought;
Never from lips of cunning fell
The thrilling Delphic oracle;
Out from the heart of nature rolled
The burdens of the Bible old;
The litanies of nations came,
Like the volcano's tongue of flame,
Up from the burning core below,—
The canticles of love and woe:
The hand that rounded Peter's dome
And groined the aisles of Christian Rome
Wrought in a sad sincerity;
Himself from God he could not free;
He builded better than he knew;—
The conscious stone to beauty grew.

Know'st thou what wove yon woodbird's nest
Of leaves, and feathers from her breast?
Or how the fish outbuilt her shell,
Painting with morn each annual cell?
Or how the sacred pine-tree adds
To her old leaves new myriads?
Such and so grew these holy piles,
Whilst love and terror laid the tiles.
Earth proudly wears the Parthenon,
As the best gem upon her zone,
And Morning opes with haste her lids
To gaze upon the Pyramids;
O'er England's abbeys bends the sky,
As on its friends, with kindred eye;
For out of Thought's interior sphere
These wonders rose to upper air;
And Nature gladly gave them place,
Adopted them into her race,
And granted them an equal date
With Andes and with Ararat.

These temples grew as grows the grass;
Art might obey, but not surpass.
The passive Master lent his hand
To the vast soul that o'er him planned;
And the same power that reared the shrine
Bestrode the tribes that knelt within.
Ever the fiery Pentecost
Girds with one flame the countless host,
Trances the heart through chanting choirs,
And through the priest the mind inspires.
The word unto the prophet spoken
Was writ on tables yet unbroken;
The word by seers or sibyls told,
In groves of oak, or fanes of gold,
Still floats upon the morning wind,
Still whispers to the willing mind.
One accent of the Holy Ghost
The heedless world hath never lost.

I know what say the fathers wise,—
The Book itself before me lies,
Old *Chrysostom*, best Augustine,
And he who blent both in his line,
The younger *Golden Lips* or mines,
Taylor, the Shakespeare of divines,
His words are music in my ear,
I see his cowled portrait dear;
And yet, for all his faith could see,
I would not the good bishop be.

DAYS

Daughters of Time, the hypocritic Days,
Muffled and dumb like barefoot dervishes,
And marching single in an endless file,
Bring diadems and fagots in their hands.
To each they offer gifts after his will,
Bread, kingdoms, stars, and sky that holds them all.

I, in my pleached garden, watched the pomp,
Forgot my morning wishes, hastily
Took a few herbs and apples, and the Day
Turned and departed silent. I, too late,
Under her solemn fillet saw the scorn.

GOOD-BYE

Good-bye, proud world! I'm going home:
Thou are not my friend, and I'm not thine.
Long through thy weary crowds I roam;
A river-ark on the ocean brine,
Long I've been tossed like the driven foam;
But now, proud world! I'm going home.

Good-bye to Flattery's fawning face;
To Grandeur with his wise grimace;
To upstart Wealth's averted eye;
To supple Office, low and high;
To crowded halls, to court and street;
To frozen hearts and hasting feet;
To those who go, and those who come;
Good-bye, proud world! I'm going home.

I am going to my own hearth-stone,
Bosomed in yon green hills alone,—
A secret nook in a pleasant land,
Whose groves the frolic fairies planned,
Where arches green, the livelong day,
Echo the blackbird's roundelay,
And vulgar feet have never trod
A spot that is sacred to thought and God.

O, when I am safe in my sylvan home,
I tread on the pride of Greece and Rome;
And when I am stretched beneath the pines,
Where the evening star so holy shines,
I laugh at the lore and the pride of man,
At the sophist schools and the learned clan;
For what are they all, in their high conceit,
When man in the bush with God may meet?

CHARACTER

The sun set, but set not his hope:
Stars rose; his faith was earlier up:
Fixed on the enormous galaxy,
Deeper and older seemed his eye;
And matched his sufferance sublime
The taciturnity of time.
He spoke, and words more soft than rain
Brought the Age of Gold again:
His action won such reverence sweet
As hid all measure of the feat.

TERMINUS

It is time to be old,
To take in sail:—
The god of bounds,
Who sets to seas a shore,
Came to me in his fatal rounds,
And said: "No more!
No farther shoot
Thy broad ambitious branches, and thy root.
Fancy departs: no more invent;
Contract thy firmament
To compass of a tent.
There's not enough for this and that,
Make thy option which of two;
Economize the failing river,
Not the less revere the Giver,
Leave the many and hold the few.

Timely wise accept the terms,
Soften the fall with wary foot;
A little while
Still plan and smile,
And, fault of novel germs,
Mature the unfallen fruit.

Curse, if thou wilt, thy sires,
Bad husbands of their fires,
Who, when they gave thee breath,
Failed to bequeath
The needful sinew stark as once,
The Baresark marrow to thy bones,
But left a legacy of ebbing veins,
Inconstant heat and nerveless reins,—
Amid the Muses, left thee deaf and dumb,
Amid the gladiators, halt and numb."

As the bird trims her to the gale,
I trim myself to the storm of time,
I man the rudder, reef the sail,
Obey the voice at eve obeyed at prime:
"Lowly faithful, banish fear,
Right onward drive unharmed;
The port, well worth the cruise, is near,
And every wave is charmed."

CHAPTER IX

WILLIAM CULLEN BRYANT

Bryant has been called the Patriarch of American poetry. The title is not inappropriate, nor the distinction unmerited. For, in point of time, Bryant ranks first of our major poets, and the quality of his verse comes up to the standard set by the best of that number. "Thanatopsis," which first proclaimed the rising of his star, was written when its author was not yet out of his teens, and at once took rank as the finest poem which American literature, up to that time, had produced. It bore striking testimony to Bryant's precocious genius and by its appeal to nature and the higher life it demonstrated his admiration for, and adherence to, the best traditions of English poetry, and proved its author a pupil of Wordsworth, the great English singer of nature. While not up to the level of Wordsworth's best verse, "Thanatopsis" is like it in kind and quality—so much so that no critic would have paid the penalty of impaired confidence in his own judgment who might have attributed the anonymous lyric to the famous English laureate. By this one brief song Bryant achieved for himself the enviable reputation of a genuine poet, and immediately established himself as the undisputed laureate of America.

Bryant spent most of his life in New York City, and because of this circumstance he is usually placed by the critics in the Knickerbocker group of writers. But he was not essentially of this group.

He belonged really to the New England school, both in respect of the character and of the quality of his poetic achievement. He was sprung from the sturdy old Puritan stock, and his ancestors came over in the *Mayflower*. He therefore enjoyed much the same literary traditions and heritage as his contemporary Longfellow, who was descended from the same stock.

Bryant was born November 3, 1794, in the village of Cummington, amid the Hampshire hills of Massachusetts. Here he passed his boyhood in this beautiful country where nature displays her infinite variety of scenery in open field, green meadow with its babbling brook and the wood-clad hills. Young Bryant found keen delight in his picturesque surroundings. With his elder brother Austin he attended the district school hard by the babbling brook and received instruction of the most elementary character. "I was an excellent, almost an infallible speller," he wrote later, speaking of his early school days, "and ready in geography; but in the Catechism, not understanding the abstract terms, I made but little progress."

Bryant's father, who was a good country physician and who served his State many years in the Legislature, encouraged his son's aptitude for letters and stimulated his desire for knowledge by allowing him to browse at will in his well-selected library. When William Cullen was in his tenth year, his grandfather gave him a nine-penny coin for turning the first chapter of Job into a rhymed version. About the same time the precocious lad wrote out a rhymed description of the district school he attended, and the lines were honored with a place in the columns of the county paper. At this early age his ambition was kindled with an all-absorbing desire to be a poet. He eagerly read all the poetry that came within his reach and still longed for more. In this manner there was early developed in him a peculiar susceptibility to the poetical aspects of nature.

"I was always," he tells us, "from my earliest years, a delighted observer of external nature—the splendors of a winter's daybreak over the wide wastes of snow seen from our windows, the glories of the autumnal woods, the gloomy approaches of the thunderstorm and its departure amid sunshine and rainbows, the return of the spring with its flowers, and the first snowfall of winter. The poets fostered this taste in me, and though at that time I rarely heard such things spoken of, it was none the less cherished in my secret mind."

It is an interesting, though unimportant, circumstance that Bryant's first original poem was called forth by a political measure—the embargo laid upon all the ports of the Republic at the instance of President Jefferson. This measure, which wrought much damage to private interests in New England, rendered Jefferson's administration extremely unpopular in that part of the Union. The Bryants were zealous Federalists. It is small wonder, therefore, that William Cullen, with his characteristic knack for rhyming, should have given expression to his partisan feeling in a satiric poem, entitled "The Embargo." This juvenile production was published in Boston, in 1808, and was intended as a severe indictment against the Democratic party and its great founder. In general, it may be said to have reflected the feelings and temper of the New England Federalists. It is a noteworthy example of the irony of fate that this youthful, ardent Federalist became, in after years, the stanchest advocate and most influential champion of those Democratic principles of which Jefferson was the first accredited exponent.

"The Embargo" of course has no value as poetry. The theme—not to mention its author's immature age—did not lend itself to poetic treatment. The piece, though possessing no merit, is prized, however, as a curiosity, which shows Bryant's facility for versification. Neither this nor any other of his numerous juvenile effusions was deemed worthy of being included in any collected edition of his poems, though they were regarded by his contemporaries as "the flowering laurel on his brow." These early productions demonstrate very clearly their author's instinctive accuracy in measure and rhyme—points which he invariably looked after with scrupulous care.

Bryant was prepared for college by a neighboring clergyman, Rev. Moses Hallock, whose fitting school (facetiously called by his pupils the "Bread and Milk College," from the frequency of these simple articles of diet in the menu) enjoyed a very favorable reputation in preparing youths for college. Young Bryant entered the sophomore class in Williams College, in 1810, being in his sixteenth year. Before the close of the session he applied for honorable dismissal, intending to matriculate at Yale. "When the time drew near," he wrote years after,— "When the time drew near that I should apply for admission at Yale, my father told me that his means did not allow him to maintain me at New Haven, and that I must give up the idea of a full course of education. I have always thought this unfortunate for me, since it left me but superficially acquainted with several branches of education which a college course would have enabled me to master and would have given me greater readiness in their application."

His father's scant means put an abrupt termination to Bryant's college education and compelled him to settle down to hard manual labor on the farm. The years spent on the farm were not, however, without some compensation. They afforded young Bryant's teeming fancy ample opportunity to build for him a world of his own liking and to mark out, at his leisure, the lines of his future activity and development. His proximity to nature incident to his rural occupation furnished his aspiring mind fresh inspiration as well as themes for poetic treatment, which were destined to expand with his growing years. It was during this formative period spent on his father's farm that he drank in that beauty and love of nature which not only kindled his imagination and compelled its expression in undying verse, but which abode with him all those long years afterwards as editor in the great metropolis and kept his heart young and aglow with interest in public affairs, even to the very end of his long life.

Yet Bryant was not entirely cut off from books during those years of enforced farm life. He fully explored his father's library, and his interest was absorbed, in turn, in chemistry, botany and literature. He narrowly missed adopting medicine as his profession and becoming a country doctor, as his paternal ancestors for three successive generations had been. His own inclination and taste marked out for him a literary career. But he was unwilling, in his impecunious condition, to risk his fortune on so capricious a profession as the vocation of letters in America then was. He, therefore, compromised on law as his second choice, and in the adjacent towns of Bridgewater and Worthington he endeavored to explore its mysteries. His heart, however, was not in law. Literature proved the engrossing rival of his legal studies and awakened in his mind a growing discontent with law. His purpose to become a lawyer, therefore, wavered. Even while he was seeking for a promising place in which to begin the practice of his profession, his absorbing love for letters asserted the supremacy and fired his poetic imagination to the production of those chaste, beautiful lines "To a Waterfowl." While wending his way, late on a December afternoon, in 1815, to the neighboring town of Plainfield, where he proposed to establish himself as a lawyer, forlorn and desolate he descried the figure of a solitary bird winging its flight along the western horizon, then flooded with a rich splendor of the gorgeous colors of sunset. Watching the lone wanderer till it faded out of sight in the twilight distance, he resumed his journey with fresh courage and with stronger faith in the unknown future. On reaching his destination, in the evening, he sat down and wrote his classic lines "To a Waterfowl."

After a year's practice of law at Plainfield and nine years more of it at Great Barrigton, Bryant, although by no means a briefless barrister, decided to abandon the legal profession as unsuited to his taste. He thereupon resolved to move to New York City and devote himself to journalism, believing it would afford him a more congenial occupation. Accordingly, in 1826, when he was in his thirty-third year, we find Bryant, after several experiments in newspaper work, permanently established in New York as the associate editor of the *Evening Post*, only three years later to succeed to the important position of editor-in-chief and joint proprietor.

From that date his life and labors were bound up with the fortunes of that sheet; and by dint of his own untiring energy and unfaltering faith he succeeded in elevating that journal to a unique place in the forefront of American newspapers.

Bryant's far-reaching influence upon American journalism cannot be estimated. It is not an exaggeration to say that under his leadership the entire character of American journalism was transformed. In the words of his colleague and biographer, John Bigelow, "Journalism when Bryant entered the profession was as little like the journalism of 1889 as Jason's fifty-oared craft *Argo* was like a modern steam packet." By virtue of his unimpeachable honesty and integrity, and by his clean business methods no less than by his extraordinary ability as an editor, Bryant furnished a striking illustration of the fact that the newspaper can be made one of the great educational forces in the world in enlightening the masses and in directing and shaping public opinion on a high moral plane. The pioneer work of Bryant in this field was infectious, and the high moral tone of his paper proved a stimulus to other New York journals which have striven to emulate the rich traditions of the *Evening Post*. Bryant's editorial career covered a half century of the most momentous period of our national existence; and during this time he spoke out, with no uncertain sound, upon the many questions of national and international politics involving the interests and welfare of the American people. The editorial columns of the *Evening Post* during those fifty years furnish a complete and unbroken record of the growth and development of political thought in the United States. There is no matter of public concern falling within the domain of journalism, during

that period, which Bryant did not deal with and
express an opinion upon in such a manner as to
command the respectful consideration of those even
who did not accept his conclusions. He was no temporizer or trimmer waiting to take his cue from his
own clientele and reflect their opinion simply. He
had the moral courage to utter his own convictions
whether indorsed by his own patrons or not, and he
considered it his duty to help create a sound,
healthy public opinion by speaking out his sentiments in advance. He took high ground in his discussion of all the important questions of the day,
such as the Bank of the United States, the tariff,
nullification, slavery and the like, and defended his
position ably and vigorously, giving forceful utterance to his convictions.

Bryant's arduous duties as editor were interrupted by occasional visits to Europe (he made six
trips in all) and the Orient, to Mexico, Cuba and the
West Indies. Nor were these mere pleasure trips.
They served the desirable end of enhancing Bryant's
capacity as a keen and acute interpreter of affairs
in general and of deepening and broadening his
culture as a man, so that in his latter days he was
regarded perhaps the most cultured man in America, and universally esteemed and respected. His
success as a journalist soon placed him beyond that
pecuniary embarrassment which so harassed his
early years; and his *audax paupertas* which he experienced while a young man struggling for recognition in the world, as in the case of Horace,
remained only as a memory in his riper years. He
bought himself a fine country home, "Roslyn," on
Long Island; and in 1865 he bought back his old
homestead at Cummington. This latter place he
purchased not so much to gratify a worthy senti-

ment as in the hope that the high altitude of the locality might benefit his wife's health, then rapidly failing.

Bryant wrote several prose volumes during his long career, including books of travel and occasional addresses. He developed a clear, concise and vigorous prose style; and his prose works afford at once engaging and stimulating reading. Like most devotees of the Muse, he made himself master of the art of expression. He was a conservator of the best traditions of English prose in all its purity and simplicity and never used a neologism if there was a classic word in the vernacular to convey his meaning. His plain, homespun diction is not the least attractive quality of his admirable style. However, his fame as a man of letters reposes not on his achievement as master of a superior prose style, nor on his brilliant pioneer work in the history of American journalism. To be sure, he is not a negligible quantity in either of these closely allied departments of literary activity. Far from this, he left behind him a record worthy of admiration in every respect, and his accomplishment as a prose writer has enriched our literature. But it is as a poet chiefly that he has won for himself a conspicuous place among our literary leaders, and it is his poetry that is destined to perpetuate his name in the history of American literature after his prose has long since been forgotten. Indeed, even now, though only a quarter of a century since his death, he is much more favorably and widely known by his verse than by his prose. Yet he was not a prolific poet. So exacting were his duties as editor that he had little time left for courting the muse of poetry. He was a poet by nature, by instinct, as is every true poet; and ever and anon he would lapse

into verse even in the editor's sanctum and produce
an occasional poem, which was far removed from
the sort technically described as *vers d' occasion*.
The total output of his muse hardly exceeded one
hundred and sixty poems, aggregating about thirteen thousand lines. Of these one-third were written before he became connected with the *Evening
Post*. In 1821 he published a pamphlet collection
of his poems, and ten years later he augmented
this number by the addition of eighty other poems
written during that decade. This collection he
caused to be introduced to British readers through
the kindly offices of his friend Washington Irving,
then residing abroad; and thus his fame spread beyond our shores to the other side of the Atlantic.
It was his custom to incorporate his new poems into
his previous collection, and not to publish them sep-
arately as an entirely new edition.

Bryant never grew old, at least in his faculties
and feelings. It is true that he attained the patriarchal age of eighty-four, but till the day of his fatal
fall his faculties, both mental and physical, were
still unimpaired, and his heart was almost as young
as on the day when he came to New York more than
fifty years before, as an adventurer seeking fame
and fortune. His famous translation of Homer—
the execution of which would naturally tax the
strength of a scholar even in the very prime of life—
was hardly begun till 1866, when its author had already rounded out the full scriptural limit of
human life. Indeed, the laborious undertaking itself, truly courageous for a man of Bryant's advanced age, bears mute testimony to the man's indomitable resolution and energy no less than to his
characteristic buoyancy of temper. The death of
his wife produced in him a growing indisposition

for severe work and a yearning for some light employment to engage his attention and thus divert his mind from his domestic sorrow. His occasional translations of some passages from Homer, previously made, furnished him the suggestion desired, and he thereupon determined to turn his attention to this new departure from his absorbing labors as a journalist. Sailing on his sixth voyage to Europe, with a copy of Homer in his pocket, he set himself the daily task of translating at least forty lines of the Iliad during the entire time of his travels. Four years later he had finished his self-imposed task, and in June, 1870, his complete translation of the Iliad in two volumes was given to the public. His own account of the labor involved in the undertaking, as expressed some years later in a letter to his friend Dana, is indicative of Bryant's cheerfulness in old age and of his sunny disposition. "I did not find the work of rendering Homer into blank verse very fatiguing," he says in this letter, "and perhaps it was the most suitable occupation for an old man like me, who feels the necessity of being busy about something and yet does not like hard work."

Bryant had no sooner seen the Iliad through the press than he took up the Odyssey. He pursued the congenial task of rendering this supplementary Homeric epic into English with even more ceaseless diligence than he did the Iliad. So eager was he to complete his energetic plan of translating the whole of Homer before death should interrupt the work, that, by the end of the year 1871, he had dispatched the concluding instalment of the Odyssey manuscript to his publishers. Though finished in its author's seventy-seventh year, the translation reveals no mark of senile work. Far from showing the defects and weaknesses incident to old age, the version is remarkably accurate, spirited, rhythmical and noble withal.

The translation of the Odyssey proved the last sheaf of Bryant's literary harvest. He did not venture to embark on another enterprise of pith and moment. For his ripe old age warned him that he must content himself with his past accomplishment in letters and that henceforth he must husband his waning strength and powers for the remnant of life. The octogenarian author was gratified to live to witness the cordial reception accorded his last work by his own countrymen. The critics and scholars were especially enthusiastic in their praise. Somehow, they felt that Homer had never before been brought so near them as in Bryant's blank verse rendering, and the conviction that our literature had been materially and permanently enriched by this new successful achievement grew apace, and was not confined to Hellenists simply, but was shared by American scholars in general. Nor was this verdict the product of sympathy for the aged poet—what Ruskin perhaps calls the pathetic fallacy—or of prejudice against Pope's translation, because he was British and Bryant American. This latter alternative would indicate sheer provincialism. Yet Bryant's version inevitably invites comparison with Pope's, and does not suffer much by the comparison. For Bryant seems, even more than Pope, to have caught the spirit of the old blind bard of Hellas, and his admirable blank verse appears to be a closer approach to the original than the effect of Pope's metre. Bryant's Homer is conceded by the critics to possess a striking fidelity to the Greek, with a minimum of rhetorical adornment or surplusage rendered imperative by the exigencies of the verse. This is hardly the place for a detailed comparison of the relative merits of these two standard translations of Homer. In dismissing the subject, suffice it to say that Bryant's version has never yet elicited from a competent critic the withering comment which Bentley passed on Pope's: "A pretty poem, Mr. Pope, but you must not call it Homer."

Bryant's death in his eighty-fourth year was the result of an accident. In the latter part of May, 1878, on a warm afternoon, he delivered an address in Central Park, on the occasion of the unveiling of a statue to the Italian patriot Mazzini. On his return the aged journalist and poet fell, while mounting the steps of the house of his friend General Wilson, and struck his head on the stones, causing concussion of the brain. After lingering in a comatose condition for two weeks, he passed away, leaving behind him as a priceless heritage to his hosts of friends and admirers the record of a pure, exalted and noble Christian life. Perhaps it is safe to affirm that no man in America commanded more universal respect and reverence than Bryant did "when his summons came to join the innumerable caravan." At his death, press and platform seemed to vie with each other in paying glowing, generous tribute to his memory.

When we come to review and analyze Bryant's poetry, in order to discover the quality and limitations of his genius, we find some notable results. To begin with, he was a born singer. Like Pope, whose verse was not without considerable influence on our author's formative period, Bryant almost lisped in numbers, and early recognized his poetic mission. He is the first American poet in whom the national consciousness is thoroughly awakened and in whom it expresses itself in such a manner as to make itself felt far and wide throughout the country. No great poet had preceded him in this vast republic on the western hemisphere. Songsters there had been, to be sure, who piped a beautiful song here and there; but there had been no singer of undisputed supremacy whose note touched the national consciousness and challenged universal admiration. Freneau, "the poet of the Revolution," was a graceful singer, the author of the "Wild Honeysuckle" and the "Home of Night," but he left behind very little to redeem his name from oblivion and was, after all, provincial. Joseph Rodman Drake, the so-called American Keats, wrote two impassioned, though immature odes which still command admiration; and John Howard Payne will long be remembered by his immortal lyrics, "Home, Sweet Home," and the "Star-Spangled Banner." But neither of these authors ever attained to the dignity and rank of a great poet or can claim the distinction of a truly national representative singer. Poe, while fully the rival and peer of Bryant in the beauty and polish of his poems, and far surpassing him in imagination and technical execution, as well as in the melody of his verse, yet has nothing distinctly national about him, nothing that smacks of the soil from which he was sprung. Moreover, Bryant's reputation was established before Poe began to write. It may be objected that Bryant was the poet of Puritanism. This cannot be gainsaid. But it is equally true that, though the poet of Puritanism, Bryant was at the same time the first American poet whose verse breathes the spirit of the national consciousness and the spirit of American nature and landscape scenery. Under the influence of Pope and Wordsworth, Bryant

learned the best traditions of English poetry and
incorporated them into his own verse, with its broad
outlook on nature and on life. Bryant, therefore,
has no successful rival to his claim as the "father
of American song." He is the first of our American
poets, in point of time, whose place in English literature is definitely assured.

No quality of Bryant's poetry is more noteworthy
than his extraordinary precocity. In poetry, as in
prose, maturity of art usually comes with years of
unremitting toil and practice. But Bryant served
no apprenticeship. His maiden poem "Thanatopsis," though thrust aside into a pigeon-hole and not
published till years after it was written, was as
faultless in quality and execution as the best production of his mature genius. The seventeen-year-
old author of "Thanatopsis," who also wrote his
lines "To a Waterfowl" before he attained his majority, even with all the practice and accumulated
experience of many years spent in productive literary work, never succeeded in striking a more melodious note or teaching a profounder philosophy than
he expressed in his first two lyrics. The key of his
song, of course, varied, but the rhythm and quality
remained almost on the same level. He enhanced
the beauty of his later poetry by broadening its
range rather than by improving its quality and he
never surpassed the high standard of excellence established by the first products of his muse. In this
respect Bryant's example sets at naught all literary
traditions, and forms an exception to the rule of
poetic development.

Bryant's chief source of inspiration is nature, and
as a poet of nature he shows his affinity and kinship
with the renowned master of the Lake school of
English poets. No element of our bard's poetry is

more characteristic or more universally appreciated than his nature poems. His love of nature was little short of passionate and, moreover, it expressed itself in a number of lyrics which constitute his finest work. A notable example is his ode "To the Fringed Gentian," to mention a specific example. In his familiar, pathetic verses on "Death of the Flowers," equally illustrative of his penetrating love of nature, he touches an elegiac chord which contributes not a little to the tender charm of the piece.

Another quality of Bryant's genius is exhibited in the meditative, reflective character of his poetry. This distinctive feature of his verse appears in his very first song, "Thanatopsis," and, like a golden thread, can be traced through the warp and woof of his entire poetic fabric. "Thanatopsis" is reputed to have been written under the immediate inspiration of Kirk White's melancholy poem "The Grave," which superinduced in young Bryant's muse a meditative, pensive mood. This seems a a sufficient explanation of the sombre, reflective vein running through this chaste and classic song. But this element is found in all of Bryant's themes and marks his genius. It was his habit to meditate on the significance of life, its moral meaning, and upon death and the hereafter. In the contemplation of such disturbing questions his deep religious nature and Puritanism afforded him consolation and peace, and he naturally gave utterance to his feelings in his song.

Like all the poets of the New England school, Bryant could hardly resist the temptation to use his song to point a moral. He felt compelled— such was his Puritan nature—to teach religious truth even in his verse, to give a moral turn to every poetic scene or thought that kindled his imagination. To him beauty did not appear a sufficient excuse for its own being, as it did to Poe, and Bryant, therefore, subordinated it to the higher end, in his eyes, of conveying religious instruction. This didactic feature is repugnant to modern canons of art; and, for this reason, some of the critics disparage Bryant's verse, relegating it to the limbo of mere religious poetry. Yet it is this very religious quality that explains, in large measure, the hold of Bryant's poetry upon the people, his widespread popularity. The American people, by and large, are not critical, and hence their literary sensibilities are not offended by a poem with "a moral tag."

Bryant's most noticeable defect is, probably, his narrowness of range, He sang mostly in one note. There are themes unlimited in number, capable of beautiful poetic interpretation and treatment, which did not, apparently, appeal to his muse. But this fault is not peculiar to Bryant: it is common to most poets. It is only the very great singers who have a wide register and are capable of running the entire gamut of song. Some critics find Bryant cold and lacking in breadth of sympathy and also in spontaneity. The criticism is not without some foundation in fact. Bryant, the man, was not a warm-hearted, impulsive, magnetic personality. He was reserved, cautious and calculating, but pure, noble and generous withal. It is but natural, therefore, that his verse, in its limitations as well as in its excellences, should reflect somewhat its author's character, his individuality. Thus Bryant's song may be viewed as interpreting himself to the world, his characteristic thought and feeling. He revealed his inner nature to the world in terms of his song.

Bryant never essayed a poem requiring prolonged effort and inspiration. Like Poe, he rejected the theory and principle of the long poem as contrary to the recognized canons of poetic invention. He contended that, on analysis, a long poem simply resolves itself into a series of short lyrics of more or less intensity of inspiration. Moreover, the ethical element in Bryant's poetry does not comport well with a long narrative or descriptive poem, and he had sufficient appreciation of the divine fitness of things not to attempt to reconcile two such incongruities. Our poet's chief triumphs are found in his simple, unimpassioned lyrics which demand no long-sustained attention. His inspiration was intermittent. Nature denied him the dramatic power of invention and constructive skill, such as a long narrative poem like "Hiawatha" implies in its author. She also denied the intensity of passion necessary for the production of erotic verse. Bryant's nearest approach to fervor and passion is perhaps found in his patriotic song, "The Battlefield," of which some lines have won a wide currency.

Bryant's choice in the use of his metres is as limited and narrow as is the range of his themes. In keeping with his simplicity of manner, he confined himself to a few familiar metres, never once inventing or using any intricate forms. In his stanzaic forms he harked back to the eighteenth century models and attempted few or none of the metrical effects, such as engaged the attention of those masters of rhythm, Poe and Swinburne. Yet Bryant was an expert in versification; and probably no poet was more skilled in the technique, the architectonics of verse, than was he. His rhymes, too, are as scrupulously accurate as his verses are correct and polished. He bestowed upon their structure unstinted care and spared not the labor of the file. Hence his verses, in respect of their polish and finish, compel our admiration, even when the sentiment seems cold and wanting in inspiration. The beauty of his blank verse excited the envy of his fellow-poets and filled them with despair. The skill with which he handled this difficult metre, as revealed in his "Thanatopsis," that famous production of his boyhood, proved the poetical marvel of his age, and even now can only be explained as conclusive evidence of his precocious genius.

It follows, therefore, that Bryant occupies no insignificant, no inconspicuous place in the history of American letters. He appears a calm, dignified, noble seer who had visions, ever and anon, of the grand divine purpose concerning man, and who felt impelled to teach the people the high moral significance of life and death as related to the Great Beyond. Like one of the ancient Hebrew prophets, he caught now and then inspiring glimpses of man's sublime destiny and interpreted it to us in terms of song.

BRYANT

TO THE FRINGED GENTIAN

Thou blossom bright with autumn dew,
And colored with the heaven's own blue,
That openest when the quiet light
Succeeds the keen and frosty night.

Thou comest not when violets lean
O'er wandering brooks and springs unseen,
Or columbines, in purple dressed,
Nod o'er the ground-bird's hidden nest.

Thou waitest late and com'st alone,
When woods are bare and birds are flown,
And frosts and shortening days portend
The aged year is near his end.

Then doth thy sweet and quiet eye
Look through its fringes to the sky,
Blue—blue—as if that sky let fall
A flower from its cerulean wall.

I would that thus, when I shall see
The hour of death draw near to me,
Hope, blossoming within my heart,
May look at heaven as I depart.

THE DEATH OF THE FLOWERS

The melancholy days are come, the saddest of the year,
Of wailing winds, and naked woods, and meadows
    brown and sere.
Heaped in the hollows of the grove, the autumn leaves
    lie dead;

They rustle to the eddying gust, and to the rabbit's
   tread;
The robin and the wren are flown, and from the shrubs
   the jay,
And from the wood-top calls the crow through all the
   gloomy day.

Where are the flowers, the fair young flowers, that
   lately sprang and stood
In brighter light and softer airs, a beauteous sister-
   hood?
Alas! they all are in their graves, the gentle race of
   flowers
Are lying in their lowly beds, with the fair and good
   of ours.
The rain is falling where they lie, but the cold November rain
Calls not from out the gloomy earth the lovely ones
   again.

The wind-flower and the violet, they perished long ago,
And the brier-rose and the orchis died amid the summer glow;
But on the hills the golden-rod, and the aster in the
   wood,
And the yellow sun-flower by the brook in autumn
   beauty stood,
Till fell the frost from the clear cold heaven, as falls
   the plague on men,
And the brightness of their smile was gone, from upland, glade, and glen.

And now, when comes the calm mild day, as still such
   days will come,
To call the squirrel and the bee from out their winter
   home;

When the sound of dropping nuts is heard, though all
    the trees are still,
And twinkle in the smoky light the waters of the rill,
The south wind searches for the flowers whose fra-
    grance late he bore,
And sighs to find them in the wood and by the stream
    no more.

And then I think of one who in her youthful beauty
    died,
The fair meek blossom that grew up and faded by my
    side.
In the cold moist earth we laid her, when the forests
    cast the leaf,
And we wept that one so lovely should have a life so
    brief:
Yet not unmeet it was that one, like that young friend
    of ours,
So gentle and so beautiful, should perish with the
    flowers.

ROBERT OF LINCOLN

Merrily swinging on brier and weed,
    Near to the nest of his little dame,
Over the mountain-side or mead,
    Robert of Lincoln is telling his name:
        Bob-o'-link, bob-o'-link,
        Spink, spank, spink;
Snug and safe is that nest of ours,
Hidden among the summer flowers.
        Chee, chee, chee.

Robert of Lincoln is gayly drest,
    Wearing a bright black wedding-coat;
White are his shoulders and white his crest.
    Hear him call in his merry note:

Bob-o'-link, bob-o'-link,
   Spink, spank, spink;
Look, what a nice new coat is mine,
Sure there was never a bird so fine.
     Chee, chee, chee.

Robert of Lincoln's Quaker wife,
   Pretty and quiet, with plain brown wings,
Passing at home a patient life,
   Broods in the grass while her husband sings:
     Bob-o'-link, bob-o'-link,
     Spink, spank, spink;
Brood, kind creature; you need not fear
Thieves and robbers while I am here.
     Chee, chee, chee.

Modest and shy as a nun is she;
   One weak chirp is her only note.
Braggart and prince of braggarts is he,
   Pouring boasts from his little throat:
     Bob-o'-link, bob-o'-link,
     Spink, spank, spink;
Never was I afraid of man;
Catch me, cowardly knaves, if you can!
     Chee, chee, chee.

Six white eggs on a bed of hay,
   Flecked with purple, a pretty sight!
There as the mother sits all day,
   Robert's singing with all his might:
     Bob-o'-link, bob-o'-link,
     Spink, spank, spink;
Nice good wife, that never goes out,
Keeping house while I frolic about.
     Chee, chee, chee.

Soon as the little ones chip the shell,
   Six wide mouths are open for food;
Robert of Lincoln bestirs him well,
   Gathering seeds for the hungry brood.

Bob-o'-link, bob-o'-link,
Spink, spank, spink;
This new life is likely to be
Hard for a gay young fellow like me.
Chee, chee, chee.

Robert of Lincoln at length is made
   Sober with work, and silent with care:
Off is his holiday garment laid,
   Half forgotten that merry air:
      Bob-o'-link, bob-o'-link,
      Spink, spank, spink;
Nobody knows but my mate and I
Where our nest and our nestlings lie.
      Chee, chee, chee.

Summer wanes; the children are grown;
   Fun and frolic no more he knows;
Robert of Lincoln's a humdrum crone;
   Off he flies, and we sing as he goes:
      Bob-o'-link, bob-o'-link,
      Spink, spank, spink;
When you can pipe that merry old strain,
Robert of Lincoln, come back again.
      Chee, chee, chee.

TO A WATERFOWL

Whither, midst falling dew,
   While glow the heavens with the last steps of day,
Far, through their rosy depths, dost thou pursue
   Thy solitary way?

Vainly the fowler's eye
   Might mark thy distant flight to do thee wrong,
As, darkly seen against the crimson sky,
   Thy figure floats along.

Seek'st thou the plashy brink
  Of weedy lake, or marge of river wide,
Or where the rocking billows rise and sink
  On the chafed ocean-side?

There is a Power whose care
  Teaches thy way along that pathless coast—
The desert and illimitable air—
  Lone wandering, but not lost.

All day thy wings have fanned,
  At that far height, the cold, thin atmosphere,
Yet stoop not, weary, to the welcome land,
  Though the dark night is near.

And soon that toil shall end;
  Soon shalt thou find a summer home, and rest,
And scream among thy fellows; reeds shall bend,
  Soon, o'er thy sheltered nest.

Thou 'rt gone, the abyss of heaven
  Hath swallowed up thy form; yet, on my heart
Deeply has sunk the lesson thou hast given,
  And shall not soon depart.

He who, from zone to zone,
  Guides through the boundless sky thy certain flight,
In the long way that I must tread alone,
  Will lead my steps aright.

THANATOPSIS

WRITTEN IN THE POET'S EIGHTEENTH YEAR

To him who in the love of Nature holds
Communion with her visible forms, she speaks
A various language; for his gayer hours
She has a voice of gladness, and a smile
And eloquence of beauty, and she glides
Into his darker musings, with a mild
And healing sympathy, that steals away
Their sharpness, ere he is aware. When thoughts
Of the last bitter hour come like a blight
Over thy spirit, and sad images
Of the stern agony, and shroud, and pall,
And breathless darkness, and the narrow house,
Make thee to shudder, and grow sick at heart;—
Go forth, under the open sky, and list
To Nature's teachings, while from all around—
Earth and her waters, and the depths of air—
Comes a still voice—

                              Yet a few days, and thee
The all-beholding sun shall see no more
In all his course; nor yet in the cold ground,
Where thy pale form was laid, with many tears,
Nor in the embrace of ocean, shall exist
Thy image. Earth, that nourished thee, shall claim
Thy growth, to be resolved to earth again,
And, lost each human trace, surrendering up
Thine individual being, shalt thou go
To mix forever with the elements,
To be a brother to the insensible rock
And to the sluggish clod, which the rude swain
Turns with his share, and treads upon. The oak
Shall send his roots abroad, and pierce thy mould.

Yet not to thine eternal resting-place
Shalt thou retire alone, nor couldst thou wish
Couch more magnificent. Thou shalt lie down
With patriarchs of the infant world—with kings,
The powerful of the earth—the wise, the good,
Fair forms, and hoary seers of ages past,
All in one mighty sepulchre. The hills
Rock-ribbed and ancient as the sun,—the vales
Stretching in pensive quietness between;
The venerable woods—rivers that move
In majesty, and the complaining brooks
That make the meadows green; and, poured round all,
Old Ocean's gray and melancholy waste,—
Are but the solemn decorations all
Of the great tomb of man. The golden sun,
The planets, all the infinite host of heaven,
Are shining on the sad abodes of death,
Through the still lapse of ages. All that tread
The globe are but a handful to the tribes
That slumber in its bosom.—Take the wings
Of morning, pierce the Barcan wilderness,
Or lose thyself in the continuous woods
Where rolls the Oregon, and hears no sound,
Save his own dashings—yet the dead are there:
And millions in those solitudes, since first
The flight of years began, have laid them down
In their last sleep—the dead reign there alone.
So shalt thou rest, and what if thou withdraw
In silence from the living, and no friend
Take note of thy departure? All that breathe
Will share thy destiny. The gay will laugh
When thou art gone, the solemn brood of care
Plod on, and each one as before will chase
His favorite phantom; yet all these shall leave
Their mirth and their employments, and shall come
And make their bed with thee. As the long train
Of ages glides away, the sons of men,

The youth in life's fresh spring, and he who goes
In the full strength of years, matron and maid,
The speechless babe, and the gray-headed man—
Shall one by one be gathered to thy side,
By those who in their turn shall follow them.

So live, that when thy summons comes to join
The innumerable caravan, which moves
To that mysterious realm, where each shall take
His chamber in the silent halls of death,
Thou go not, like the quarry-slave at night,
Scourged to his dungeon, but sustained and soothed
By an unfaltering trust, approach thy grave
Like one who wraps the drapery of his couch
About him, and lies down to pleasant dreams.

CHAPTER X

HENRY WADSWORTH LONGFELLOW

It has been now somewhat more than a score of years since the death of Longfellow. Perhaps we are not yet far enough removed from his day to form an impartial estimate of the rank and place in our literature which this deservedly popular poet is destined to occupy. It requires a considerable lapse of time to dispel the illusion and glamour which his charming poetry cast over the minds of his readers; and it may be that we are not yet prepared to examine his verse in the cold and dispassionate light of criticism.

Longfellow was born in Portland, Maine, in 1807. He came of one of the first New England families, and his father, who was a successful lawyer, spared no expense to equip his son fully for a literary life. The way, therefore, was made smooth for Henry Wadsworth Longfellow to attain to the eminent distinction of being America's most popular poet at the time of his death. It seems fitting to review his poetic achievement and inquire whether the foremost American poet of a generation ago is still holding his own. It is possible that his popularity has been eclipsed by the fame of some bard whose star had not risen two decades ago.

In his own time, as just stated, Longfellow enjoyed a wider fame than any other poet, alive or dead, on this side of the Atlantic. Emerson was doubtless a profounder thinker and more philosophical, and appealed more powerfully to a select circle

of readers.   But he was the recognized exponent of
a certain school, and his audience was therefore
limited.' Whittier's verse smacked too much of a
party, or of a section, to be universally admired.
Profoundly stirred by the evils of slavery, he came
to regard himself, for the nonce, as the poetic
mouthpiece of the Abolition party, and when his
party passed away together with the cause which
called it into being, Whittier's poetry lost much of
its power and charm, even for his most zealous co-
partizans.   Lowell was perhaps more brilliant and
versatile than Longfellow; but he was rather bookish, and his poetry is not infrequently open to the
charge of pedantry.   Bryant was chaste and finished and grand even; but his poetry was as lifeless and as cold as marble.   There was no fire or
passion in it: it came from the head, not from the
heart.   Longfellow, however, "looked into his own
heart and wrote"; and he touched in his song those
chords which awaken an echo in every heart.   For
this reason his poetry approximates that class of
literature which critics sometimes denominate
"universal."   Not that Longfellow deserves to rank
with the world's great poets, for he does not: nor
would the most ardent admirers of his genius make
any such claim for him.   But his poetry has more
in it that appeals to the human heart than has the
poetry of any of his American contemporaries.

Longfellow's fame is not confined to America.
He is favorably known in Europe.   No other
American poet, with the possible exception of Poe,
is so widely known on the other side of the Atlantic.
Indeed, it is questionable that Poe forms an exception.   For while Poe is much read on the Continent,
especially in France, still it is his tales rather than
his poetry that foreigners read.   Longfellow's

poetry has been far more extensively translated. His recent biographer is authority for the statement that there have been one hundred versions, in whole or in part, of Longfellow's work, extending into eighteen foreign languages. What other American author can equal, much less surpass, this flattering record of appreciation?

Longfellow has been aptly called the people's poet; and, in the judgment of many discriminating critics, the title is well founded in fact. For his sympathies and affections were ever with the people; for them he wrought, for them he sang. By education and culture, by his happy faculty of literary expression and by his unfailing good taste he was peculiarly qualified and equipped for this office; and herein lies the secret of his unbounded popularity and success. His message was not erudite or esoteric; nor did it presuppose any extraordinary degree of mental acumen in those to whom it was addressed, to appreciate it. But it was such as a man of average intellectual endowment could comprehend and appreciate. In this respect our poet was poles removed from Browning, whose poetry fully yields its hidden meaning only to the most acute and best trained intellects. But Longfellow's simplicity of utterance makes his poetry readily "understanded of the people" and renders a commentary unnecessary. His verse is at once lucid and clear and melodious and beautiful. Indeed, his distinguishing virtue consists in his power of expressing in chaste, lucid and musical verse what everybody has felt, but few can say with such felicity of phrase. He possessed the rare faculty of re-clothing old, familiar truths in a poetic dress in such a manner as to give them the appearance of entirely new and original creations. *Difficile est proprie communia dicere,* says Horace, himself a master in the art of literary expression; but, somehow, Longfellow seems to have acquired the secret of this difficult art of putting commonplace things happily.

Longfellow was of a poetic temperament. His taste and feelings were essentially those of a poet. This is evident from the glamour and witchery of phrase, which we have just observed as characteristic of his style. He first felt the poem in his own soul, and then he translated it into terms of surpassing grace, beauty and music. Herein lies the secret of his genius.

Some critics are willing to concede Longfellow facility, beauty and charm; but they deny him originality. There is a sense in which this criticism is true; but, like all half truths, the dictum is misleading and does the poet an injustice. Longfellow, it is true, was not original in the sense in which Poe was original; nor was he original in the sense in which Browning was original. It is not probable that Longfellow possessed as high a degree of originality perhaps as either of these poets. Yet, if by originality is meant creative genius, then Longfellow was unquestionably original. For does it not require a high order of creative genius to give to the prosy, commonplace sentiments and experiences of everyday life poetic form and beauty and spontaneity as well? Now, this, as has been observed, is just what Longfellow has done. Let us have done therefore with the cant that he was not an original poet.

Longfellow achieved his greatest triumphs in lyrical poetry. As a dramatic poet he was not a success. But this is no great disparagement. It only proves that, like most authors, our poet had his limitations. For few, indeed, are the poets of the last century who have won laurels in the province of the drama.   Not even Tennyson with all the glamour of his name could make one of his dramas hold the stage.   Longfellow produced two successful narrative poems.   But it is not chiefly these that have won him his enviable reputation as the poet of the people.   It is rather his sonnets, his shorter poems, in which he excelled.   Of these perhaps the best known is his "Psalm of Life," now as familiar as a household word.   This contains a larger number of lines, long since become familiar quotations, than any other of our poet's lyrics.   In point of furnishing quotable lines, as well as in point of spontaneity and general excellence, it challenges comparison with Gray's beautiful Elegy.   Longfellow gave conclusive proof of his good taste and sound literary judgment in resisting the temptation to make of his theme a mere didactic poem.   He speaks to us through the lines of this psalm as standing, not on a plane above and beyond us, but on the same level with us and as being himself one of our own number.   The poem is a stirring and inspiriting appeal for sympathy, of a man who aspires with us, to a higher and nobler life.   There is nothing of didacticism about it.   On the contrary, it is imaginative and spontaneous and pulsates with emotion and sympathy.

Worthy of special mention among our poet's lyrics are "Excelsior," "The Reaper and the Flowers," "Footsteps of Angels," "Maidenhood" and "Resignation."   These are all excellent and have attained a wide currency.   They are poems instinct with tender sentiment and make a strong, albeit mute, appeal to gentle and pensive natures. Equally beautiful in technical execution, though not so pathetic perhaps, are such snatches of song as "Land of the Desert," "The Lighthouse," "The Jewish Cemetery," and "The Arsenal." In the production of such sonorous trifles (if that is not too frivolous a word to apply to these songs), Longfellow stands unexcelled in American literature. Indeed, few English singers have surpassed him in this kind of verse.

In his ballads, such as "The Skeleton in Armor" and kindred lyrics, Longfellow made a new departure and entered the domain of romance. This and the sad sea ballad, "The Wreck of the Hesperus," are perhaps his finest. But however much critics may praise these ballads, we feel nevertheless that the romantic vein was not their author's forte. Probably the most felicitous sea poem that Longfellow wrote was "The Building of the Ship." This furnishes a noteworthy example of his metrical skill. Moreover it is full of energy and patriotic fervor and challenges comparison with Horace's graceful, patriotic ode, which was its prototype. The glowing apostrophe to the Union, at the close, is a far more impassioned appeal to patriotism than Horace's pæan of victory over the defeated Cleopatra.

In his narrative poems Longfellow blazed out an entirely new path in our literature. Accordingly, he deserves the distinction of being the first American poet to compose a long narrative poem the interest of which is sustained throughout. In this respect Longfellow essayed a bold undertaking, but the generous and cordial welcome which "Evangeline" received fully justified the author's daring attempt. The pathetic story of "Evangeline" is well told, and the delicate descriptive passages here and there throughout the poem indicate the presence of the hand of a master artist. The concep-

tion, too, of the heroine, in her noble and inspiring
example of sacrifice for the sake of her lost lover,
is as beautiful as it is tender and pathetic. The
author was happy both in conception and execution, and the result is that "Evangeline" is an exquisite idyl which deserves to take rank as a classic
by the side of Goldsmith's "Deserted Village."
Still, notwithstanding its beauty and pathos,
"Evangeline" is not a poem which rivets our attention and compels our unqualified admiration. Considered from the point of view of art, the poem has
blemishes and imperfections that impair its charm
and beauty not a little. The characters are not
portrayed with that skill and power which one
could desire. They do not stand out upon the page
with distinctness and with clearness of outline.
Moreover, there are long stretches of narrative
which do not contribute materially to the development and interest of the story. There are few
dramatic episodes, though the poem affords numerous glimpses of interesting and picturesque characters.

Perhaps we ought to take "Evangeline," however,
as the author probably intended it, viz., as a tender
and graceful idyl fashioned out of a beautiful and
pathetic legend of early American history. Viewed
in that light it cannot fail to charm and entertain
the reader. But if we attempt to apply to it the
canons of the drama, or of the novel, it is immediately open to serious criticism.

Longfellow culled the pathetic legend of "Evangeline" from the gray dawn of our country's history
and suffused it with a soft glow of his poetic imagination, thus imparting to it its charm and romantic
interest, and made of it "the flower of American
idyls." But the poem is much indebted to the clas-

sic measure the author chose, for its beauty and for
the delightful spell it casts over the reader.   The
selection of the hexameter for the meter of "Evangeline" seems a stroke of genius, because this meter,
somehow, is specially well adapted to the bucolic
love story.   And the author handled this difficult
measure with rare skill and deftness—so much so,
indeed, that his hexameters challenge comparison
with the most graceful in our language.   Longfellow has hardly yet received his due meed of praise
for his service in helping to domicile a form of verse
which is almost universally condemned by the
critics as an exotic and as unadapted to the exigencies of English poetry.   The critics poured out
the vials of their wrath upon his head for such a
bold attempt, and almost exhausted their vocabulary of censure.   All this Longfellow anticipated,
but he felt that the hexameter was the measure for
his idyl, and so he adopted it despite the storm of
criticism it was destined to call forth.   In no point
of literary art did our bard show more conclusive
evidence of the courage of his convictions than in
his deliberate choice of the meter for his "Evangeline."   The popularity of this delightful bucolic
love story has justified his choice and fully vindicated the soundness of his judgment.   For many
of the familiar lines of the "Evangeline" have won
their currency chiefly through the sonorous cadence
and roll of the hexameter.

The "Courtship of Miles Standish" formed a companion piece to the author's favorite idyl, "Evangeline."   The former is a Pilgrim idyl in which
Priscilla, John Alden and the bluff old captain
form the principal figures.   It is so familiar as to
render an analysis of it superfluous.   Though not
so popular as "Evangeline," the "Courtship of

Miles Standish" marks a distinct advance upon its predecessor in constructive skill and in the delineation of the characters. The figures stand out with greater definiteness and distinctness of outline. Not the least noteworthy feature of this entertaining idyl is the broad humour that lights up the conventional conception of the Pilgrim character in those far-off times in our history. We do not usually invest that character with much charm or romance. But Longfellow's conception glows with a warm imagination and a romantic interest more in keeping with the impulsive character of the Virginia cavalier than with the cold, impassive character of the Pilgrim.

In his narrative poem of "Hiawatha" Longfellow achieved a notable success. This poem, as is well known, deals with the manners, customs and legends of the various tribes of our North American Indians. The one idea which, like a golden cord, runs through the twenty-two different legends and binds them all together, giving them unity and harmony, is the life of Hiawatha. The "Song of Hiawatha" is a distinctive American product and smacks of the soil whence it sprang. It breathes the wild outdoor odor of forest and stream in every line. Its strange wildness and grim weirdness, as reflected in the interplay of the savage aborigines upon the rugged background of nature, combine to impart to the poem the beauty and fascination of a fairy tale. The characters of Hiawatha and of his Indian wife, the laughing Minnehaha, are both masterful poetic conceptions, such as only a true poet would or could conceive. In the creation of these characters Longfellow gave indisputable proof of his inventive genius and originality, for nothing approaching "Hiawatha" even remotely had been

attempted before in our literature, and nothing has
been done since that equals it. "Hiawatha," therefore, stands alone in American literature; and
English literature offers no parallel to it.

The meter conspired with the subject matter of
"Hiawatha" to make the poem unique and original.
For the characteristic verse—rhymeless trochaic
dimeter—had never before been employed in a long
poem, and was, in fact, almost unknown in English
literature. It is a difficult meter to handle; and
for this reason it required consummate skill on the
part of the poet to prevent the verse from degener-
ating into commonplace chant, or mere singsong.
The grotesque Indian names are woven into the
poem with a musical effect little short of marvelous, and impart to the story a decided epic quality.
Had the meter been other than it is, it were impossible to say what the result would have been. Longfellow so blended the meter and the substance into
a poem, at once beautiful and melodious, as to make
it impossible to divorce them without marring the
artistic effect. "Hiawatha," therefore, is the form
the Indian legends assumed as the poem was crystallized in the poet's imagination.

Not the least important service which Longfellow
rendered American letters was his excellent and
scholarly interpretation of the great Italian poet of
the Middle Ages. His translation of Dante proved
a touchstone of his own invention and art; and the
result is a metrical version both musical and accurate. To be sure, the translation is not absolutely
impeccable, or faultily faultless. (Nor would it
be true to say, as an enthusiastic German critic said
of Tieck and Schlegel's version of Shakespeare, that
the translation is better than the original.) But
the faults are such as almost necessarily follow

from a scrupulous effort to give a faithful and literal rendering. No American man of letters was probably better fitted by taste, natural endowment and training for the difficult and delicate work. Longfellow, moreover, addressed himself to his arduous task with the proper conception of translation, viz., to produce a "literal and lineal rendering." As might have been expected, therefore, he caught the spirit and thought of the great Florentine and reproduced them with remarkable grace, smoothness and accuracy. The translation immediately took rank with the best in our tongue.

Like Tennyson and many other poets who have achieved distinction in the field of lyric verse, Longfellow was ambitious to win laurels in the province of the drama. But it does not follow that because a poet is successful as a lyricist that he is also a dramatist. This fact Longfellow of course knew at first theoretically, and he subsequently had it verified in experience. Emboldened by the partial success of his romance "Hyperion" and by that of his first dramatic effort, "The Spanish Student," he set out resolutely to score an unqualified and complete success in a new and original drama. Accordingly, he at length gave to the world his Trilogy of "Christus," which he regarded as the high-water mark of his dramatic genius and art. But his hopes were doomed to disappointment, for the Trilogy fell flat and proved a signal failure. Justice to the poet, however, requires us to modify this remark and add that a part of the Trilogy did possess merit. Of this more anon.

The "Christus" was a very unequal production. The first part, "The Divine Tragedy," and the third part, "The New England Tragedies," are decidedly tame and weak and little short of inane. The subjects selected may be such as to offer great possibilities to a dramatist of real genius, but in the hands of Longfellow the treatment is feeble and altogether inadequate. The work may have the proper personages and situations and the form of a play, but it lacks the action, fire and passion. The author has evidently overestimated his power and chosen a theme beyond his capacity and range.

Of the second part of the Trilogy, however, a favorable word may be spoken. This part, which, by the way, was published a score of years before the "Divine Tragedy," was entitled the "Golden Legend" and is the oasis in the desert. It is the sole redeeming part of the Trilogy. The "Golden Legend" is a fascinating romance cast in dramatic form, and, according to some critics, it reflects the author's versatile genius at its best. John Ruskin wrote of it at the time of its production: "Longfellow, in his 'Golden Legend,' has entered more closely into the temper of the monk, for good or for evil, than ever yet theological writer or historian, though they may have given their life's labor to the analysis." But even the "Golden Legend," brilliant as it is in parts, was not sufficient to redeem from a speedy oblivion the first and third parts of "Christus," and so the Trilogy remains to-day unread—a striking monument of the poet's misdirected ambition.

The fact is, Longfellow lacked dramatic skill; he was not, and never could become, a playwright. This was one of his limitations, and a limitation which he was very slow to recognize. Indeed, he never fully realized it, as his posthumous drama "Micheal Angelo" attests. If the energy and effort which he expended upon the drama had been given to lyric poetry, Longfellow would have won even greater triumphs than those he did achieve and would have left behind him a more enduring name.

If Longfellow had consulted his reputation as a poet, he would probably have withheld from publication his "Tales of a Wayside Inn." These he published in instalments extending through a decade, but they did not enchance his fame. They possess rather meagre literary merit. The poems which compose the collection are too diffuse and rambling, and the work lacks unity. They are a series of short stories gleaned from various foreign literatures and are strung together somewhat after the manner of Ovid's *Metamorphoses*. There seems, too, to be no obvious principle of classification. To be sure, there are some fine passages here and there, but the tales, as a whole, make upon the reader the wearisome impression of being long-drawn-out and prolix. The author was presumably led into this error by his extraordinary lyrical facility and by his superior qualities as a *raconteur*. He was therefore handicapped by the defects of his qualities.

It has been said that Longfellow was the poet of the people, and the remark is true. In England he is regarded as the poet of the middle classes. Now, this was also the class for whom Tennyson wrote. It is a noteworthy fact that these two poets possessed much in common. But we need not dwell upon this point. Neither Longfellow nor Tennyson was a "poet of passion or pain." This phrase, however, is a more apt characterization of the great English poet than of the gifted American singer. Longfellow never touched any very deep chord either of joy or of sorrow. His register did not include either of these extremes. He pursued the even tenor of his song, never rising to the height of ineffable joy, on the one hand, nor descending to the depth of unutterable anguish, on the other. Still, he was not "an idle singer of an empty day." Being neither rich nor poor, he occupied a fortunate intermediate station in life; and following his own exhortation, he wrote out of his own heart and experience.

Longfellow had a keen appreciation of nature. Probably nature would have appealed to him with something of the power and force with which she appealed to Wordsworth, if his lot had been cast among other surroundings. A college professor has a great deal of drudgery connected with his arduous duties, and the class-room does not afford the most glorious aspects of nature. But Longfellow's love of nature was by no means an absorbing, passionate love. It has not that May-morning freshness about it, such as we find in the father of English poesy and in those who have drawn their inspiration from the same source as he. Like his contemporary Lowell, Longfellow could never quite forget his books; but unlike Lowell, Longfellow did not allow his learning to obtrude itself unduly, and thus render his art over-literary. A good illustration of what is meant is found in the poet's commemoration ode, "Morituri Salutamus," written for the fiftieth anniversary of his graduating class. As Mr. Stedman has pointed out in his appreciative sketch of Longfellow in his "Poets of America," this ode contains more than twenty learned references within the brief compass of three hundred lines, and yet the allusions are so deftly wrought into the poem that the effect is simple, natural and artless. Had Lowell essayed to do the same thing, he would almost inevitably have produced the impression of airing his erudition and parading his art.

Longfellow learned the art, as happy as it is rare, of veiling his learning, and he knew the value of simplicity and artlessness. Above all things he strove to be natural. Affectation and display were foreign to his nature. He never posed for effect. His motto in art as in life was, *Esse quam videri malim*. His poetry was but the natural expression of his sterling character, which despised sham and pretense in whatever form masquerading, and was as sincere and chaste as his own pure soul.

Longfellow's genius was lyrical. His inspiration he sought more often in the heart than in the head. Tenderness, sympathy and love, combined with melody and charm, are the distinctive qualities of his verse. He aimed to look, not upon the dark, threatening exterior of the cloud, but upon its bright silver lining. In a word, he was an optimist, and looked out upon life through roseate glasses. There was nothing morbid about him, as there was, for instance, about Poe. He is thoroughly sane and wholesome as well as chaste and pure. He put himself into his work and through his verse gave himself to the world. Guileless, pure and true, he would no sooner have written a line which he felt to be untrue than he would have told a glaring falsehood. Of the sacredness and importance of the office of the poet no man ever entertained a more exalted opinion. His poetry is the flower and fruit of his noble life.

LONGFELLOW

MORITURI SALUTAMUS

"O Caesar, we who are about to die
Salute you!" was the gladiators' cry
In the arena, standing face to face
With death and with the Roman populace.

O ye familiar scenes,—ye groves of pine,
That once were mine and are no longer mine,—
Thou river, widening through the meadows green
To the vast sea, so near and yet unseen,—
Ye halls, in whose seclusion and repose
Phantoms of fame, like exhalations, rose
And vanished,—we who are about to die
Salute you; earth and air and sea and sky,
And the Imperial Sun that scatters down
His sovereign splendor upon grove and town.
Ye do not answer us! ye do not hear!
We are forgotten; and in your austere
And calm indifference, ye little care
Whether we come or go, or whence or where.
What passing generations fill these halls,
What passing voices echo from these walls,
Ye heed not; we are only as the blast,
A moment heard, and then forever past.

Not so the teachers who in earlier days
Led our bewildered feet through learning's maze;
They answer us—alas! what have I said?
What greetings come there from the voiceless dead?
What salutation, welcome, or reply?
What pressure from the hands that lifeless lie?
They are no longer here; they all are gone
Into the land of shadows,—all save one.

Honor and reverence, and the good repute
That follows faithful service as its fruit,
Be unto him, whom living we salute.

The great Italian poet, when he made
His dreadful journey to the realms of shade,
Met there the old instructor of his youth,
And cried in tones of pity and of ruth:
"Oh, never from the memory of my heart
Your dear, paternal image shall depart,
Who while on earth, ere yet by death surprised,
Taught me how mortals are immortalized;
How grateful am I for that patient care
All my life long my language shall declare."

To-day we make the poet's words our own,
And utter them in plaintive undertone;
Nor to the living only be they said,
But to the other living called the dead,
Whose dear, paternal images appear
Not wrapped in gloom, but robed in sunshine here.

*   *   *   *   *   *   *

CHAPTER XI

OLIVER WENDELL HOLMES

Few years in the history of English and American literature have been more signalized by the birth of great men than the year 1809. Nature distributed her gifts with a lavish hand to her babes of that year, for among those babes were Gladstone, Lincoln, Darwin, Tennyson, and Poe, to mention only a few, the bare recital of whose names quickens the pulse and kindles the imagination. There was another born at Cambridge, Massachusetts, during that *annus mirabilis*, Oliver Wendell Holmes, who made for himself a name and, when he died in 1894, left behind him a record destined to stimulate and inspire our American youth for years to come. He was not a powerful factor, like Gladstone or Lincoln in the councils of State, in shaping the destinies of nations; nor was he, like Darwin, a brilliant investigator of nature, devoting himself to the advancement of science with an energy and zeal almost unparalleled in the world's history. Yet he was inspired by a spirit somewhat akin to that which fired Darwin's soul and started him on the line of his daring researches into the secrets of nature. For he devoted himself to the noble profession of medicine, and lent his healing art to the relief of suffering humanity, and though he made no brilliant discoveries, he yet strove to advance the bounds of human knowledge and to contribute to man's comfort and welfare. But it is not this phase of Holmes' life that we propose to consider.

Our object here is to discuss Holmes as a man of letters, in which capacity he achieved as great distinction as he did as a follower of Æsculapius.

Young Holmes was intended by his father, himself a Congregational clergyman, for the ministry, but nature decreed otherwise. "I might have been a minister myself, for aught I know," wrote Holmes in later life, "if a certain clergyman had not looked and talked so like an undertaker." Again, speaking in a satiric vein of the impressions the ministers visiting his father's house made upon his youthful mind, he says:

"But now and then would come along a clerical visitor with a sad face and a wailing voice, which sounded exactly as if somebody must be lying dead upstairs, who took no interest in us children except a painful one as being in a bad way, with our cheery looks, and did more to unchristianize us with his woe-begone ways than all his sermons were likely to accomplish in the other direction."

Thus the boy was repelled rather than attracted to the ministry by a well-meaning clergyman, and did not yield to his father's wishes. Upon his graduation from Harvard, in 1829, Holmes felt some inclination to the law, but he pursued it only a short time when he discovered that he had not yet "found himself," and that law was not to his taste. He then addressed himself to medicine, which he felt to be his calling. After the completion of his medical course, which he pursued mainly in Paris, he returned to his native State of Massachusetts and began the practice of his profession. In 1838 he was called to a professorship of anatomy in Dartmouth College, and a few years afterwards he was called thence to Harvard, his *alma mater*. Here he remained and continued to lecture till his resignation of his professorship in 1882. The evening of life he devoted exclusively to his literary pursuits.

The Little Man of Boston, as Dr. Holmes was familiarly called, enjoyed an enviable reputation as a *raconteur* and wit and became a familiar figure upon the lyceum platform. In 1884, he visited Europe—fifty years or more after his first prolonged visit when a student—and was cordially received wherever he went, for his writings had already made his name famous, and the literati vied with each other in doing him homage. Oxford and Cambridge conferred upon him their highest honors. Upon his return to America he described his trip in an entertaining volume of travels, "Our Hundred Days in Europe." Holmes then settled down in Beacon Street to spend a peaceful and happy old age, accompanied with "honor, love, obedience and troops of friends."

After this brief biographical sketch it is in order to review Holmes's writings, prose and poetry, and to determine his place, as best we may, among American men of letters. For convenience of treatment his prose works will be considered first and afterwards his poetry.

I.

Holmes is, no doubt, quite as favorably known by his prose as by his poetry. He is not of the number of authors who excelled in only one of the great departments of literature. As in case of his life-long friend, James Russell Lowell, it is difficult to affirm whether Holmes advanced his reputation as an author more by his prose or by his poetry. Both his prose and verse exhibit very much the same qualities of wit, humor, piquancy, and good taste. Perhaps, however, his genial originality is the most distinctive characteristic of his work. It shines forth from every page that he wrote, just as it is said to have flashed and sparkled in the conversation of the man himself.

Holmes showed a decided *penchant* for literature early in life. Even during his college days he began to write. But most of his early work was verse—metrical essays, of light banter, with an occasional poem in a sober, serious vein. He was fast approaching the meridian of life before he seems to have developed any special aptitude for prose composition. At any rate, if he possessed it before, he does not appear to have appreciated it.

When *The Atlantic Monthly* was projected in 1857, James Russell Lowell was asked to become the editor. This he reluctantly consented to do, but only on condition that Holmes should become a regular contributor and be "the first contributor to be engaged." Referring to this honor that Lowell paid him, Holmes afterwards said:

"I, who felt myself outside the charmed circle drawn around the scholars and poets of Cambridge and Concord, having given myself to other studies and duties, wondered somewhat when Mr. Lowell insisted upon my becoming a contributor. I looked at the old portfolio and said to myself, 'Too late! too late! This tarnished gold will never brighten, these battered covers will stand no wear and tear; close them and leave them to the spider and the bookworm.' "

With this famous magazine, which was indebted for its name to a suggestion of our author, a new star swam into the ken of the American reading public. That star was Holmes, who, as Howells said, not only named, but made *The Atlantic* the foremost literary magazine in America.   It was the publication, in that journal of those inimitable papers, the "Breakfast Table" series, that gave the monthly caste and established its reputation.

The first of this well-known series to appear in the columns of *The Atlantic* was "The Autocrat of the Breakfast Table."   But this was not the author's maiden effort.   More than a score of years before he had dashed off two papers in a similar vein, which he had published under the same *nom de plume* in the short-lived *New England Magazine*. In the "Autocrat's Autobiography," Holmes says of these two early essays that "the recollection of the crude products of his uncombed literary boyhood suggested the thought that it would be a curious experiment to shake the same bough again, and see if the ripe fruit were better or worse than the early windfalls."   But the world, if it had tasted his early windfalls, had forgotten them; and so the "Autocrat" series appeared with all the freshness and attendant interest of the discovery by the public of a new author.

It is related that when the management of the magazine announced the title of the series as "a drawing card," the proprietor of a well-known religious weekly took it for granted that it was a cook book, and that a Frenchman, perplexed at the odd title, exclaimed, "L' Autocrate à la table du déjeuner, titre bizarre!"   The series was eagerly expected and read far and wide when it appeared, and it elicited no little comment, both favorable and unfavorable.   Some critics, enraged at the daring views set forth, applied uncomplimentary, not to say sulphurous, epithets to the Autocrat.   Some in mild protest called him undignified and "an inordinate egotist"; and one even suggested that the poems with which the essays close "showed as ill as diamonds among the spangles of the court fool." The religious press in general took umbrage at the universalist opinions which the book reflected, and voided its rheum upon the author. It is probably a safe statement that no book published in those times created a greater sensation in the American literary world.

"The Autocrat of the Breakfast Table" was really a unique book and an entirely new departure. Nothing quite like it, or indeed approaching it, had ever before appeared in this country. It is usually regarded as the best of Holmes's prose works, and is slightly above the level of the subsequent volumes of the series. But the entire "Breakfast Table" series is excellent. It is a New England product, and smacks of the soil. Like Hawthorne's Puritan romances, the "Breakfast Table" books could not have been written by any other than one born and bred in New England. (Both authors had a good deal of the Puritan in them, Hawthorne more than Holmes.) The characters of the books are distinctively local and correspondingly provincial; they were drawn from New England models. Their language, their way of thinking, their general bearing, and the local color withal, conspire beyond question to betray their origin, and to stamp them peculiarly New England creations.

It is to be observed by way of parenthesis that Holmes rendered American literature a vast service in thus presenting and preserving for all time these various types of New England character; and for this reason alone his work merits high praise. For the "Breakfast Table" series is, in its way, as true and admirable a portrayal of New England charac-

ter as Lowell's equally famous "Biglow Papers." It
is true that Lowell's creation is more valuable in
preserving the language, since in this respect it is a
veritable treasure-trove for the student of the Yankee dialect.   But barring this difference, the two
works are almost equally valuable as exhibiting a
faithful and vivid portrayal of fast-disappearing
types of New England character.   That character
and that country were dear to the heart of Holmes;
and old Boston, with all its historic associations and
memories, was dear to his heart above all the other
spots in his beloved Massachusetts.   Indeed, few
men have loved their native place more passionately
than did he.   No Roman could have loved Rome
with more ardor, and no ancient Hebrew the Holy
City with more devotion, than Holmes loved Boston.   "I would not," exclaims he in an impassioned
outburst of patriotism, when speaking of his native
city, "I would not take all the glory of all the greatest cities in the world for my birthright in the soil
of little Boston!"   It is true that Boston represented the best in New England life and character;
and Holmes, being of the people of that locality and
a New Englander to the core, regarded himself as an
exponent of this peculiar type of American civilization, and conceived it to be his special mission to
give expression to it for the benefit of our literature.
That he was truly representative of New England
cannot be questioned.   Indeed, he was a more faithful exponent of the place and the people than was
Lowell, or perhaps even Hawthorne; for these both
resided abroad long enough to rub off considerable
of their provincialism, and in their diplomatic
capacities and contact with men of various nationalities they took on something of a cosmopolitan
veneer and finish; but Holmes remained New England till his death.

"The Autocrat of the Breakfast Table" was followed by "The Professor at the Breakfast Table," which, like its predecessor, also first appeared as a serial in *The Atlantic*. This book is of course, very much in the same manner as "The Autocrat," though perhaps not quite up to the level of the latter. After its publication the author refrained for more than a decade from writing any more of those charming essays. During this period, when our country was in the throes of civil war, he turned his attention to fiction, and wrote two novels. After the fire and smoke of civil strife had passed away, Holmes resumed his essays and produced the third volume of his series, entitled "The Poet at the Breakfast Table," which appeared in 1872. This book is similar, in plan and scope, to those that preceded it, but in the conversation of the characters it plainly reflects some of the many changes which took place during that momentous period in our country's history. "The Poet at the Breakfast Table" was generally regarded as the last volume of the series. But in 1891, well-nigh twenty years after, another volume, somewhat different in character, though bearing a general family resemblance, appeared. This youngest child of his creative genius the author, now in the evening of life, very appropriately christened "Over the Teacups."

Holmes lived to see his early critics undergo a change of heart with reference to the merits of his "Breakfast Table" series. "The Autocrat" had divided the reading public into two camps; "Over the Teacups" found the hostile camp deserted, and all the quondam foes now friends. The author's early views and convictions were, to a considerable extent, in advance of the times, but the world soon came to adopt, in large measure, his way of thinking. "Over the Teacups," his last hostage to fortune, was therefore kindly received; and since the author had rounded out the scriptural limit of threescore years and ten, the book was looked upon as "sad autumn's last chrysanthemum." But there is no mark of senility to be found in the book. It holds the reader's attention as closely as the first volume of the series, published over thirty years before. It is generally conceded, however, that "The Autocrat" is the best of the series. But all the volumes are interesting and entertaining; yea more, they are really fascinating. There is not a dull, prosaic page in any of them, and some of the papers are brilliant. There is an atmosphere of freshness and piquancy pervading every volume, as one might naturally expect in a kind of writing entirely unique and original as the "Breakfast Table" series was. Holmes scored a phenomenal success in this new departure, and upon it established his reputation as a writer of a racy and charming English prose style. As a specimen of graceful, facile English the papers of the "Breakfast Table" series are unexcelled in American literature, and surpassed only by Addison's and Lamb's inimitable essays in English literature.

Like most prose writers, Holmes, when he learned that he held the attention of the public, decided to try his hand at the alluring art of novel-writing. But this fact will elicit little surprise in his case if we reflect that in "The Professor at the Breakfast Table" were contained the elements of a good story. Accordingly, in 1861, he gave the world his first novel, "The Professor's Story," which he subsequently christened "Elsie Venner," the name by which the novel is generally known. The novel was greeted with a storm of criticism on all sides, but this adverse criticism caused the book to be all the more widely read. Though thus criticised, it may

be called a popular novel, and is even now occasionally read. Still, if one may make such a distinction,
the book was not a success, at any rate from an
artistic point of view. Its conception was, upon the
whole, unhappy.

"Elsie Venner" is of that class of fiction known
as the "purpose novel." This fact of itself heavily
discounts it with many readers. Of the novel with
a purpose we may distinguish at least two classes.
The first class includes those novels that are designed by their authors to correct certain social
abuses, or to bring about certain reforms. Of this
class are Dickens's "Bleak House" and "Little Dor-
rit," and Sir Walter Beasant's best-known novel,
"All Sorts and Conditions of Men," the agitation
engendered by which resulted in the establishment
of that philanthropic institution, the People's
Palace, in London. The second class includes those
novels which are written to set forth some pet
theory of the novelist, and may be called psychological novels. "Elsie Venner" belongs to this class.
Its purpose is theoretical, and involves a psychological problem. For this reason it falls legitimately in the province of science, rather than of art.

The problem of "Elsie Venner" is twofold. First,
supposing a prospective mother to be bitten by a
rattlesnake, can the venom infused into the mother
be so communicated to the unborn babe as to affect
its nature and influence its disposition? Secondly,
granted that this theory of prenatal poisoning be
true, to what extent is such a child morally responsible? This is the theory underlying "Elsie Venner," of which the story is the outgrowth. It will
be seen that the conception itself is not attractive;
on the contrary, the thought is positively repellent.
The novel, therefore, in its very essence, creates a
prejudice in the reader's mind, for the normally

constituted man or woman has an aversion to snakes, and does not take much interest in any such unnatural hybrid creature as Holmes made the heroine of his story.

"Elsie Venner" has come to be recognized as one of the chief snake stories in English literature. From what source the author got the suggestion is not clear. It is possible that the biblical account of Eve's encounter with the serpent may have suggested the idea to him. We are told that Holmes, in order to make the effect more vivid and realistic, made a special study of serpents, and kept a rattlesnake in a cage, closely observing its every habit and movement. These he reproduced in Elsie Venner, with all the accuracy and skill at his command, under the limitations of her hybrid nature. The result is that Elsie Venner is a girl whose nature is tainted by the trail of the serpent—a character to many readers uninviting, not to say repulsive. Yet such was the popularity of the story that shortly after its appearance an attempt was made to dramatize it. As a play it proved a signal failure. This is but what might have been expected, for it is an extremely difficult task to dramatize with good effect a psychological story. The psychology is likely to volatilize in the process, and the play to degenerate into a mere burlesque. In the novel, Elsie Venner, with her small, beady, snake-like eyes and her cold, unnatural touch, may cast an illusion over the reader's imagination; but the illusion is dispelled directly the attempt is made to put her upon the stage. Indeed, the illusion is not always perfect even in the novel, and you feel at times that the author transcends the limit of art and comes perilously near to the farcical.

But Holmes never intended this novel for a farce. Nor did he conceive it in any frivolous spirit. Far from it. As the author wrote a friend of his, the story was conceived in the fear of God and the love of man. The problem at the bottom of the novel in Holmes's mind was the extent of moral responsibility in a creature like Elsie Venner. In connection with this thought he suggests the cognate thought as to how far are children, born of wicked, degraded parents and reared amid squalid, immoral associations, morally responsible for their conduct. This is a theological question; and after all it was theology, so his biographer tells us, that engaged Holmes's attention more profoundly and more constantly than anything else. Medicine he loved and literature he loved, but he loved theology above all. Yet, strange to say, the clergy were disposed to regard him as an infidel. He attacked the religion of certain clergymen, not because he did not believe in the Saviour, but because he did not believe in the religion that they preached. He felt that their religion had become incrusted with human errors and superstitions, and these he would tear away in order that he might get nearer to the essentials of Christianity—to its heart. He believed in pruning off all human excrescences which had grown up around our religion, and in throwing them away as being false, and therefore worthless. This part of religion he rejected as spurious, but the divine part he clung to tenaciously. But enough of this phase of the discussion of our author's novel.

"Elsie Venner," as has been said, was not a success from the point of view of art. True, it abounds in brilliant passages here and there, and the local color is admirable and the description fine. But this is not enough to make a successful novel. There must be clear-cut characterization and a strong plot. Now, "Elsie Venner" is not above criticism on either of these scores. The characters are not real enough;

they do not live and move as men and women of flesh and blood. But it is only the great novelists that possess this power of creation. Again, the plot is weak, and the incidents are not sufficiently striking. This is a notably weak spot in Holmes's equipment as a novelist. He is tolerably good at portraying characters and reproducing the local color, in creating an atmosphere and giving the proper setting to a story, but in the construction and working out of the plot he is lamentably weak.

The reader will observe that we have dwelt quite at length upon this first novel of our author. We have done so for two reasons. In the first place, it is considered Holmes's best-known and strongest story; in the second place, it is representative of his method and art as a writer of fiction. As it is not our purpose to speak in detail of his other novels, the detailed consideration of "Elsie Venner," already given, may serve to indicate to the reader Holmes's excellences and limitations as a novelist.

Holmes's second novel, which appeared in 1868, was entitled "The Guardian Angel." It is in some respects a stronger story than the author's first adventure, and shows an improvement over it, considered as a work of art. It is probably more brilliant, and, as a critic has said, fairly sparkles "with gems of wisdom, wit, and humor." It is like its predecessor in being a novel with a purpose, but it is less fantastic, not so improbable in conception and more inviting in fact. Holmes's third and last novel was "A Mortal Antipathy," produced during the declining years of his life and published in 1885. It is somewhat in the same vein as his other two works of fiction, but far inferior in detail and execution. If the author had consulted his literary reputation, he would not have published this feeble story. As a work of fiction, it falls but little short of a failure. Even Holmes himself seemed to realize this, after the publication of the book, and perhaps would fain have recalled it. But as Horace centuries ago said, *Nescit vox missa reverti.* Of Holmes's two memoirs, "Emerson" and "Motley," it is not worth while to speak, except to remark that they were both well done and contain some of the author's terse, epigrammatic, and pungent sentences.

II

It is time now to speak of Holmes's poetry. It is a question whether Holmes's prose or poetry will contribute more to perpetuate the memory of his name. However that may be, no just estimate of his place in American letters can be formed without taking into consideration his verse as well as his prose, for the two cannot be divorced. They were born together. It is of course well known that it was the author's practice to insert his poetic effusions in the "Breakfast Table" chat, and especially to close his papers with a song or an ode. Hence many of his best poems appeared first in this series; and, indeed, "The Autocrat" contains the finest poetic work he ever did. His prose and verse are therefore intimately associated in the popular mind, and have both united to establish his reputation as an author.

Holmes seems to have developed very early a facility for verse-making. While we are not told that he lisped in numbers, still he possessed a natural fondness, an instinct, for song, and had a sensitive ear for musical, rhythmical sounds. His verse was not of the studied and tortuous sort. It flowed forth without any apparent effort, and with all the naturalness and ease of a gentle brook. It seemed to well up out of his heart like the water from a limpid, sparkling fountain. He had no recourse to those devices adopted by some poets to conceal a poverty of invention or a deficiency of inspiration. His poetry, like his prose, abounds in cleverness, wit, and humor. Of course a vein of genial originality runs through it all. His early verse teems with a broad humor, which closely verges on mere fun, and it makes no claim to seriousness or beauty. By this early work he came to be known as a clever, witty, satiric versifier. This is, in the main, the character of the volume of "Humorous Poems" he published in 1865, and of his metrical escapades which first appeared in *The Collegian*. Into his famous "Old Ironsides," however, published about the same time, he infused a spirit of impassioned eloquence which made the ballad far more serious and sober than anything he had hitherto written.

Holmes's facility and versatility combined with his wit and humor to make him a favorite writer of society verse. No other American has probably equaled Holmes in this department of verse. His services were greatly in demand at banquets, class reunions, and social gatherings of all sorts; for he enjoyed the rare distinction of being unrivaled as a writer of *vers d' occasion*. Some of his *jeux d' esprit* are very happy, and would be worthy of quotation did space permit. The greater part of his poetic output is of this light kind of verse, and as a writer of such verse he occupies a place quite his own in our literature.

But Holmes could also write verse of a graver nature and of a nobler type. Some few of his serious efforts are lyrics of genuine poetry, and deserve to be placed by the side of our finest short poems. Witness here those beautiful flights of inspiration, "The

Chambered Nautilus" and "The Living Temple."
The latter poem is one of the finest things of the
kind in our literature. Indeed, it is but little inferior to Addison's sublime paraphrase of the nineteenth Psalm, than which few sacred lyrics in our
language are finer. Another excellent hymn of his
that might be mentioned here is that beginning,

"O Love divine! that stooped to share
Our sharpest pang, our bitterest tear."

This is eminently worthy to be in an anthology of
our best sacred lyrics, and has already found its
way into some of the hymnals of our Churches.
Equally exquisite is the "Sunday Hymn," beginning,
"Lord of all being! throned afar."

As illustrating Holmes's power and range in the
domain of serious poetry, we venture to quote "The
Living Temple," partly because it may not be so
well known and partly because of its beauty and
sustained loftiness of thought:

"Not in the world of light alone,
Where God has built his blazing throne,
Nor yet alone in earth below,
With belted seas that come and go,
And endless isles of sunlit green,
Is all thy Maker's glory seen;
Look in upon thy wondrous frame,—
Eternal wisdom still the same!

"The smooth, soft air with pulse-like waves
Flows murmuring through its hidden caves,
Whose streams of brightening purple rush,
Fired with a new and livelier blush,
While all their burden of decay
The ebbing current steals away,
And red with Nature's flame they start
From the warm fountains of the heart.

"No rest that throbbing slave may ask,
Forever quivering o'er his task,
While far and wide a crimson jet
Leaps forth to fill the woven net
Which in unnumbered crossing tides
The flood of burning life divides,
Then kindling each decaying part
Creeps back to find the throbbing heart.

"But warmed with that unchanging flame
Behold the outward moving frame,
Its living marbles jointed strong
With glistening band and silvery thong,
And linked to reason's guiding reins
By myriad rings in trembling chains,
Each graven with the threaded zone
Which claims it as the master's own.

"See how yon beam of seeming white
Is braided out of seven-hued light,
Yet in those lucid globes no ray
By any chance shall break astray.
Hark how the rolling surge of sound,
Arches and spirals circling round,
Wakes the hushed spirit through thine ear
With music it is heaven to hear.

"Then mark the cloven sphere that holds
All thought in its mysterious folds,
That feels sensation's faintest thrill
And flashes forth the sovereign will;
Think on the stormy world that dwells
Locked in its dim and clustering cells!
The lightning gleams of power it sheds
Along its slender glassy threads!

"O Father! grant thy love divine
To make these mystic temples thine!
When wasting age and wearying strife
Have sapped the leaning walls of life,

When darkness gathers over all,
And the last tottering pillars fall,
Take the poor dust thy mercy warms
And mold it into heavenly forms."

This it must be admitted, is excellent of its kind. "The Last Leaf," however, is by some considered finer still. It is probably more popular, and appeals to some more forcibly than to others. Hundreds of persons are said to know it by heart, which speaks highly for its excellence. But it is not worth while to discuss the relative merits of Holmes's poems further.

Was Holmes a great poet? No; we are forced to confess, after all, that he was not. He wrote no one poem, nor any collection of poems, that stands out preëminently and conspicuously in the body of our literature. Nothing that he did in verse is quite sufficient to insure him a lasting fame and make his name immortal. He attempted only lyrics, odes, and ballads—nothing of a dramatic or epic sort. His poetic work is not quite such as to entitle him to rank with Poe, Longfellow, or Bryant. But, while he is not of this number, he is not far below them. His proper place is perhaps just a little below these, with Lowell and poets of his class—poets who have written excellent poetry, but whose work is not of a character to entitle them to stand in the front rank of American poets. In some respects Holmes occupies a unique place in our literature. We refer to his facility in writing *vers d' occasion*. But this is not the highest form of verse, not poetry of the first water. Some little of this latter kind of poetry he did write, but not enough to place him among our immortals.

Taken all in all, Holmes's prose seems to be of a higher order of merit than his poetry. The literary

qualities that he possessed would, in the very nature
of things, achieve distinction for an author more
readily in the domain of prose than in that of
poetry. His racy, witty, humorous, original style
places him easily among the very first of our American prose writers. His style is what might be
called the essay style. He therefore appears at his
best in the "Breakfast Table" series, where he is
unsurpassed. In this department of prose he is
superior to Lowell, if one may compare the two, for
Holmes's prose flows on with fewer interruptions
and turns than Lowell's and has more of an outdoor
air about it. Lowell could never quite forget his
library, and his prose is consequently somewhat
bookish. Now, as a critic Lowell is far better, because Holmes made no pretentions to criticism and
himself disparaged the art. As a novelist Holmes
can hardly be called successful. His prose in his
stories is up to the high level he maintains in his
essays, and is sometimes even more brilliant, but
the plot is weak, and leaves much to be desired from
an artistic point of view.

Such, then, in our judgment, is Holmes's relative
standing among American men of letters. His prose
is of a more uniformly high order than his poetry.
Nevertheless, he wrote a few lyrics of rare beauty
and excellence which have already found their way
into our anthologies and are counted among our
most highly prized poems. Surely it is no small
achievement to have won for oneself a place among
the very first of our American prose writers and to
be rated only a little below our best poets.

HOLMES

GREAT TREES

(The Autocrat of the Breakfast-Table.)

—I wonder how my great trees are coming on this summer.

—Where are your great trees, sir?—said the divinity-student.

Oh, all round about New England. I call all trees mine that I have put my wedding-ring on, and I have as many tree-wives as Brigham Young has human ones.

—One set's as green as the other,—exclaimed a boarder, who has never been identified.

They're all Bloomers,—said the young fellow called John.

[I should have rebuked this trifling with language, if our landlady's daughter had not asked me just then what I meant by putting my wedding-ring on a tree.]

Why, measuring it with my thirty-foot tape, my dear,—said I. —I have worn a tape almost out on the rough barks of our old New England elms and other big trees.—Don't you want to hear me talk trees a little now? That is one of my specialties.

[So they all agreed that they should like to hear me talk about trees.]

I want you to understand, in the first place, that I have a most intense, passionate fondness for trees in general, and have had several romantic attachments to certain trees in particular. Now, if you expect me to hold forth in a "scientific" way about my tree-loves, —to talk for instance, of the *Ulmus Americana,* and describe the ciliated edges of its samara, and all that, —you are an anserine individual, and I must refer you to a dull friend who will discourse to you of such

matters. What should you think of a lover who
should describe the idol of his heart in the language
of science, thus: Class, Mammalia; Order, Primates;
Genus, Homo; Species, Europeus; Variety, Brown;
Individual, Ann Eliza; Dental Formula,

$$i\ \frac{2-2}{2-2}\ c\ \frac{1-1}{1-1}\ p\ \frac{2-2}{2-2}\ m\ \frac{3-3}{3-3}, \text{ and so on?}$$

No, my friends, I shall speak of trees as we see
them, love them, adore them in the fields, where they
are alive, holding their green sun-shades over our
heads, talking to us with their hundred thousand
whispering tongues, looking down on us with that
sweet meekness which belongs to huge but limited
organisms,—which one sees in the brown eyes of oxen,
but most in the patient posture, the outstretched arms,
and the heavy-drooping robes of these vast beings
endowed with life, but not with soul,—which outgrow
us and outlive us, but stand helpless,—poor things!—
while Nature dresses and undresses them, like so many
full-sized but under-witted children.

Did you ever read old Daddy Gilpin? Slowest of
men, even of English men; yet delicious in his slow-
ness, as is the light of a sleepy eye in woman. I always
supposed "Dr. Syntax" was written to make fun of
him. I have a whole set of his works, and am very
proud of it, with its gray paper, and open type, and
long *ff*, and orange-juice landscapes. Père Gilpin
had a kind of science I like in the study of Nature,
—a little less observation than White of Selborne, but
a little more poetry.—Just think of applying the Lin-
næan system to an elm! Who cares how many stamens
or pistils that little brown flower, which comes out
before the leaf, may have to classify it by? What we
want is the meaning, the character, the expression of
a tree, as a kind and as an individual.

There is a mother-idea in each particular kind of
tree, which, if well marked, is probably embodied in
the poetry of every language. Take the oak, for

instance, and we find it always standing as a type of strength and endurance. I wonder if you ever thought of a single mark of supremacy which distinguishes this tree from those around it? The others shirk the work of resisting gravity; the oak defies it. It chooses the horizontal direction for its limbs so that their whole weight may tell,—and then stretches them out fifty or sixty feet, so that the strain may be mighty enough to be worth resisting. You will find, that, in passing from the extreme downward droop of the branches of the weeping-willow to the extreme upward inclination of those of the poplar, they sweep nearly half a circle. At 90° the oak stops short; to slant upward another degree would mark infirmity of purpose; to bend downwards, weakness of the organization. The American elm betrays something of both; yet sometimes, as we shall see, puts on a certain resemblance to its sturdier neighbor.

It won't do to be exclusive in our taste about trees. There is hardly one of them which has not peculiar beauties in some fitting place for it. I remember a tall poplar of monumental proportions and aspect, a vast pillar of glossy green, placed on the summit of a lofty hill, and a beacon to all the country round. A native of that region saw fit to build his house very near it, and, having a fancy that it might blow down some time or another, and exterminate himself and any incidental relatives who might be "stopping" or "tarrying" with him,—also laboring under the delusion that human life is under all circumstances to be preferred to vegetable existence,—had the great poplar cut down. It is so easy to say, "It is only a poplar," and so much harder to replace its living cone than to build a granite obelisk!

I must tell you about some of my tree-wives. I was at one period of my life much devoted to the young lady-population of Rhode Island, a small but delightful State in the neighborhood of Pawtucket. The number of inhabitants being not very large, I had leisure, during my visits to the Providence Plantations, to inspect the face of the country in the intervals of more fascinating studies of physiognomy. I heard some talk of a great elm a short distance from the locality just mentioned. "Let us see the great elm,"—I said, and proceeded to find it,—knowing that it was on a certain farm in a place called Johnson, if I remember rightly. I shall never forget my ride and my introduction to the great Johnson elm.

I always tremble for a celebrated tree when I approach it for the first time. Provincialism has no *scale* of excellence in man or vegetable; it never knows a first-rate article of either kind when it has it, and is constantly taking second and third rate ones for Nature's best. I have often fancied the tree was afraid of me, and that a sort of shiver came over it as over a betrothed maiden when she first stands before the unknown to whom she has been plighted. Before the measuring tape the proudest tree of them all quails and shrinks into itself. All those stories of four or five men stretching their arms around it and not touching each other's fingers, of one's pacing the shadow at noon and making it so many hundred feet, die upon its leafy lips in the presence of the awful ribbon which has strangled so many false pretensions.

As I rode along the pleasant way, watching eagerly for the object of my journey, the rounded tops of the elms rose from time to time at the roadside. Wherever one looked taller and fuller than the rest, I asked myself, "Is this it?" But as I drew nearer, they grew smaller, or it proved, perhaps, that two standing in a line had looked like one, and so deceived me. At last, all at once, when I was not thinking of it,— I declare to you it makes my flesh creep when I think of it now,—all at once I saw a great green cloud swelling in the horizon, so vast, so symmetrical, of such Olympian majesty and imperial supremacy among the lesser forest-growths, that my heart stopped short, then jumped at my ribs as a hunter springs at a five-barred gate, and I felt all through me, without need of uttering the words, "This is it!"

You will find this tree described, with many others, in the excellent "Report upon the Trees and Shrubs of Massachusetts." The author has given my friend the Professor credit for some of his measurements, but measured this tree himself carefully. It is a grand elm for size of trunk, spread of limbs, and muscular development,—one of the first, perhaps the first, of the first class of New England elms.

The largest actual girth I have ever found at five feet from the ground is in the great elm lying a stone's throw or two north of the main road (if my points of compass are right) in Springfield. But this has much the appearance of having been formed by the union of two trunks growing side by side.

The West-Springfield elm and one upon Northampton meadows belong also to the first class of trees.

There is a noble old wreck of an elm at Hatfield, which used to spread its claws out over a circumference of thirty-five feet or more before they covered the foot of its bole up with earth. This is the American elm most like an oak of any I have ever seen.

The Sheffield elm is equally remarkable for size and perfection of form. I have seen nothing that comes near it in Berkshire County, and few to compare with it anywhere. I am not sure that I remember any other first-class elms in New England, but there may be many.

—What makes a first-class elm? — Why, size, in the first place, and chiefly. Anything over twenty feet of clear girth, five feet above the ground, and with a spread of branches a hundred feet across, may claim that title, according to my scale. All of them, with the questionable exception of the Springfield tree above referred to, stop, so far as my experience goes, at about twenty-two or twenty-three feet of girth and a hundred and twenty of spread.

Elms of the second class, generally ranging from fourteen to eighteen feet, are comparatively common. The queen of them all is that glorious tree near one of the churches in Springfield. Beautiful and stately she is beyond all praise. The "great tree" on Boston Common comes in the second rank, as does the one at Cohasset, which used to have, and probably has still, a head as round as an apple-tree, and that at Newburyport, with scores of others which might be mentioned. These last two have perhaps been over-celebrated. Both, however, are pleasing vegetables. The poor old Pittsfield elm lives on its past reputation. A wig of false leaves is indispensable to make it presentable.

[I don't doubt there may be some monster-elm or other, vegetating green, but inglorious, in some remote New England village, which only wants a sacred singer to make it celebrated. Send us your measurements, —(certified by the postmaster, to avoid possible imposition),—circumference five feet from soil, length of line from bough-end to bough-end, and we will see what can be done for you.]

—I wish somebody would get us up the following work:—

"SYLVA NOVANGLICA.

Photographs of New England Elms and other Trees, taken upon the Same Scale of Magnitude. With Letter-Press Descriptions, by a distinguished Literary Gentleman. Boston: —— —— & Co. 185—."

The same camera should be used, as far as possible, at a fixed distance. Our friend, who has given us so many interesting figures in his "Trees of America," must not think this Prospectus invades his province; a dozen portraits, with lively descriptions, would be a pretty complement to his large work, which, so far as published, I find excellent. If my plan were carried out, and another series of a dozen English trees photographed on the same scale, the comparison would be charming.

It has always been a favorite idea of mine to bring the life of the Old and the New World face to face, by an accurate comparison of their various types of organization. We should begin with man, of course; institute a large and exact comparison between the development of *la pianta umana,* as Alfieri called it, in different sections of each country, in the different callings, at different ages, estimating height, weight, force by the dynamometer and the spirometer, and finishing off with a series of typical photographs, giving the principal national physiognomies. Mr. Hutchinson has given us some excellent English data to begin with.

Then I would follow this up by contrasting the various parallel forms of life in the two continents. Our naturalists have often referred to this incidentally or expressly; but the *animus* of Nature in the two half globes of the planet is so momentous a point of interest to our race, that it should be made a subject of express and elaborate study. Go out with me into that walk which we call "the Mall," and look at the English and American elms. The American elm is tall, graceful, slender-sprayed, and drooping as if from languor. The English elm is compact, robust, holds its branches up, and carries its leaves for weeks longer than our own native tree.

Is this typical of the creative force on the two sides of the ocean, or not? Nothing but a careful comparison through the whole realm of life can answer this question.

There is a parallelism without identity in the animal and vegetable life of the two continents, which favors the task of comparison in an extraordinary manner. Just as we have two trees alike in many ways, yet not the same, both elms, yet easily distinguishable, just so we have a complete flora and a fauna, which, parting from the same ideal, embody it with various modifica-

tions.   Inventive power is the only quality of which
the Creative Intelligence seems to be economical; just
as with our largest human minds, that is the divinest
of faculties, and the one that most exhausts the mind
which exercises it.   As the same patterns have very
commonly been followed, we can see which is worked
out in the largest spirit, and determine the exact limitations under which the Creator places the movement
of life in all its manifestations in either locality.   We
should find ourselves in a very false position if it
should prove that Anglo-Saxons can't live here, but
die out, if not kept up by fresh supplies, as Dr. Knox
and other more or less wise persons have maintained.
It may turn out the other way, as I have heard one of
our literary celebrities argue,—and though I took
the other side, I liked his best,—that the American
is the Englishman reinforced.

— Will you walk out and look at those elms with
me after breakfast?—I said to the schoolmistress.

[I am not going to tell lies about it, and say that
she blushed,—as I suppose she ought to have done,
at such a tremendous piece of gallantry as that was
for our boarding-house.   On the contrary, she turned
a little pale, but smiled brightly and said,—Yes, with
pleasure, but she must walk towards her school.—
She went for her bonnet.   The old gentleman opposite followed her with his eyes, and said he wished
he was a young fellow.   Presently she came down,
looking very pretty in her half-mourning bonnet, and
carrying a schoolbook in her hand.]

CHAPTER XII

JOHN GREENLEAF WHITTIER

Of all our American singers, Whittier deserves preëminently the distinction of being the poet of the people. By sheer force of his moral character, coupled with his facile lyrical gift, this poor New England country boy worked his way up from obscurity and, by his poetical achievement, left behind him, in the domain of American letters, a name of which any author might justly feel proud. As a poet of the people the Quaker bard reflects in his verse the feelings and sentiments, the ideals and aspirations, at least in a measure, of the American nation. But, like Wordsworth, Whittier is a very unequal poet. At his best he is noble and uplifting and his message stirs and stimulates the reader to inspiring conceptions and purposes. When his genius deserts him and inspiration is wanting, his muse is decidedly pedestrian and lapses into mere doggerel. On such occasions he exhibits some glaring defects which materially mar the beauty and melody of his verse, such as his atrocious rhymes, his slipshod habit of pronunciation, and his unpardonable tenuity and tediousness. Yet, despite these serious blemishes, his poetry took firm hold upon the affections of his countrymen and won for its author a permanent and enduring name in our literature.

Whittier came of good sturdy New England stock. His ancestors for several generations back had lived in the Merrimac Valley of Eastern Massachusetts, and were known as honest, law-abiding,

God-fearing tillers of the soil, who served their native State faithfully in their humble sphere. Thomas Whittier, one of our poet's forebears, settled in Salisbury, near Amesbury, Massachusetts, as early as 1638. Nine years later he removed to Haverhill, and there this thrifty, upright son of Anak, with his own hands, hewed out the oak timbers for the house in which John Greenleaf Whittier was destined to be born on the 17th of December, 1807. The poet's ancestors on the mother's side—the Greenleafs—were of the same plain, substantial country folk.

Whittier's father was a hard-working tiller of the soil, and he desired his son, John Greenleaf, to follow the same independent vocation. But nature had endowed the boy with an insatiable thirst for knowledge; and his mother, who understood his temperament better than his father, fostered her son's ambition, herself instructing him and caring for his spiritual development. The chief text-book used in that Quaker home was the Bible; and its teachings entered into the very warp and woof of Whittier's early life, imparting to it a distinctly moral and religious coloring.

Whittier had inherited a frail body and a weak constitution. His health therefore was never robust, and he was compelled to husband his strength. When a boy, unlike his brothers, he was not able to do the hard work of the farm, and for this reason he was assigned light tasks on the farm and performed chores about the house. He has given us a vivid and striking picture of his experiences as a New England lad in his autobiographical idyl, "Snow-Bound." He was fond of domestic animals,—dogs, horses and cattle,—and his sensitive nature responded readily to the wholesome influence of his home life. "I found," said he in later life, in reply to questions as to his early life,—"I found about equal satisfaction in an old rural home, with the shifting panorama of the seasons, in reading the few books within my reach and dreaming of something wonderful and grand somewhere in the future. . . . The beauty of outward nature early impressed me, and the moral and spiritual beauty of the holy lives I read of in the Bible and other good books also affected me with a sense of my falling short and longing for a better state."

The region along the Merrimac in Essex County in which Whittier passed his boyhood is an attractive and typical New England landscape. It commands a distant view of the mountains and is yet within sound of the sea. The scenery is diversified by field and woodland, hill and dale, meadow and stream. Remote from the pulsating, bustling life of the crowded city, Amesbury was still near enough to Newburyport to feel the stimulating effect even of that small center of trade and commerce. The locality, too, is rich in history and legendary lore, which circumstance kindled and quickened the young poet's imagination, filling his mind with noble plans and purposes.

Amid these charming surroundings then Whittier spent his boyhood days. Here he attended the little district school and acquired the rudiments of an education. He went to school intermittently till his nineteenth year, being kept at home at frequent intervals to work on the farm. The poverty of his father precluded his enjoying the educational advantages of that famous center of learning and culture only thirty-four miles distant from Amesbury. Indeed, Whittier seems to have visited Boston only once before he was twenty, though it was so near; and even then he returned the day after, a bewildered and depressed country lad, glad to escape, he tells us, the bustle and excitement of that teeming city.

In his father's home young Whittier had access to but few books, perhaps thirty-odd volumes in all, and these mostly sermons and biographies of noted Friends.   These few books he read again and again. He informs us that he was acquainted with "Pilgrim's Progress," and that its graphic pictures of the conflict of Christian with Apollyon made a lasting impression on his youthful imagination.   He cheerfully acknowledged his indebtedness to a worn and thumb-stained copy of Murray's "English Reader" and of Bingham's "American Preceptor." He occasionally borrowed a volume of adventures and travels.   Once he stumbled upon a volume of Scott which, he says, he read with his sister stealthily at night, the candle invariably expiring before the climax of the story was reached.   Of good poetry there was a woeful lack in his father's meager library; but he records "how at an early age, the solemn organ roll of Gray's 'Elegy' and the lyric sweep and pathos of Cowper's 'Lament for the Royal George' moved and fascinated me with a sense of mystery and power, felt rather than understood."   It was truly a red-letter day in his early life when a copy of Burns fell into his hands, opening up to him a new world of sentiment and song.

It was a casual circumstance, almost a sheer accident, by which a copy of the passionate Scotch poet fell into young Whittier's hands.   Yet it fired his ambition and proved the Ithuriel's spear which touched and revealed Whittier's true poetic genius. Though a mere lad of fourteen, Whittier now began to indite verses.   To be sure, these juvenile effusions were pure doggerel; but the author soon passed to the second stage of versifying, and produced imitative work after the model of the lines published in the local newspaper and in his school reader. These imitations soon found favor with the weeklies of the neighboring towns, and the prospective poet was delighted to behold his maiden verses in print, adorning the poetical corner of some Essex County weekly. One of these "original poems" appeared in the Newburyport *Free Press,* a short-lived journal edited by William Lloyd Garrison, with the result that the noted Abolitionist very soon discovered the young Quaker poet and introduced him to the world. Upon the urgent advice of Garrison, who recognized Whittier's lyrical gift, the boy was rather reluctantly sent by his father to the Haverhill Academy. Here he spent two terms, working during vacation, alternately at teaching and making slippers, in order to eke out the frugal support allowed by his father's scant means.

His residence at Haverhill Academy afforded Whittier, for the first time, access to a library; and he reveled in the privilege, eagerly devouring book after book. By diligent and untiring application at the academy he succeeded in compounding, at least somewhat, for his sad lack of books in his earlier years, and broadened and deepened his intellectual equipment for his future work as a journalist, reformer and poet. But he received there only the rudiments of a sound education. His preparation was meager at best and was not to be compared with the thorough collegiate training which his fellow-poets, Longfellow, Lowell, Holmes and Emerson, carried with them each into his work as a man of letters. Even Bryant with his slight mental training entered the race of life with a lighter handicap than did Whittier. But Whittier accepted the conditions which his father's scant fortune had imposed upon him, and himself strove to supplement his lack of formal preparation by unremitting effort and energy. His poetic accomplishment is therefore all the more creditable and praiseworthy because he is a self-made man.

Whittier meanwhile continued, with unabated zeal, to write verse. His effusions, moreover, were eagerly sought after by the local papers, especially the Haverhill *Gazette*, in which as many as one hundred of his poems are reputed to have appeared, besides numerous prose articles, during the years 1827 and 1828. But the columns of other papers also were gladly thrown open to the productions of his muse. Contributions from his pen were invited by the Essex *Gazette*, the Boston *Philanthropist* and the *Statesman*. The author not infrequently had the gratification of seeing his poems copied far and wide by other papers, which was, if not a sign of popular favor, at least a sincere form of flattery.

Of these schoolboy poems it may be said that they were, for the most part, imitative and possessed little originality. They were written chiefly in imitation of the Irish melodist Moore and of Mrs. Hemans. The taste of the rural editors, somehow, turned to Mrs. Hemans in those days. It was quite natural then that Whittier should have taken her moral and didactic lyrics as his favorite model when he felt impelled to write for the poetical corner in the country newspaper. The cordial approbation accorded Whittier by his neighbors and by the local editors did not fail, however, to elicit some minor note of criticism. The critics challenged his originality and alleged that the Amesbury bard borrowed largely from other poets. But the editors speedily took up the cudgels in behalf of the boy poet, and before the discussion ended, they even projected the publication of a volume of poems by "Adrian"—a pseudonym under which Whittier frequently wrote. The project came to naught, albeit the poet was convinced thereby of the uniform approval of his verse, and the sting of the adverse criticism was removed.

In 1828, just as Whittier had arrived at his majority and was confronted with the question as to his life-work, which every thoughtful young man must face at the opening of his career, his first patron, William Lloyd Garrison, who had been editor of the Boston *Philanthropist,* named him to the proprietor of that journal as the man best fitted to succeed him as editor. This position, so opportunely tendered him without the least solicitation on his part, Whittier gladly accepted because it afforded him a livelihood in a field quite to his taste. This was the turning-point in young Whittier's life. If that opportunity had not come at that juncture, Whittier might have been an obscure village school teacher, or an unsuccessful farmer compelled by his indigent circumstances to dissipate his "divine energy" in the prosy task of wresting a bare subsistence from a reluctant soil. Neither of these vocations was to his taste. The former, after two years' experience, he had become utterly disgusted with; and the latter imposed upon his infirm constitution a heavier burden than he could bear. So, with high spirits and under favorable auspices, Whittier entered upon his life career of journalism, which was destined to be checkered, eventful and strenuous. Nor was it the least source of gratification to him that this new field of activity had opened up to him mainly in consequence of the early distinction of his verse.

When Whittier arrived in Boston, however, he learned that it was not the *Philanthropist* that he was to edit, but the *American Manufacturer,* which the proprietor of the former sheet intended to establish, in order to further the interests of Clay's "American system" and the new protective tariff. In the capacity of editor of a trade journal it fell to Whittier's lot to write upon subjects pertaining to political economy and to point out the advantages of the tariff to the manufacturing interests of the country. For this kind of writing the promising young editor possessed no special aptitude or qualification. Yet he shaped his office so as to include in the columns of the *Manufacturer* some verse and much prose that did not strictly fall within the province of a journal of its class. Of Whittier's prose it may be observed here that it is so far eclipsed by his verse that it may be practically ignored in the present study, which essays to determine his place as one of the standard American poets.

Upon the death of his father, in 1830, Whittier, on whom devolved the management of the ancestral farm, severed his connection with the *Manufacturer* and became editor of the Haverhill *Gazette*. This new post proved more congenial. However, he soon resigned this, too, to accept the editorship of the Hartford *New England Review* as successor to the talented journalist George D. Prentice. This journal afforded Whittier a much broader field for literary work, and his experience was very stimulating and helpful to him. Yet he did not continue his relation with the *Review* long, for in 1831 we find him again with the *Gazette*. From 1837-1840 he was editor of the *National Enquirer;* afterwards he associated himself with various journals, in turn, in Philadelphia, Washington, New York and Massachusetts. In 1857 he assisted in establishing that famous literary monthly, *The Atlantic,* and for the first decade of its existence contributed very liberally to its columns.

But Whittier had not confined his attention strictly to journalism. He was fast developing into a politician. National politics especially possessed for him an absorbing interest. Congress was the immediate goal of his political ambition when his failing health warned him that he was not equal to the arduous labors of the usual campaign, and that he must therefore forego this object of his aspiration. However, in 1831, he was sent as a delegate to the Whig National Convention. Two years later, after mature consideration, he took a step which marked an epoch in his life. He identified himself with the Abolitionists, then quite unpopular throughout the entire Union, in the hope that he might contribute to the amelioration of the condition of the negro slaves in the South. He was sent as a delegate to the Anti-Slavery National Convention. Among the stormiest incidents of his life were those growing out of his activity in the cause of the Abolitionists. But Whittier is believed to have been actuated by a strong sense of duty when he went over to the ranks of Garrison's party, and to have been prompted by stern conviction when he advocated the principles of the Abolitionists. For that movement in the thirties was extremely unpopular even in the North, and one can hardly believe that the Quaker poet would have courted social unpopularity and bodily harm as he did by his avowed course of action, if he had not been moved by a profound sense of duty. He was willing therefore to take the risk of personal violence which his course of conduct invited. Even when he was assaulted by the mob, he felt that he was acting in the line of duty.

Whittier, it is interesting to observe, did not at first take an active part in the slavery agitation. A Quaker by descent as well as by choice, he naturally

shared the sentiment for peace characteristic of
that sect. But the more he studied slavery, the
more heartily and unreservedly he threw himself
into the movement for the emancipation of the
negro slaves in the United States. By pen and
tongue, in public and private, he condemned slavery
as an institution, and kept agitating the question
year in and year out, till the national conscience
was at last aroused and the issue was settled by the
arbitrament of war. Long before the Civil War,
however, Whittier strove by his impassioned lyrics
to crystallize public sentiment throughout the entire country, and especially in New England, in
favor of negro emancipation.

But Whittier did not surrender himself, during
that long period from the early thirties to the outbreak of the Civil War, unreservedly and absolutely to his exacting duties as a social reformer.
The instincts of the author in him were stronger
than those of the reformer. Though he wrote much
that was directly inspired by the emancipation
movement, he produced more that is of the class
of pure literature. Close upon the heels of his
maiden volume, "Legends of New England," he
sent out into the world an anonymous poem, "Moll
Pitcher." In 1836 he published his longest poem,
"Mogg Megone," and the following year the first
collection of his poems under the unattractive
title, "Poems written during the Progress of the
Abolition Question in the United States between
the Years 1830 and 1838." Not to give a cata-
logue of his separate poems, suffice it to say that
his muse was regarded rather prolific and that the
poet, from the very incipiency of his career, enjoyed a reputation rather popular than critical.
Most of this early verse of our poet is of the class
termed occasional, and is not above the dead level

of mediocrity. It lacks spontaneity and genuine inspiration, and like its author's juvenile effusions, is to a considerable extent imitative. In the work of this formative period Whittier's models were evidently Mrs. Hemans, Scott and Byron, of each of whom there are striking reminiscences. The bard's struggle to throw away his crutches and walk alone is little short of pathetic. But he still lacked confidence in himself and felt that he must lean on some one. His verse, too, was frequently marred and defaced by glaring indications of hasty workmanship. Indeed, most of his mature work even is open to criticism on this score.

But despite its obvious blemishes Whittier's poetry was beginning to be appreciated by the reading public. The sales of his books, though by no means large, were somewhat remunerative. The author now for the first time began to enjoy some relief from his hitherto chronic condition of financial embarrassment. He was not yet in affluence, however, and his income was still not liberal enough to relieve him of the necessity of economizing. But the pinch of poverty was not so acute, and his future was bright with the bow of hope.

Upon the death of his father, Whittier sold the paternal homestead and moved to Amesbury, where he bought a neat, unpretentious cottage. This modest house was destined to be the home of the poet, for the most part, during the remaining half century of his life. Under its roof he did most of his literary work from 1840 on, cheered and inspired by the presence of his aged mother and his affectionate sister Elizabeth, who proved a veritable "angel in the house." The poet was devoted to his mother and sister, and never married, though he had many and warm friendships with women of congenial tastes. In his early life he sued for the hand and heart, it is said, of the talented poetess Lucy Hooper, who died a premature death at 24; and his beautiful, pensive lyric "Memories" is thought to have been inspired by this affection. If this be true, the circumstance adds a touch of pathos to his life of celibacy.

As to his personal appearance, Whittier was considered an engaging and impressive figure. He is described as tall and slight, with a quick, elastic step, his eyes brown and penetrating, and his entire demeanor serene and rather grave. In the conventional Quaker costume which he wore he presented a distinguished appearance.

In the year 1857 Whittier suffered a severe bereavement in the death of his mother, and his spirit was almost crushed by the blow. Yet a month later, in his sorrow and grief, he penned those beautiful lines, "Telling the Bees." Not many years after, he had to sustain the death of his favorite sister, and his home was broken up. Again, amid his tears and anguish he transmuted his deep affliction into a lyric of exquisite beauty and pathos, "The Vanishers," which has brought untold comfort and inspiration to thousands of readers. A peculiar interest attaches to these productions of Whittier's muse because of the pathetic circumstances immediately preceding their composition. Like many another bard, Whittier had learned in sorrow what he uttered in song.

In 1843, when he was well-nigh forty, Whittier gave to the world a volume of poems entitled "Lays of My Home." The book met with a flattering reception and, what was almost as gratifying to the indigent laureate, it had a moderately wide sale. This was the first book to bring its author considerable pecuniary compensation as well as poetic fame. If Whittier had published less and bestowed more pains upon the product of his art, his work would probably have been more remunerative. But the truth is, he had the habit of writing mostly for newspapers, and the press in that day offered but small honorarium to its contributors. Much of the work, too, that he turned out was but little above hack-work. But Whittier, it is evident, had caught the public ear, and his poems were quoted far and wide in the newspapers. As the political troubles which resulted in the bitter struggle of the sixties loomed up larger and larger, absorbing public attention, Whittier's interest in the agitation for the emancipation of the negro grew deeper and more intense; and naturally he was profoundly stirred by many an incident of those times. It is to one of those stirring incidents—the Latimer fugitive slave case —that his fiery lyric "Massachusetts to Virgina" was indebted for its inspiration. His poem "Texas: Voice of New England" had a similar origin. It was born of the times, when the country was deeply agitated by the question of the admission of that republic as a free state into the Union. The antebellum political questions and discussions furnished the inspiration and theme of most of our author's occasional verse and fugitive poems which appeared in "Voices of Freedom," "Songs of Labor," and in the other collections published prior to 1860. Having thrown his whole heart into the anti-slavery agitation, Whittier wrote and sang out of the deep-seated conviction that he was but doing his duty. Nor can it be denied that in this fray he shot many a fire-tipped dart straight to the mark. No other American poet enlisted his sympathies and powers so unreservedly in this great struggle. Even Lowell, with his fervid patriotism, can hardly be regarded a close second. Small wonder, then, that the Quaker poet by universal consent was voted the

laureate of the emancipation movement, which he
soon saw sweep to its full consummation.

In 1857 appeared a complete collection of Whittier's poems, called the "Blue and the Gold" edition.
This same year is also notable in our author's career
as the year in which our foremost literary journal—
The Atlantic Monthly—was founded, and Whittier
was urgently solicited, among other leading American men of letters, to contribute to its columns.
This public recognition of Whittier's gift of song
was, his biographers tell us, a source of unfeigned
pleasure and appreciation to him; and he responded
generously, contributing his fine poem "The Gift of
Tritemius" to the initial number. He made the
columns of this magazine, as previously stated, the
medium for his best work during the period of 1857-
70. His connection with this monthly, it is interesting to note in passing, incidentally presented
Whittier with an opportunity which he gladly accepted, of becoming acquainted with the recognized
literati of New England.

Toward the close of the war Whittier published a
collection of poems, under the title "In War Time,"
and this success he followed up the next year, when
his collection of "National Lyrics" appeared. Of
the former poems "Barbara Frietchie" is the most
widely known. Though based upon an incorrect
newspaper report of the incident which inspired
this song, "Barbara Frietchie" is a beautiful lyric
and fairly glows with patriotism. It has taken
firm hold upon the popular imagination and is a
favorite with anthologists. When the cause which
lay so near Whittier's heart became an accomplished
fact, his muse relaxed somewhat its strenuous office
and the bard now came to consider himself "the
idle singer of an empty day." It was at this period
when the poet was beginning to enjoy relief from

the strain and stress he had borne for many years that he produced his famous "Snow-Bound," harking back to the familiar scenes of his boyhood for its inspiration. The success of this poem, generally conceded to be its author's masterpiece, was immediate and generous, and stamped Whittier as a national poet. Burroughs, himself no mean authority on nature-writing, claims that "Snow-Bound" is the most faithful picture of our northern winter that has yet been put into poetry. By virtue of its genuine merit this "Winter Idyl," (if one may use the sub-title) is worthy to rank in the class with "Evangeline," the "Biglow Papers" and "The Cotter's Saturday Night." It is an artistic production and its sentiment and melody appeal to all. The sexagenarian bard, the critics are agreed, never again quite equaled the standard he attained in this sweet idyl of his childhood.

Whittier's lyre continued active till the very sunset of his life, ever and anon giving tangible proof of his activity in such collections of song as "The Tent on the Beach," "Among the Hills," "The King's Missive" and "At Sundown." But this enumeration is far from complete. A pathetic interest attaches to the collection entitled "At Sundown." It was Whittier's swan-song and was published in 1892, when the shadows of evening were gathering thick and fast about the bard. This collection furnishes unimpeachable evidence that the octogenarian singer still retained his mastery of the lyre and that age had not impaired his touch or dulled his ear. But the singer's voice was soon to be stilled. He survived the publication of "At Sundown" only a few months, the end coming somewhat unexpectedly. In the early summer of 1892 Whittier had gone to Hampton Falls, New Hampshire, to remain till autumn. He had been there

only a short while, however, before he was taken ill.
He died on the seventh of September, after a lingering illness, and his body was buried in the picturesque Friends' burying ground at Amesbury, by the
side of his beloved mother and sister.

Whittier's latter years, though he could hardly
claim to have a local habitation in the sense of a
home, after the death of his favorite sister, were
yet not entirely unhappy.   There was some compensation to mitigate and alleviate the depressing burden of his bereavement.   The liberal sale of his
books had completely removed the pinch of poverty
which he had experienced during his early life.
Besides, he enjoyed the satisfaction and comfort of
knowing that he had hosts of admiring friends
throughout the whole country who delighted to
honor him and rejoiced in his friendship.   By his
unswerving purpose and at the cost of unflagging
application he had at last achieved an enviable, if
not a brilliant, success in American letters, and
now in his old age he stood out in the public eye
as a conspicuous example of that praiseworthy product, the self-made man.   Educational institutions
were not slow to recognize his noble effort and accomplishment, and Brown and Harvard, notably,
lavished their academic honors upon him.   These
tokens of regard could not, of course, have been
without influence to assuage the bitterness of his
latter years.

But it is time to attempt some critical estimate
of Whittier as a man of letters.   To begin with, it
may be premised that we shall consider our author
only as a poet.   Whittier's prose is really a negligible quantity.   It is not above mediocrity, has
little to commend it and has therefore fallen into
oblivion.   The author himself never intended or
hoped to win for himself a lasting reputation by

his prose. He relied upon his poetry to perpetuate
his name in the republic of letters, and time has
vindicated his confidence.

It is obvious to the student of Whittier's verse
that the bent of his genuis was toward the ballad.
He gave unmistakable indication of this in his early
ballad "Cassandra Southwick," as well as in his
other legendary ballads. These ballads reveal in
their author the metrical instinct. His later ballads are even more significant as indicating Whittier's varying excellence and wide range of theme.
Of these, "Maud Muller," "Telling the Bees" and
"Skipper Ireson's Ride" may be mentioned as enduring favorites and deservedly popular. They are
unique of their kind of verse and are unsurpassed
in American song. Whittier scored no small triumph in his favorite rôle of a bucolic poet who
portrayed in sincere, ingenuous verse and with enviable skill and effect the simple pastoral life of
the Merrimac valley. While such lyrics do not
reveal, it must be admitted, that intellectual insight
and that depth of feeling which are invariably associated with poetry of the first water, still it is
these familiar household songs that have contributed much to confirm Whittier's reputation and to
establish more thoroughly his claim as the poet of
the people. Certainly no other American has so
good a claim to this distinction as the Quaker bard.
For his verse more than that of any other of our
singers is plain, simple, artless, homely and vigorous, and smacks of the soil.

Another secret of Whittier's hold upon the esteem
and affection of his countrymen is found in the
spiritual nature of his poetry. In his uplifting
spiritual lays he exhibits a religious aspect of his
nature which commends him strongly to the love
and favor of the common people. Whittier was, no

doubt, a good and pure man, and his deep piety found appropriate expression in those beautiful sacred lyrics with which he has enriched American song. Some of our hymn-book compilers have shown their good taste by incorporating a few of Whittier's exquisite sacred melodies into their hymnals. These melodies are restrained, dignified and inspiring and unquestionably conduce to pensive musing and pious meditation. Where can you find in American literature a more exquisite ode of the kind than Whittier's "Eternal Goodness"? Some of the verses of this sweet lyric have sung themselves into the heart of the nation and are as familiar almost as the twenty-third Psalm or the Sermon on the Mount.

Whittier's patriotic poetry was a notable element of his contemporaneous popularity. His verse was nothing if not patriotic. In this aspect of his muse he is unapproached. To be sure, this species of poetry is not the highest type, but it appeals mightily to the affections of the people, who naturally have a warm spot in their heart for such a singer. The cause which inspired most of Whittier's patriotic poetry lay very near his heart and was with him a passion as well as a purpose. When he attuned his lyre to the theme of home and country, he poured out his heart in impassioned song. But much of his patriotic verse had as its theme the anti-slavery agitation, and that is now a thing of the past, as is most of the poetry which it called forth. This class of poetry is designated by the critics as "occasional" and lacks, for the most part, those qualities that make for permanence and immortality. No portion of Whittier's poetry now seems more flat and jejune than his miscellaneous poems which had their *raison d' être* in the anti-slavery agitation; and there are but few grains of gold in this profusion of dross. This ephemeral verse probably fulfilled its author's design. But it is now relegated to the limbo of oblivion, since it did not possess the elements of verse that are permanent and abiding.

Whittier was a gifted singer, but he was not an artist. His facility was his besetting sin. Like most facile writers he refused to prune down sufficiently the products of his genius. Consequently he has suffered not a little in reputation. He sacrificed art and technique to his "fatal facility," with the result that a considerable part of his poetic output is very slightly removed from inane effusions —mere verbiage. Even his best verse is sadly marred by a surplusage of words which the reader must work through before he arrives at the golden grain. Relying on his innate gift of melody, Whittier gave but scant attention to the art of poetry, to technique. Some of his poems sin egregiously against the canons of art and good taste. Moreover, his ear was untrustworthy and failed to detect the false rhymes of his hasty composition; and too frequently he foisted upon an eager and indulgent public rhymes that are simply atrocious. Whittier was too sparing of the labor of the file and gave too little care to the finish and polish of his verses. This criticism does not apply, of course, to a few of his finer lyrics, which rival even Bryant's verse in artistic finish.

But despite the palpable blemishes and the manifest incompleteness of his poetry, Whittier is conceded, in the judgment of the most discriminating critics, to be entitled to a prominent place in the Valhalla of American poets. His song is fraught with a deep and tender spiritual message reinforced by the singer's inborn love of righteousness and by his noble, true, and pure life that compelled admira-

tion even from those out and out opposed to his
activity in the abolition movement. It is just this
union of a high moral purpose with his natural
lyric gift that explains in large measure the secret
of the honor universally accorded the Quaker poet
in his latter days, and the popular favor which he
enjoys now at the beginning of the twentieth century. Whittier will always live in American literature as the poet of the hearth and home, the singer
who by his instinctive lyric utterance has transformed the commonplace things and experiences of
every-day life into poetry of genuine melody and
beauty.

WHITTIER

MAUD MULLER

Maud Muller, on a summer's day,
Raked the meadow sweet with hay.

Beneath her torn hat glowed the wealth
Of simple beauty and rustic health.

Singing she wrought, and her merry glee
The mock-bird echoed from his tree.

But when she glanced to the far-off town,
White from its hill-slope looking down,

The sweet song died, and a vague unrest
And a nameless longing filled her breast,—

A wish, that she hardly dared to own,
For something better than she had known.

The Judge rode slowly down the lane,
Smoothing his horse's chestnut mane.

He drew his bridle in the shade
Of the apple-trees, to greet the maid,

And asked a draught from the spring that flowed
Through the meadow across the road.

She stooped where the cool spring bubbled up,
And filled for him her small tin cup,

And blushed as she gave it, looking down
On her feet so bare, and her tattered gown.

"Thanks!" said the Judge; "a sweeter draught
From a fairer hand was never quaffed."

He spoke of the grass and flowers and trees,
Of the singing birds and the humming bees;

Then talked of the haying, and wondered whether
The cloud in the west would bring foul weather.

And Maud forgot her brier-torn gown,
And her graceful ankles bare and brown;

And listened, while a pleased surprise
Looked from her long-lashed hazel eyes.

At last, like one who for delay
Seeks a vain excuse, he rode away.

Maud Muller looked and sighed: "Ah me!
That I the Judge's bride might be!

"He would dress me up in silks so fine,
And praise and toast me at his wine.

"My father should wear a broadcloth coat
My brother should sail a painted boat.

"I'd dress my mother so grand and gay,
And the baby should have a new toy each day.

"And I'd feed the hungry and clothe the poor,
And all should bless me who left our door."

The Judge looked back as he climbed the hill,
And saw Maud Muller standing still.

"A form more fair, a face more sweet,
Ne'er hath it been my lot to meet.

"And her modest answer and graceful air
Show her wise and good as she is fair.

"Would she were mine, and I, to-day,
Like her, a harvester of hay:

"No doubtful balance of rights and wrongs,
Nor weary lawyers with endless tongues,

"But low of cattle and song of birds,
And health and quiet and loving words."

But he thought of his sisters proud and cold,
And his mother vain of her rank and gold.

So, closing his heart, the Judge rode on,
And Maud was left in the field alone.

But the lawyers smiled that afternoon,
When he hummed in court an old love-tune;

And the young girl mused beside the well
Till the rain on the unraked clover fell.

He wedded a wife of richest dower,
Who lived for fashion, as he for power.

Yet oft, in his marble hearth's bright glow,
He watched a picture come and go;

And sweet Maud Muller's hazel eyes
Looked out in their innocent surprise.

Oft, when the wine in his glass was red,
He longed for the wayside well instead;

And closed his eyes on his garnished rooms
To dream of meadows and clover blooms.

And the proud man sighed, with a secret pain,
"Ah, that I were free again!

"Free as when I rode that day,
Where the barefoot maiden raked her hay."

She wedded a man unlearned and poor,
And many children played round her door.

But care and sorrow, and childbirth pain,
Left their traces on heart and brain.

And oft, when the summer sun shone hot
On the new-mown hay in the meadow lot,

And she heard the little spring brook fall
Over the roadside, through the wall,

In the shade of the apple-tree again
She saw a rider draw his rein.

And, gazing down with timid grace,
She felt his pleased eyes read her face.

Sometimes her narrow kitchen walls
Stretched away into stately halls;

The weary wheel to a spinnet turned,
The tallow candle an astral burned,

And for him who sat by the chimney log,
Dozing and grumbling o'er pipe and mug,

A manly form at her side she saw,
And joy was duty and love was law.

Then she took up her burden of life again,
Saying only, "It might have been."

Alas for maiden, alas for Judge,
For rich repiner and household drudge!

God pity them both! and pity us all,
Who vainly the dreams of youth recall.

For of all sad words of tongue or pen,
The saddest are these: "It might have been!"

Ah, well! for us all some sweet hope lies
Deeply buried from human eyes;

And, in the hereafter, angels may
Roll the stone from its grave away!

THE ANGELS OF BUENA VISTA

[A letter-writer from Mexico during the Mexican war, when detailing some of the incidents at the terrible fight of Buena Vista, mentioned that Mexican women were seen hovering near the field of death, for the purpose of giving aid and succor to the wounded. One poor woman was found surrounded by the maimed and suffering of both armies, ministering to the wants of Americans as well as Mexicans with impartial tenderness.]

Speak and tell us, our Ximena, looking northward far
    away,
O'er the camp of the invaders, o'er the Mexican array,
Who is losing? who is winning? are they far or come
    they near?
Look abroad, and tell us, sister, whither rolls the storm
    we hear.

"Down the hills of Angostura still the storm of battle
    rolls;
Blood is flowing, men are dying; God have mercy on
    their souls!"

Who is losing? who is winning?   "Over hill and over
    plain,
I see but smoke of cannon clouding through the moun-
    tain rain."

Holy Mother! keep our brothers!   Look, Ximena, look
    once more.
"Still I see the fearful whirlwind rolling darkly as be-
    fore,
Bearing on, in strange confusion, friend and foeman,
    foot and horse,
Like some wild and troubled torrent sweeping down
    its mountain course."

Look forth once more, Ximena!   "Ah! the smoke has
    rolled away;
And I see the Northern rifles gleaming down the ranks
    of gray.
Hark! that sudden blast of bugles! there the troop of
    Minon wheels;
There the Northern horses thunder, with the cannon at
    their heels.

"Jesu, pity! how it thickens! now retreat and now ad-
    vance!
Right against the blazing cannon shivers Puebla's
    charging lance!
Down they go, the brave young riders; horse and foot
    together fall;
Like a ploughshare in the fallow, through them ploughs
    the Northern ball."

Nearer came the storm and nearer, rolling fast and
    frightful on!
Speak, Ximena, speak and tell us, who has lost, and
    who has won?
"Alas! alas! I know not; friend and foe together fall,
O'er the dying rush the living: pray, my sisters, for
    them all!

"Lo! the wind the smoke is lifting. Blessed Mother,
   save my brain!
I can see the wounded crawling slowly out from heaps
   of slain.
Now they stagger, blind and bleeding; now they fall,
   and strive to rise;
Hasten, sisters, haste and save them, lest they die before our eyes!

"O my heart's love! O my dear one! lay thy poor head
   on my knee;
Dost thou know the lips that kiss thee? Canst thou
   hear me? canst thou see?
O my husband, brave and gentle! O my Bernal, look
   once more
On the blessed cross before thee! Mercy! mercy! all is
   o'er!"

Dry thy tears, my poor Ximena; lay thy dear one down
   to rest;
Let his hands be meekly folded, lay the cross upon his
   breast;
Let his dirge be sung hereafter, and his funeral masses
   said;
To-day, thou poor bereavèd one, the living ask thy aid.

Close beside her, faintly moaning, fair and young, a
   soldier lay,
Torn with shot and pierced with lances, bleeding slow
   his life away;
But, as tenderly before him the lorn Ximena knelt,
She saw the Northern eagle shining on his pistol belt.

With a stifled cry of horror straight she turned away
   her head;
With a sad and bitter feeling looked she back upon
   her dead;

But she heard the youth's low moaning, and his struggling breath of pain,
And she raised the cooling water to his parching lips
again.

Whispered low the dying soldier, pressed her hand and
faintly smiled;
Was that pitying face his mother's? did she watch beside her child?
All his stranger words with meaning her woman's
heart supplied;
With her kiss upon his forehead, "Mother!" murmured
he, and died!

"A bitter curse upon them, poor boy, who led thee forth,
From some gentle, sad-eyed mother, weeping, lonely, in
the North!"
Spake the mournful Mexic woman, as she laid him with
her dead,
And turned to soothe the living, and bind the wounds
which bled.

Look forth once more, Ximena! "Like a cloud before
the wind
Rolls the battle down the mountains, leaving blood and
death behind;
Ah! they plead in vain for mercy; in the dust the
wounded strive;
Hide your faces, holy angels! O thou Christ of God,
forgive!"

Sink, O Night, among thy mountains! let the cool, gray
shadows fall;
Dying brothers, fighting demons, drop thy curtain over
all!
Through the thickening winter twilight, wide apart the
battle rolled,
In its sheath the sabre rested, and the cannon's lips
grew cold.

But the noble Mexic women still their holy task pur-
sued,
Through that long, dark night of sorrow, worn and
faint and lacking food.
Over weak and suffering brothers, with a tender care
they hung,
And the dying foeman blessed them in a strange and
Northern tongue.

Not wholly lost, O Father! is this evil world of ours;
Upward, through its blood and ashes, spring afresh
the Eden flowers;
From its smoking hell of battle, Love and Pity send
their prayer,
And still thy white-winged angels hover dimly in our
air!

SKIPPER IRESON'S RIDE

Of all the rides since the birth of time,
Told in story or sung in rhyme,—
On Apuleius's Golden Ass,
Or one-eyed Calender's horse of brass,
Witch astride of a human back,
Islam's prophet on Al-Borák,—
The strangest ride that ever was sped
Was Ireson's, out from Marblehead!
    Old Floyd Ireson, for his hard heart,
    Tarred and feathered and carried in a cart
    By the women of Marblehead!

Body of turkey, head of owl,
Wings a-droop like a rained-on fowl,
Feathered and ruffled in every part,
Skipper Ireson stood in the cart.
Scores of women, old and young,
Strong of muscle, and glib of tongue,
Pushed and pulled up the rocky lane,
Shouting and singing the shrill refrain:

"Here 's Flud Oirson, fur his horrd horrt,
Torr'd an' futherr'd an' corr'd in a corrt
By the women o' Morble'ead!"

Wrinkled scolds with hands on hips,
Girls in bloom of cheek and lips,
Wild-eyed, free-limbed, such as chase
Bacchus round some antique vase,
Brief of skirt, with ankles bare,
Loose of kerchief and loose of hair,
With conch-shells blowing and fish-horns' twang,
Over and over the Mænads sang:
"Here 's Flud Oirson, fur his horrd horrt,
Torr'd an' futherr'd an' corr'd in a corrt
By the women o' Morble'ead!"

Small pity for him!—He sailed away
From a leaking ship in Chaleur Bay,—
Sailed away from a sinking wreck,
With his own town's-people on her deck!
"Lay by! lay by!" they called to him.
Back he answered, "Sink or swim!
Brag of your catch of fish again!"
And off he sailed through the fog and rain!
Old Floyd Ireson, for his hard heart,
Tarred and feathered and carried in a cart
By the women of Marblehead!

Fathoms deep in dark Chaleur
That wreck shall lie forevermore.
Mother and sister, wife and maid,
Looked from the rocks of Marblehead
Over the moaning and rainy sea,—
Looked for the coming that might not be!
What did the winds and the sea-birds say
Of the cruel captain who sailed away?—
Old Floyd Ireson, for his hard heart,
Tarred and feathered and carried in a cart
By the women of Marblehead!

Through the street, on either side,
Up flew windows, doors swung wide;
Sharp-tongued spinsters, old wives gray,
Treble lent the fish-horn's bray,
Sea-worn grandsires, cripple-bound,
Hulks of old sailors run aground,
Shook head, and fist, and hat, and cane,
And cracked with curses the hoarse refrain:
   "Here 's Flud Oirson, fur his horrd horrt,
   Torr'd an' futherr'd an' corr'd in a corrt
     By the women o' Morble'ead!"

Sweetly along the Salem road
Bloom of orchard and lilac showed.
Little the wicked skipper knew
Of the fields so green and the sky so blue.
Riding there in his sorry trim,
Like an Indian idol glum and grim,
Scarcely he seemed the sound to hear
Of voices shouting, far and near:
   "Here 's Flud Oirson, fur his horrd horrt,
   Torr'd an' futherr'd an' corr'd in a corrt
     By the women o' Morble'ead!"

"Hear me, neighbors!" at last he cried,—
"What to me is this noisy ride?
What is the shame that clothes the skin
To the nameless horror that lives within?
Waking or sleeping, I see a wreck,
And hear a cry from a reeling deck!
Hate me and curse me,—I only dread
The hand of God and the face of the dead!"
   Said old Floyd Ireson, for his hard heart,
   Tarred and feathered and carried in a cart
     By the women of Marblehead!

Then the wife of the skipper lost at sea
Said, "God has touched him! why should we!"
Said an old wife mourning her only son,
"Cut the rogue's tether and let him run!"

So with soft relentings and rude excuse,
Half scorn, half pity, they cut him loose,
And gave him a cloak to hide him in,
And left him alone with his shame and sin.
  Poor Floyd Ireson, for his hard heart,
  Tarred and feathered and carried in a cart
  By the women of Marblehead!

CHAPTER XIII

JAMES RUSSELL LOWELL

More than a decade of years have gone by since
James Russell Lowell, the foremost of American
men of letters, passed away. His death naturally
called forth numerous expressions of sincere appreciation, from writers on both sides of the Atlantic,
both as to his character and as to his works. The
English were no less generous in their glowing trib-
utes to his memory as a man and an author than
were the Americans, whom he so strongly loved and
who reciprocated that love. No doubt the personal
element prompted and entered into the encomiums,
written by those who, in the rude shock of death,
could not but record their keen personal loss in the
passing of a warm, true friend.

Time is needed to heal the wounds our friendship
has to sustain in the death of those whom we have
learned to love and to admire. The heart is too
profoundly agitated at the death of a true friend
for the intellect to weigh critically and pass judgment upon the literary merits of that friend. Time
must intervene to heal our wounded affections and
to separate us sufficiently far from his day, before
we can trust our judgments to render an unbiased
verdict upon his standing in the realm of letters.
Moreover, in the words of an author there is generally something, often much, which is of an
ephemeral character; and with the lapse of time
all that is transient and of passing interest tends
to be sifted and winnowed out, so that only what is
of permanent value finally remains. Such being the

case, we may hope now, over a decade after Lowell has been in his grave, to consider dispassionately and to form something of a critical estimate of this gifted, versatile American as a man of letters.

It is not proposed here to give a detailed account of Lowell's life, or indeed to consider his life at all, except incidentally where it throws light upon his work as an author. It may be observed, however, that he was born at Cambridge in 1819, of good Puritan stock, and that the Puritan teachings were woven into the very fiber and tissue of his being. His life was pure and sweet. Nor did it, like the life of such a poet as Byron or Shelley, stand in need of any "biographical chemistry to bleach out any dark spots in his character." Lowell's father and grandfather were both ministers of the gospel; and his mother was a gifted woman, well versed in English literature and acquainted with several foreign languages. From her, doubtless, young Lowell, like the great German poet Goethe, inherited his passion for song and letters. From his father he inherited his broad culture, his sturdy character, his moral fervor, and his Puritan love of righteousness. This combination of qualities which Lowell united in himself conspired to make him, as has been truly said, one of the prophets of the nineteenth century, the Milton of his times.

Lowell was a born scholar. Even while a student at Harvard he showed a decided *penchant* for literature. His subsequent career as the most brilliant critic that American scholarship has produced is but the fulfilment of the great promise of his early years. As a student, he preferred to follow the bent of his genius rather than the college curriculum which the Harvard authorities had prescribed; and so, at his graduation in 1838, he was under discipline for breach of order, when he delivered the class poem. After graduation he studied law, but, like not a few other young lawyers, soon found it uncongenial to his literary taste: he therefore abandoned the law, and came shortly to be numbered among the votaries of the muses. His first offering upon their altar was a slender volume of poetry, published in 1841, which he entitled "A Year's Life." This graceful little volume was dedicated to "Una," who first awakened in him the gift of song and then became his companion. The author afterwards referred to these early poems as the "firstlings of his muse, the poor windfalls of unripe experience." When he gave to the public the standard collection of his "Early Poems," the book was found to contain a few of the choicer songs, culled from "A Year's Life."

In these early poems the poet shows traces of the influence of Tennyson and Shelley. His sonnets to Wordsworth and Keats indicate also that he had been browsing on these high table-lands of poetry. It is especially interesting to note that, as a youth, Lowell was brought up on Pope, "in the old superstition," to quote his own words, "that he was the greatest poet that ever lived." But he early broke with Pope, and repudiated his claim to the primacy in the republic of letters. Conventional verse of the drawing-room type had lost its charm for young Lowell, who now turned to the fields of beauty and romance, to fresh outdoor subjects, for his inspiration. These early poems are immature, it is true, but they reveal the presence of a deep vein of poetic wealth which was destined to be improved and developed with increasing years. It is to be observed in passing that even in this early collection, "the first heir of his invention," Lowell sounded in his sonnets to Phillips and Giddings the anti-slavery note, which later swelled into a veritable trum-

pet blast in the "Biglow Papers" and other patriotic poems of the author's.   But of this more
anon.

Passing over Lowell's unsuccessful attempt to
found *The Pioneer,* a literary journal of brilliant,
though short-lived fame; and leaving out of consideration his poem of the "Legend of Brittany,"
which Poe said was "the noblest poem yet written
by an American," we come to his little idyl
"Rhœcus," as beautiful as it is artistic, and to the
"Poems" of 1848, which established Lowell's reputation as a poet of original genius, both at home and
abroad.   All his former efforts, though by no means
insignificant as indicating the rise of a new star in
the poetic heavens, were eclipsed by the luster of
this collection.   This book was the logical outcome
of the author's wholesome dread of dilettanteism
and affectation, to which, as to a luring temptation, many a promising young author has
fallen victim.   No poet, perhaps, ever felt more
sensibly the siren power of dilettanteism than did
Lowell; and he resolved, if possible, to escape from
it.   To the execution of this purpose, on his part,
the "Biglow Papers," the "Fable for Critics," and
"Sir Launfal" stand to-day indebted for their existence.   In these poems Lowell made a distinct departure from the well-beaten path of current poetic
fashion; and he achieved a notable triumph.   Yea,
he did more: he added something entirely unique
and original to the literature of his day.   For nothing like the "Biglow Papers" had ever been produced before in America, or anywhere else, for that
matter.   Lowell blazed out three new paths in
American literature: first, political satire, as in the
"Biglow Papers"; secondly, literary criticism, as in
the "Fable for Critics"; and thirdly, romantic and
religious sentiment, as in "Sir Launfal."   And in

each of these fields he scored a decisive and immediate success.

First, as to the "Biglow Papers." Nothing like these had ever been attempted before; nothing equal to them has ever been produced since. In them Lowell's genius has caught and portrayed with remarkable vividness and vigor the spirit of that sturdy Yankee character which, in a certain sense, is the salt and the peculiar product of Puritan New England. The first series (for there are two series of these papers) sets forth the feelings, as to the invasion of Mexico, of that intelligent party of the minority in New England as faithfully and fully as it reflects the Yankee character in its coarse shrewdness, its keen wit, its dry humor, and its plain, homespun English. The "Papers" showed, moreover, the moral stamina of their author—his Puritan inheritance—in giving expression, in such a bold manner, to the feelings of his party, then largely in the minority. Aside from the realistic portrayal of the Yankee character, the book had much to commend it as a work of art. "Never sprang the flower of art," as Stedman truly observes,"from a more unpromising soil; and yet these are eclogues as true as those of Theocritus or Burns." The wide-reaching success the "Papers" met with was marvelous. Nothing before in the history of American literature, with the possible exception of Poe's "Raven," had equaled the enthusiastic reception accorded Mr. Hosea Biglow's reflections. Lowell leaped at once into fame as suddenly as Byron with the publication of "Childe Harold," or Poe with his "Raven." The shrewd Yankee common sense, combined with the keen wit and breezy humor, sent the satire cutting straight to the mark; and many a trimmer and temporizer in New England, when they discovered that they were made the butt of ridicule, must have winced under the shafts of that ridicule. Strange to say, these "Papers" won for their author a reputation as a humorist—a reputation not confined to this side of the Atlantic. Indeed, it was these "Papers" that first won for Lowell a name in England and bespoke for him a warm place in the heart of the English people when he was appointed our Minister at the Court of St. James.

The "Biglow Papers" furnish the best political satire that American literature has produced. Indeed, English literature has produced nothing superior to their satire since the days of Swift and Butler. Lowell's satiric poetry, but for its dialect, might be rated above Dryden's, which it surpasses both in range and variety of style. Of course, it is not to be taken as giving a true picture of the times. It is characteristic of political satire to exaggerate the facts and to misrepresent men, and Mr. Biglow's crude verses form no exception to the rule. His soul was deeply stirred by the injustice of the Mexican war and by the cant of the party that attempted to justify it; and he was as severe and unrelenting in satirizing the North as the South. Witness his outburst of intense wrath against Massachusetts in his first poem:

> Massachusetts, God forgive her,
>   She's a-kneelin' with the rest,
> She, thet ough' to ha' clung ferever
>   In her grand old eagle-nest;
> She thet ough' to stand so fearless
>   W'ile the wracks are round her hurled
> Holdin' up a beacon peerless
>   To the oppressed of all the world!

Surely, every true son of the old Bay State, the hotbed of abolitionism, must have been profoundly

stirred by these lines. The political effect of such
lines, as might be expected, was great and immediate in crystallizing anti-slavery sentiment in New
England. Lowell did not himself comprehend the
influence his verses exerted. In the preface to the
second series of the "Biglow Papers" he says with
reference to this:

> The success of my experiment soon began not only
> to astonish me, but to make me feel the responsibility
> of knowing that I held in my hand a weapon, instead
> of the mere fencing-stick I had supposed. Very far
> from being a popular author under my own name, so
> far, indeed, as to be almost unread, I found the verses
> of my pseudonym copied everywhere; I saw them pinned
> up in workshops; I heard them quoted and their
> authorship debated; I once even, when rumor had at
> length caught up my name in one of its eddies, had the
> satisfaction of overhearing it demonstrated, in the
> pauses of a concert, that *I* was utterly incompetent
> to have written anything of the kind.

But enough of the "Biglow Papers" for the present. The second achievement in verse that Lowell
won, in 1848, was the "Fable for Critics." This
clever poem was probably inspired by Pope's example. It was not, however, conceived in that spirit
of rancor and ill-will that prompted the scathing,
drastic satire of the famous Queen Anne wit.
Lowell's satire was mere banter; it had no envenomed sting, and did not deserve the sharp attack
which Poe made upon its author. It was intended
merely as a mild satiric poem to hit off the art and
manner of the contemporary bards, Lowell himself
included. The author's characterization of his own
art and method, while not comprehensive, still reveals a considerable measure of intuitive insight
and critical analysis. The interest of the poem is

not well sustained, though showing here and there
a nice appreciation of his contemporaries' merits.
The parts are not compactly joined together; and
the poem, as a whole, shows marks of rather careless workmanship, especially in the versification.
Yet, with all its defects, the "Fable for Critics" is
a very clever *jeu d' esprit*, and as good as anything
of its kind done before in America.

The poem of really high literary merit which
Lowell published in 1848 was the "Vision of Sir
Launfal." Here the poet, though only thirty,
touched a note which he hardly surpassed in his
maturest years. (Indeed, it is quite remarkable
that work of such high order as that we have been
considering should have been done by a man of only
thirty.) There is a tradition that Lowell dashed
off this beautiful poem in the brief period of forty-
eight hours, during which time he was in a kind of
poetic ecstasy. The theme is that of the search for
the Holy Grail, rendered already familiar through
its frequent treatment by artist and poet alike. We
need not pause to analyze the poem or to comment
on the poet's handling of his subject, "Sir Launfal"
is so familiar to us all. It may be said, however, in
passing, that the disproportionately long prelude
appears to many critics as an artistic blemish, but
it does not materially mar the beauty of the poem.
In it are found some of Lowell's best lines, a few of
which have passed into household words; as,

"And what is so rare as a day in June?"

In this poem, too, the author gives unmistakable
evidence of his ardent love of nature, which
amounted almost to a passion with him. It permeates all that he wrote, prose as well as poetry.
Indeed, some critics think that "Sir Launfal" owes

its charm and beauty quite as much to the glowing
feeling for nature which pervades the entire poem
as to its legendary religious theme.

But Lowell was not only a poet. Nor did he
strive to force always into poetic form the thoughts
and feelings that flashed through his mind. He was
also a critic and an essayist, and the practitioner
of an excellent prose style, which has not been surpassed, if indeed it has been equaled, by any other
American man of letters. His essays and critiques
have contributed no less to his fame than his poetry
has. He was above all things a scholar, and filled
with rare grace and exceptional ability the chair at
Harvard, formerly occupied by Longfellow. He
lived all his life long surrounded by books, and
moved in a scholarly atmosphere. It was as editor
of the two leading American literary magazines, the
Atlantic and the *North American Review,* that he
wrote and published most of his essays on literature
and life. These charming essays he afterwards
collected and published under the titles, "Among
My Books" (two series), "Fireside Travels," and
"My Study Windows," making four volumes. Lowell's first prose volume, "Conversations on Some
of the Old Poets," appeared in 1844; and, while not
showing any great critical acumen, the book is yet
replete with remarks which give evidence of genuine
appreciation of literature. The young poet was
only beginning to feel his way along as a critic of
the Elizabethan dramatists. He had not yet
attained that sureness of touch and mastery of his
art which, like a skillful musician, he makes us
instinctively feel in his later essays. In these he
speaks as one having authority, as one having a developed, critical faculty which discerns with an unerring judgment and literary taste the weaknesses
and excellencies alike in an author. His fondness

for literature, which he had exhibited even in his
callow days, had now ripened into a rare and broad
scholarship, which was by no means confined to
English, but embraced the leading Continental languages as well. He could write with equal grace
and erudition, no matter whether the subject of his
essay was Chaucer, Lessing, Rosseau, or Dante. His
register, to use a musical term, was unusually
good; and the range of his essays embraced a rich
selection of authors, showing his familiarity not
only with English literature in all its periods, but
also with French, Spanish, Italian, and German.
In addition to his critical essays, Lowell wrote with
a glamour rivaled only by Lamb, upon such topics
as "A Good Word for Winter," and "A Certain
Condescension in Foreigners," etc.

Dr. Johnson, the great Cham, said of Addison,
the prince of essayists, that he never touched anything with his pen that he did not adorn it. The
same may, with equal propriety, be said of Lowell.
Not that Lowell and Addison have the same style
or the same manner of expressing an idea. They
have not; nor is Lowell's style modeled after the
Addisonian school. But Lowell possesses something
of the same attractive manner, something of the
same felicity of expression, and very much the same
indefinable charm. He lacks, however, Addison's
lightness of touch and airiness.

In 1865 Lowell gave the public the second series
of his "Biglow Papers." This, like the first series,
was inspired by war. It was called into being by
the author's reflections upon the causes which
brought on the Civil War. Here his voice again
rang out like a shrill clarion in behalf of the anti-
slavery cause, and he threw himself into the struggle with all the moral fervor and earnestness of a
true patriot. That he was partisan goes without

saying. Yet, it appears that he was perfectly sincere in his warm championship of the abolitionist movement. He had the deep and abiding conviction that slavery was a great evil and a festering sore which threatened the very existence of our national life. Nor did he lack the moral courage to speak out his convictions; and he hurled many a dart, tipped with biting wit and ridicule, against those Northern statesmen who counseled a temporizing policy or anything short of emancipation. The second series is written in the same manner and in the same dialect as the first. The author prefaced the collected papers with a treatise on the Yankee dialect which has proved a veritable treasure-trove to the student of that *patois*. Conceived on the same general plan and executed with equal skill, the second series of the "Biglow Papers" made as telling a hit as the first, published almost twenty years before, and was quite as far-reaching in influence and quite as potent in crystallizing anti-slavery sentiment.

It is rather noteworthy that some of Lowell's most impassioned poems were inspired by the question of slavery. Witness his poems "On the Capture of the Fugitive Slaves near Washington" and "Lines on the Present Crisis," which for intensity and ardor of feeling (even if we do not subscribe to the sentiment) are almost unexcelled by anything of their kind in English during the last half-century. Mr. Stead said of these verses that "they as nearly approach the prophetic fire of Isaiah and Ezekiel as any writing in prose or verse of modern times."

In 1868 Lowell published "Under the Willows," which poems, as the appended note stated, were written at intervals during many years. Two years later appeared "The Cathedral," a beautiful, though

unequal blank-verse poem.   In both of these we see
the same rich imagination and deftness of touch.
True, there are occasional lapses which we find in
well-nigh all of Lowell's poetry.   But one should
not take these to be earmarks of hasty composition;
on the contrary, they seem rather to be the defects
of his genius.   These latter poems are not so vigorous or intense as his patriotic verse; they are
more subdued in tone, the outgrowth of a mellowed
experience which has not lost its faith in man and
God, or its love for nature.   "Under the Willows"
shows that same love of nature which their author
had exhibited in his early work, and has all the
freshness of a spring morning.   Here the poet again
revels in the beauties of June with all the zest of a
child, as he did over twenty years ago in "Sir Launfal."   His heart was still young, though he had
already passed the meridian of life.   The truth is,
Lowell always retained, even up to the evening of
his life, his tender, sympathetic love of nature.   Nor
did Wordsworth, whose disciple Lowell would
probably have acknowledged himself to be, scarcely
love her more passionately.   "Under the Willows"
contains some of Lowell's finest specimens of pure
poetry, such as "Auf Wiedersehen" and "Palinode."
By way of illustration, take a few lines from that
exquisite little poem, "In the Twilight":

> "Sometimes a breath floats by me,
>   An odor from Dreamland sent,
> That makes the ghost seem nigh me
>   Of a splendor that came and went,
> Of a life lived somewhere, I know not
>   In what diviner sphere,
> Of memories that stay not and go not,
>   Like music once heard by an ear
> That cannot forget or reclaim it—

A something so shy, it would shame it
    To make it a show,
A something too vague, could I name it,
    For others to know,
As if I had lived it or dreamed it,
As if I had acted or schemed it,
      Long ago!

"And yet, could I live it over,
    This life that stirs in my brain,
Could I be both maiden and lover,
Moon and tide, bee and clover,
    As I seem to have been, once again,
Could I but speak and show it,
    This pleasure, more sharp than pain,
    That baffles and lures me so,
The world should not lack a poet,
      Such as it had
      In the ages glad
        Long ago!"

Lowell could, when occasion required, also write heroic verse, which voices a nation's feelings. Indeed, few modern poets have excelled him in this field. Most state poems are little better than failures. Lowell's, however, must be numbered among the exceptions; for where can we find a poem more stately, and at the same time more beautiful, than his "Harvard Commemoration Ode," or "Under the Old Elm"? These memorial poems are admired by all, and are among the finest things of the kind in American literature—yea, in English literature.

In 1877 Lowell was appointed Minister to Spain, and three years later was transferred to the Court of St. James. Here he had opportunity to cultivate his gift of oratory, and as a diplomat to serve his country. In this responsible post he proved himself most acceptable to the English people, who show-ered honors upon him; and he did more than any other American to weld together the two great branches of the Anglo-Saxon race. The addresses delivered during the years of his official duties he afterwards collected and published under the title of "Democracy and Other Essays." This was followed two years later by another volume of "Political Essays," which appeared in 1888. The same year he collected his occasional poems and published a slender volume, entitling it "Heart's-ease and Rue." This was "sad autumn's last chrysanthemum." The course of lectures on the old English dramatists, which he delivered at the Lowell Institute in 1877, was not published till after his death, in 1891.

It is time to ask the question, What is Lowell's place in literature? Lowell as a man of letters stands before the world to-day as both poet and critic; and it would be difficult to say whether he is more favorably known by his poetry or by his criticism. Without attempting to give an answer to this query, let us now endeavor to form an estimate of him in each of these rôles. And, first, as to his place as a poet.

Lowell's poetic range, as has been already said, is remarkably wide. He could write poems as diverse in conception and finish and as far removed in style and sentiment as the polished "Sir Launfal" and the rustic effusions of Hosea Biglow. But no matter how different in character, all his poetry is imaginative. Not all of his verse, however, is beautiful, though the poet himself possessed a keen innate sense of beauty which was strengthened and developed by a lifelong study of the best literature. There is very little verse in the "Biglow Papers," which can be called beautiful, either in form or phrase. Indeed, so far is this political satire from

being beautiful that most critics see almost nothing
in it to admire except its passion and vigor of expression. It is very grotesque, and has no felicity
of phrase to commend it. But it is useless to make
these strictures on the poem. The poet chose the
coarse, unpolished Yankee dialect as part and
parcel of his conception of Hosea Biglow, who
would not have been true to the shrewd Yankee
character if he had spoken in any other tongue. We
ought to feel indebted to Lowell's genius for thus
portraying that character in its proper setting, as
well as for fashioning such vigorous and passionate
verses out of such a homely dialect. Lowell made
no claim to lofty poetry in the "Biglow Papers."
He intended them to be taken merely as a kind of
serio-comic satire in which he gave impassioned
utterance to his own feelings upon the distinct issue
of his times. And that is all we are to take the
"Papers" for. It is by Lowell's more serious poetry
that we are to judge of his standing as a poet.
Leaving out of consideration, therefore, his satiric
verse, let us form an estimate by such poetry as his
"Sir Launfal," "Under the Willows," "Heart's-ease
and Rue," "Memorial Odes," and "Early Poems."
Lowell's gifts were preëminently lyrical; and his
lyrics are, for the most part, beautiful in conception, in sentiment, and in workmanship. We must
search far and wide in American literature before
we find anywhere a more imposing, passionate, and
graceful poem than the "Commemoration Ode," or
"Under the Old Elm," or "Sir Launfal." Some of
his shorter, less pretentious lyrics are equally beautiful. But this is far from claiming that they are
perfect. Beauty, charm, felicity of diction—all
these qualities Lowell's poems possess; but we feel
that they nevertheless lack the supreme quality of
melody, spontaneity. They do not, in the now trite

phrase of Matthew Arnold, "rise like an exhalation": they do not sing themselves. They do not gush spontaneously from the heart, as water welling from the fountain, or as the liquid notes float out upon the air from the throat of the nightingale. They lack that lilt, that melody which we feel in the poetry of Shelley, and of our own Poe. But how few is the number of poets that possess it!

Lowell was a critic *par excellence*. It was the critical faculty, it seems, that was most fully developed in him. And no doubt it was the critic in the man that put a check upon his creative genius, upon his poetic utterance. His training, his instincts, his tastes, his scholarship—all these combined to fit him for the office of critic. His criticism is at once subtle, penetrating, independent, and catholic. His critical writings, therefore, have a real and permanent value. When he pronounced upon an author, his judgment has generally been sustained by the popular verdict. No American man of letters has ever put pen to paper who was better equipped for the work of a critic than was Lowell. Poe, though superior to him in the domain of pure poetry, was far inferior as a critic. Poe, to be sure, deserves great credit for his pioneer work in literary criticism in America, but he never had the thorough qualification and innate gift of criticism which Lowell possessed. Poe was too easily led astray by prejudice to render an unbiased and trustworthy judgment; and he could not always resist the temptation to display his learning, which sometimes was little better than arrant ignorance masquerading in the guise of pedantry. Lowell never laid himself open to censure on this score. He had a thorough knowledge of all that fell within his province to review. He was somewhat bookish, perhaps a little pedantic. There is an air of erudition about

all his work; he could never quite rid himself of it.
He makes you feel that he is a scholar, and he was.
He is saturated with the spirit of literature, and
this, like the odor of nicotine, clings to all that he
wrote. Yet it would be manifestly unjust to call
him a pedant. He was close enough in touch with
the world to develop an almost unerring faculty
for detecting counterfeit and sham wherever they
lurked; and we feel that when he censures, the censure is just.

Lowell was a critic of broad sympathies. Where
can we find a better illustration of this fact than is
afforded by his sympathetic treatment of poets so
widely removed from one another in temperament
and style as Dryden and Dante? How charmingly
he writes upon authors of our own literature so remote from one another in time as Chaucer and
Shakespeare! And, too, his English is so excellent,
and his writing such easy reading! Such a volume
as "My Fireside Travels," or "Among My Books,"
is positively refreshing, a genuine tonic to an appetite jaded from reading many of our present-day
books, with their slipshod English, with which the
rushing printing presses are flooding our land. Not
that Lowell's English is absolutely impeccable, or
"faultily faultless." He was no purist; on the contrary, like most virile writers, he has certain con-
ceits, such as his occasional use of polysyllables and
newly coined words. So sparse is the sprinkling,
however, that these do not mar his page. But, to
quote his own words in reference to another, he has
"that exquisite something called style, which makes
itself felt by the skill with which it effaces itself,
and masters us at last with a sense of indefinable
completeness." His page, too, is warm with a genial
humor, flashes with pungent wit, and refreshes us
with a breezy, winsome style. Lowell is beyond

question the most brilliant and scholarly of our critics. In him American literary criticism reached its high-water mark. No other man of letters on this side of the Atlantic has equaled him; and, perhaps, only one of his contemporaries in England has surpassed him, namely, Matthew Arnold. It is, assuredly, a great distinction thus to have impressed one's personality upon one's age.

Lowell's genius would hardly be considered prolific. Other American men of letters have exceeded his output. As previously said, it was perhaps his critical faculty that prevented a fuller flowering of his poetic gifts; and doubtless his public duties precluded the employment, to its greatest extent, of his genius for criticism. He never undertook, so far as is known, a *magnum opus*. He expended his energies upon the themes suggested by the issues of the day, and thus produced a very creditable, though not voluminous, amount both of prose and poetry. His fancy strikes us sometimes as being a little exuberant, and we almost wish that at times he had exercised some restraint, especially upon his flow of language. But generally he has his powers entirely under control, and exhibits a very terse art of expression. He has presumably given us his best; and it is useless to criticise an author for not giving us better than his best. What he has left us is, indeed, of a very high order, and ranks with the best in our literature. We have reason then to be content with the rich legacy he has bequeathed to American literature, and to believe with Mr. Stedman that in him we have "a poet who is our most brilliant and learned critic, and who has given us our best native idyl, our best and most complete work in dialectic verse, and the noblest heroic ode that America has produced—each and all ranking with the first of their kind in English literature of the modern time."

LOWELL

BOOKS AND LIBRARIES

*　*　*　*　*　*　*　*　*

Every book we read may be made a round in the ever-
lengthening ladder by which we climb to knowledge,
and to that temperance and serenity of mind which, as
it is the ripest fruit of Wisdom, is also the sweetest.
But this can only be if we read such books as make us
think, and read them in such a way as helps them to
do so, that is, by endeavoring to judge them, and thus
to make them an exercise rather than a relaxation of
the mind. Desultory reading, except as conscious
pastime, hebetates the brain and slackens the bow-
string of Will. It communicates as little intelligence
as the messages that run along the telegraph wire to
the birds that perch on it. Few men learn the highest use of books. After lifelong study many a man
discovers too late that to have had the philosopher's
stone availed nothing without the philosopher to use
it. Many a scholarly life, stretched like a talking
wire to bring the wisdom of antiquity into communion with the present, can at last yield us no better
news than the true accent of a Greek verse, or the
translation of some filthy nothing scrawled on the
walls of a brothel by some Pompeian idler. And it
is certainly true that the material of thought reacts
upon the thought itself. Shakespeare himself would
have been commonplace had he been paddocked in a
thinly-shaven vocabulary, and Phidias, had he worked
in wax, only a more inspired Mrs. Jarley. A man is
known, says the proverb, by the company he keeps,
and not only so, but made by it. Milton makes his
fallen angels grow small to enter the infernal council
room, but the soul, which God meant to be the spacious

chamber where high thoughts and generous aspirations might commune together, shrinks and narrows
itself to the measure of the meaner company that is
wont to gather there, hatching conspiracies against
our better selves. We are apt to wonder at the
scholarship of the men of three centuries ago, and at
a certain dignity of phrase that characterizes them.
They were scholars because they did not read so many
things as we. They had fewer books, but these were
of the best. Their speech was noble, because they
lunched with Plutarch and supped with Plato. We
spend as much time over print as they did, but instead of communing with the choice thoughts of
choice spirits, and unconsciously acquiring the grand
manner of that supreme society, we diligently inform
ourselves, and cover the continent with a cobweb of
telegraphs to inform us, of such inspiring facts as
that a horse belonging to Mr. Smith ran away on
Wednesday, seriously damaging a valuable carryall;
that a son of Mr. Brown swallowed a hickory nut
on Thursday; and that a gravel bank caved in and
buried Mr. Robinson alive on Friday. Alas, it is we
ourselves that are getting buried alive under this
avalanche of earthy impertinences. It is we who,
while we might each in his humble way be helping
our fellows into the right path, or adding one block
to the climbing spire of a fine soul, are willing to
become mere sponges saturated from the stagnant
goose-pond of village gossip. This is the kind of
news we compass the globe to catch, fresh from
Bungtown Centre, when we might have it fresh from
heaven by the electric lines of poet or prophet! It is
bad enough that we should be compelled to know so
many nothings, but it is downright intolerable that
we must wash so many barrow-loads of gravel to find
a grain of mica after all. And then to be told that
the ability to read makes us all shareholders in the
Bonanza Mine of Universal Intelligence!

One is sometimes asked by young people to recom-
mend a course of reading. My advice would be that
they should confine themselves to the supreme books
in whatever literature, or still better to choose some
one great author, and make themselves thoroughly
familiar with him. For, as all roads lead to Rome,
so do they likewise lead away from it, and you will
find that, in order to understand perfectly and weigh
exactly any vital piece of literature, you will be
gradually and pleasantly persuaded to excursions and
explorations of which you little dreamed when you
began, and will find yourselves scholars before you
are aware. For remember that there is nothing less
profitable than scholarship for the mere sake of
scholarship, nor anything more wearisome in the at-
tainment. But the moment you have a definite aim,
attention is quickened, the mother of memory, and
all that you acquire groups and arranges itself in an
order that is lucid, because everywhere and always it
is in intelligent relation to a central object of constant and growing interest. This method also forces
upon us the necessity of thinking, which is, after all,
the highest result of all education. For what we
want is not learning, but knowledge; that is, the
power to make learning answer its true end as a
quickener of intelligence and a widener of our intellectual sympathies. I do not mean to say that every
one is fitted by nature or inclination for a definite
course of study, or indeed for serious study in any
sense. I am quite willing that these should "browse
in a library," as Dr. Johnson called it, to their hearts'
content. It is, perhaps, the only way in which time
may be profitably wasted. But desultory reading
will not make a "full man," as Bacon understood it,
of one who has not Johnson's memory, his power of
assimilation, and, above all, his comprehensive view of
the relations of things. "Read not," says Lord Bacon
in his *Essay of Studies,* "to contradict and confute;
nor to believe and take for granted; nor to find talk

and discourse; but to weigh and consider. Some books are to be tasted, others to be swallowed, and some few to be chewed and digested; that is, some books are to be read only in parts; others to be read, but not curiously, and some few to be read wholly and with diligence and attention. *Some books also may be read by deputy.*" This is weighty and well said, and I would call your attention especially to the wise words with which the passage closes. The best books are not always those which lend themselves to discussion and comment, but those (like Montaigne's *Essays*) which discuss and comment ourselves.

I have been speaking of such books as should be chosen for profitable reading. A public library, of course, must be far wider in its scope. It should contain something for all tastes, as well as the material for a thorough grounding in all branches of knowledge. It should be rich in books of reference, in encyclopædias, where one may learn without cost of research what things are generally known. For it is far more useful to know these than to know those that are *not* generally known. Not to know them is the defect of those half-trained and therefore hasty men who find a mare's nest on every branch of the tree of knowledge. A library should contain ample stores of history, which, if it do not always deserve the pompous title which Bolingbroke gave it, of philosophy teaching by example, certainly teaches many things profitable for us to know and lay to heart; teaches, among other things, how much of the present is still held in mortmain by the past; teaches that, if there be no controlling purpose, there is, at least, a sternly logical sequence in human affairs, and that chance has but a trifling dominion over them; teaches why things are and must be so and not otherwise, and that, of all hopeless contests, the most hopeless is that which fools are most eager to challenge,—with the Nature of Things; teaches, perhaps more than anything else, the value of personal character as a chief factor in what used to be called destiny, for that cause is strong which has not a multitude but one strong man behind it. History is, indeed, mainly the biography of a few imperial men, and forces home upon us the useful lesson how infinitesimally important our own private affairs are to the universe in general. History is clarified experience, and yet how little do men profit by it; nay, how should we expect it of those who so seldom are taught anything by their own! Delusions, especially economical delusions, seem the only things that have any chance of an earthy immortality. I would have plenty of biography. It is no insignificant fact that eminent men have always loved their Plutarch, since example, whether for emulation or avoidance, is never so poignant as when presented to us in a striking personality. Autobiographies are also instructive reading to the student of human nature, though generally written by men who are more interesting to themselves than to their fellow-men. I have been told that Emerson and George Eliot agreed in thinking Rousseau's *Confessions* the most interesting book they had ever read.

     *   *   *   *   *   *   *   *   *   *

CHAPTER XIV

SIDNEY LANIER

Poetry in the South since the Civil War has been almost a neglected field of literature. Prose writers such as Joel Chandler Harris, George W. Cable, James Lane Allen, Richard Malcolm Johnston, Thomas Nelson Page and others of less note have flourished and seem to have absorbed the entire interest of the reading public. But of poetry there has been a dearth. Of the few poets who have warbled forth their songs only two or three have risen to anything like a conspicuous place in American literature.

Whether Poe's conviction that there was no equal chance for the native Southern poets be the true explanation of this fact or not, it would be idle here to discuss. The fact remains that since the Civil War there has been but one poet of renown in the South, and that poet was Sidney Lanier. Perhaps the ardent admirers of Timrod and of Paul Hamilton Hayne, "the poet laureate of the South," as his enthusiastic devotees, with more zeal than knowledge, are pleased to style him, would not permit this statement to pass unchallenged. Timrod's claim may be dismissed with the remark that he cannot properly be considered, as his premature death, in 1867, closed his brief, but promising career almost synchronously with the war. Of Hayne it may be said that he is not known outside of his own country and not very widely known even in America. It is significant to note here that when a few years ago Mr. Edmund Grosse, an eminent English

critic and literateur, contributed to the *Forum* an
essay upon the somewhat invidious question, "Has
America produced ᶦᵤ poet?" he made no mention
whatsoever of Hayne (or of Timrod either, for the
matter of that), but he did consider Lanier's claim
to the distinction of being a poet.

Lanier was born at Macon, Georgia, on the third
of February, 1842. From his parents he inherited
his passion for music and poetry, for both on
father's and mother's side the love of these two
kindred arts dates so far back in the families as to
amount to a traditional characteristic. So pronounced was Sidney's love for music that when only
a child, his biographer tells us, "he learned to play
almost without instruction, on every kind of instrument he could find; and while yet a boy he played
the flute, organ, piano, violin, guitar and banjo,
especially devoting himself to the flute in deference
to his father, who feared for him the powerful fascination of the violin. For it was the violin-voice
that, above all others, commanded his soul. He has
related that during his college days, it would sometimes so exhalt him in rapture that presently he
would sink from his solitary music-worship into a
deep trance, thence to awaken, alone, on the floor of
his room, sorely shaken in nerve. It is not, therefore, surprising that Lanier followed music as his
profession in life, since his love for it even from
childhood amounted to a passion. The effect, too,
of his all-absorbing passion for music upon his
poetry is quite pronounced. Whether he would
have devoted himself wholly to music or to poetry,
had he found some Maecenas to provide for his
material wants, it would be impossible to say.
Certain it is that his impecunious condition prevented the full fruition of his passionate love of
either music or poetry, by degrading the products

of his genius to the sordid level of their commercial value, in order to enable him to eke out a living for himself and his family. Alas, too often has nature imposed so severe a condition of existence upon her sons of genius.

Even in his college days (he attended Oglethorpe College, in his native state), he felt the drawing influence of the two kindred arts of music and poetry upon his soul; and concerning his vocation in life he says in his college note-book: "The point I wish to settle is merely, by what method shall I ascertain what I am fit for, as preliminary to ascertaining God's will with reference to me; or what my inclinations are as preliminary to ascertaining what my capacities are; that is, what I am fit for. I am more than all perplexed by this fact, that the prime inclination, that is, natural bent (which I have checked, though) of my nature is to music; and for that I have the greatest talent; indeed, not boasting, for God gave it to me, I have an extraordinary musical talent and feel it within me plainly that I could rise as high as any composer. But I cannot bring myself to believe that I was intended for a musician, because it seems so small a business in comparison with other things which, it seems to me, I might do."

It was Lanier's weakness, if that is not too strong a word to use, that he could not definitely make up his mind whether he was intended for a musician or a poet. He felt both passions in his soul struggling for utterance. Or, as Stedman has beautifully expressed it, "in him the sister-spirits of Music and Poesy contended with a rivalry as strong as that between 'twin daughters of one race,' both loving and both worshipped by one whom death too soon removed while he strove to perfect their reconciliation." Had he been able to determine in his early life, once for all, that nature intended him for a musician, like Paganini, he might have moved vast audiences to rapturous delight by the soul-stirring music of his violin. But then we should have been deprived of much fine, graceful poetry which adorns and enriches American literature. On the other hand, if he had followed, untrammelled, his literary bent and poetic taste, he would probably have produced more copious and spontaneous verses and of supernal beauty. In short, had he been less of a musician, he would probably have been more of a poet. Even as it was, he has left us much poetry that is destined to something more than a fugitive existence, yea to an immortality as enduring as the republic of American letters, and has won for himself a place among the first poets of America. He is not, then, of that class of poets who, as Wordsworth said with keen poetic insight, "ne'er have penned their inspiration."

But Lanier was not permitted to devote himself, uninterrupted, to his chosen pursuits. From cultivating the Muse he was called by his duty to his country to enlist in the Confederate army, and with his company from his native Georgia, he was sent to do service, brave soldier that he was, upon the battle-scarred soil of Virginia. But the life of a soldier was not to his taste, just as it has not been to the taste of many another literary man from the days of the genial Horace down to the present. In "Tiger Lilies," a novel he wrote a year after the close of the war, he has given us a picture of his experiences in Point Lookout prison, where he was kept in close confinement for five months during the latter part of his career as a soldier. Even during his imprisonment he had with him his indispensable flute, which he had concealed under his sleeve when he entered the prison. On his release he made his way, on foot, back to his home in Georgia, only to be prostrated, upon his arrival, by a desperate illness, from which he recovered with shattered health. It was during the war that he felt the premonitions of that fell disease consumption, with which the rest of his life was a pathetic struggle, and to which, like the poet "whose name was writ in water," he was in the end to succumb.

To provide for the material needs of himself and his little family, he addressed himself successively to teaching and the practice of law. But neither of these professions, though they might have yielded him bread enough for his wife and babes, satisfied the poet-spirit in the man. His artistic nature was starving, and the keen pangs of that hunger were torturing his sensitive soul. It was during this period that he wrote to his friend, Bayard Taylor, those pathetic lines, "I could never describe to you what a mere drought and famine my life has been. . . . Perhaps you know that, with us the younger generation in the South, since the war, pretty much the whole of life has been merely not dying." He resolved to seek a more congenial atmosphere where his feeling for art might expand and develop. Accordingly, in December, 1873, he moved to Baltimore and procured for himself an engagement as first flute for the Peabody Symphony Concerts. It was several years after this that he was appointed lecturer on English literature in the Johns Hopkins University.

The lectureship at the Johns Hopkins University afforded Lanier abundant opportunity for study and he eagerly embraced it, addressing himself to the congenial task with all the diligence and earnestness of his noble nature. But his feeble body gradually wasting away with consumption proved unequal to the labor involved and his frequent hem-

orrhages warned him that he must desist. Yet he
knew that he was under the stern necessity of working to provide bread for his wife and babes, and was
too high-spirited to be an object of charity. At the
same time he felt that he had to write in order to
give expression to the thoughts of his poetic imagination that pressed for utterance, since dread disease was threatening to seal his lips in death. This
chapter in Lanier's life is a story of as brave and
pathetic a struggle as any to be found in the history
of literary biography. So he struggled on, working
often, literally, at fever heat, till the end came in
the autumn of 1881, in the mountains of North
Carolina, whither he had fled temporarily to prolong
his life.

During his residence in Baltimore, in addition to
the fugitive poems contributed to such magazines
as *Lippincott's, Scribner's* and the *Independent,*
Lanier wrote two books of exceptional value and
individuality,—"The English Novel" and the
"Science of English Verse." These treatises were the
product of the stimulus of his staff appointment and
were delivered as lectures at the Johns Hopkins
University. The "Science of English Verse" shows
marked originality and deep insight and is frequently quoted by scholars in that field as worthy of
profound consideration. The several books of tales
from our old literature such as "Malory's King
Arthur" and the "Welsh Mabinogian" which Lanier
edited for boys, about this same time, deserve no
special mention except that the work was admirably done.

To his father who desired him to return to Georgia and settle with him and share his income, the
poet wrote:

My dear father, think how, for twenty years, through poverty, through pain, through weariness, through sickness, through the uncongenial atmosphere of a farcical college and of a bare army and then of an exacting business life, through all the discouragement of being wholly unacquainted with literary people and literary ways—I say, think how, in spite of all these depressing circumstances, and of a thousand more which I could enumerate, these two figures of music and poetry have steadily kept in my heart so that I could not banish them. Does it not seem to you as to me, that I begin to have the right to enroll myself among the devotees of these two sublime arts, after having followed them so long and so humbly, and through so much bitterness?

But Lanier had faith in his mission; and it was this indomitable, never-failing faith in his own mission that inspired his heart amid all the sufferings he had endured for the present and nerved that heart against the ominous future his frequently recurring hemorrhages boded. Under the inspiration of this implicit confidence in his mission he wrote to his wife, after one of his hemorrhages, "Were it not for some circumstances which make such a proposition seem absurd in the highest degree, I would think that I am shortly to die, and that my spirit hath been singing its swan-song before dissolution. All day my soul hath been cutting swiftly into the great space of the subtle, unspeakable deep, driven by wind after wind of heavenly melody." And again, to comfort his wife and dispel a lurking suspicion she entertained that he had, after all, perhaps made a mistake in devoting his life to literature, he wrote:

Know, then, that disappointments were inevitable, and will still come until I have fought the battle which

every great artist has had to fight since time began.
This —dimly felt while I was doubtful of my own vocation and powers— is clear as the sun to me now that I
know, through the fiercest tests of life, that I am in
soul, and shall be in life and utterance, a great poet.

Now this is written because I sit here in my room
daily, and picture *thee* picturing *me* worn, and troubled,
or disheartened; and because I do not wish thee to
think up any groundless sorrow in thy soul. Of course
I have my keen sorrows, momentarily more keen than I
would like any one to know; but I thank God that in
a knowledge of Him and of myself which cometh to me
daily in fresh revelations, I have a steadfast firmament
of blue, in which all clouds soon dissolve. I have
wanted to say this several times of late, but it is not
easy to bring one's self to talk so of one's self, even to
one's dearer self.

Have, then . . . . . no fears nor anxieties
in my behalf; look upon all my disappointments as
mere witnesses that art has no enemy so unrelenting as
cleverness, and as rough weather that seasons timber.
It is of little consequence whether *I* fail; the *I* in the
matter is a small business: *"Que mon nom soit fletri.
que la France soit libre!"* quoth Danton; which is to
say, interpreted by my environment, Let my name perish—the poetry is good poetry and the music is good
music, and beauty dieth not, and the heart that needs
it will find it.

Here, then, we have Lanier's confession of his
own conviction that he was a poet, nay a great
poet—a conviction that grew with his years. Perhaps it is time for us to inquire, Was Lanier a great
poet? The unbiased answer to this question must
be in the negative, if by a great poet is meant one
who is entitled to rank with the world's great poets,
such as Dante, Goethe, Shakespeare, Milton, Wordsworth, Byron and Tennyson, to mention only mod-

356 MAKERS OF AMERICAN LITERATURE

erns. But while Lanier is not entitled to rank with
these world-poets, so to say, nor even with such
lesser lights as Shelley or Keats, he is yet a poet
whose work has in it elements of permanency and
will bear comparison with the best poetic product
that America has produced. Let us, then, if we
may, review his poetic output and examine more in
detail its quality.

The first poem of Lanier which won for him the
admiring attention of the reading public was
"Corn," written in 1874. Most of his work prior to
this time was not above mediocrity, and therefore
hardly need be passed in review. It was the prestige that this poem gave its author that subsequently won for him the distinction of being invited
to write the Centennial Cantata. (That poem, however, did not add to his reputation.) The theme
of "Corn" is, in its nature, prosaic enough; and yet
the author invested this commonplace subject with
a poetic air and coloring, weighing the respective
claims of both corn and cotton upon the attention
of the farmer and pointing out the disastrous results of speculation. Lanier could hardly resist the
temptation which his theme offered of pointing a
moral. Here, as so frequently in his poems, like
Wordsworth when not at his best, he lapses into
didacticism, apparently oblivious of the fact that
didacticism is a relentless foe to poetry of the first
water. Lanier was not, however, the first to write
upon such a theme as corn. The path had been
blazed out before by Whittier. But it is to be said
to Lanier's credit that he surpassed his predecessor
in poetic conception and technical execution.

"Corn" was quickly followed by "The Symphony," a poem no less unique than beautiful, in
which the author expresses through the musical
instruments as speakers his own feelings and senti-

ments. Here he portrays, under the guise of a dialogue between the instruments, the deadening effect
of the trade-spirit upon the human heart and affections and suggests as the remedy for the heartless-
ness of trade more love for humanity. Indeed, the
key-note of the poem is love, which is struck by the
violins in the very first couplet:

> "O Trade! O Trade! would thou wert dead!
> The Time needs heart—'tis tired of head."

Love is the specific for all the ills of trade. It
is this point that reconciles the poor even to their
contracted and narrow life, as they long for a
broader, a fuller life. It is this that brings man in
closer touch with nature and puts him also in harmony with nature's God. It is this that leads to
purity, not only in woman but also in man, and
beckons and allures both man and woman to a
higher and nobler life. In a word, the poem is an
attempt to put in graceful, poetic form the second
great commandment of the Gospel, "Love thy
neighbor as thyself;" and the musician-poet closes
it with that beautiful line,

> "Music is love in search of a word."

Lanier felt, and felt keenly, the sentiment he
expressed in "The Symphony." In a letter to Judge
Bleckley he says concerning the trade-spirit:
"Trade has now had possession of the civilized
world for four hundred years; it controls all things,
it interprets the Bible, it guides our national and
almost all our individual life with its maxims; and
its oppressions upon the moral existence of man
have come to be ten thousand times more grievous
than the worst tyrannies of the feudal system ever

were. Thus, in the reversal of time, it is now the *gentleman* who must rise and overthrow Trade. That chivalry which every man has, in some degree, in his heart; which does not depend upon birth, but which is a revelation from God of justice, of fair dealing, of scorn of mean advantages; which contemns the selling of stock which one *knows* is going to fall to a man who *believes* it is going to rise, as much as it would contemn any other form of rascality, or of injustice, or of meanness; it is this which must in these latter days organize its insurrections and burn up every one of the cunning moral castles from which Trade sends out its forays upon the conscience of modern society."

In his "Song of the Chattahoochee," published in 1877, the poet showed his mastery of an art as beautiful as it is rare. The charming lilt and melody of this song place it second only to Tennyson's "Brook," and its music haunts the memory almost as powerfully as Poe's "Ulalume." In the last stanza is seen an example of the poet's intense moral earnestness:

"But oh, not the hills of Habersham,
    And oh, not the valleys of Hall
Avail: I am fain for to water the plain.
Downward the voices of Duty call—
Downward, to toil and be mixed with the main,
The dry fields burn, and the mills are to turn,
And a myriad flowers mortally yearn,
And the lordly main from beyond the plain
    Calls over the hills of Habersham,
    Calls through the valleys of Hall."

In the "Revenge of Hamish," published a year after the "Song of the Chattahoochee," Lanier essayed a new field of poetic art, that of the ballad; and in this new venture he achieved, by the vividness of the conception and the musical flow of the language, such high success as to challenge comparison with the very finest ballads in English literature. But it was in the "Marshes of Glynn" that he produced his most original poem, at least in conception. The theme itself is surely unpoetic enough —a dreary marsh such as one may see in Southern Georgia—and yet the poet, by his glowing imagination and sympathetic love of nature, has idealized it, and out of this vast dreary waste of water has built up an inspiring poem upon the illimitable greatness of God.

"As the marsh-hen secretly builds on the watery sod,
   Behold I will build me a nest on the greatness of God:
I will fly in the greatness of God as the marsh-hen flies
   In the freedom that fills all the space 'twixt the marsh
      and the skies,
   By so many roots as the marsh-grass sends in the sod
I will heartily lay me a hold on the greatness of God:
   Oh, like to the greatness of God is the greatness within
   The range of the marshes, the liberal marshes of
      Glynn."

Another poem which is indebted for its inspiration to the same source as the "Marshes of Glynn" is "Sunrise," a wonderful poem if we consider the circumstances of its composition, written when the author's fever temperature registered one hundred and four degrees and he was nearing the end of his brief life. "Sunrise" shows to a still more astonishing extent even than the "Marshes of Glynn" the poet's mastery of the technical beauties of rhythm and his unfailing love of nature, which amounted almost to a passion. In the concluding stanza of this poem Lanier gives expression to his unswerving devotion to art:

"And ever my heart through the night shall with knowledge abide thee,
And ever by day shall my spirit, as one that hath tried
thee,
Labor, at leisure, in art—till yonder beside thee
    My soul shall float, friend Sun,
    The day being done."

He saw that sun with a clear vision, undimmed
by the mists and damps of his hard-cast life, when
his day was done.   And that sun to him was God,
just as it was to Turner, the great English landscape painter, who, as he lay dying and beheld the
sun through the London mists, exclaimed, "The Sun
is God."

One of Lanier's most exquisitely beautiful and
delicate poems is that to his wife's eyes, "My
Springs."   Indeed, there is scarcely a finer poem of
its kind in the whole range of English literature.
It is too long to quote in its entirety, and to give
simply a selection would be to mutilate it.   Another
snatch of song, written in his early days, is the "Be-
trayal," which may be here quoted:

"The sun has kissed the violet sea,
    And burned the violet to a rose.
O Sea! Would'st thou not better be
    Mere violet still?   Who knows? who knows?
        Well hides the violet in the wood;
        The dead leaf wrinkles her a hood,
        And winter's ill is violet's good;
        But the bold glory of the rose,
        It quickly comes and quickly goes—
        Red petals whirling in white snows,
            Ah, me!

"The sun has burnt the rose-red sea:
    The rose is turned to ashes gray.
O Sea, O Sea, mightst thou but be
    The violet thou hast been to-day!

The sun is brave, the sun is bright,
The sun is lord of love and light;
But after him it cometh night.
Dim anguish of the lonesome dark!
Once a girl's body, stiff and stark,
Was laid in the tomb without a mark,
  Ah, me!

Lanier's poetry was inspired by the muse of Christendom. Not that it breathes an introspective or mystical air, which, as Heyne thought, tended to chill and ultimately to freeze the Homeric gods; nor that it is what is technically called religious poetry, such as the work of Watts or Wesley. Lanier drew his inspiration from the New Testament; his poetry teaches an evangel of love. His entire work is so shot through with this sentiment as to render selections for illustration quite unnecessary. It furnishes the *motif* of his poem, "How Love Looked for Hell," and occurs in "Absence," where he says that love is the redeeming quality of life that makes it worth living.

"When life's all love, 'tis life; aught else, 'tis naught."

Endowed with so noble a gift of heart, he ever strove to inculcate a broader and more catholic love and a larger tolerance on the part of Christians. Witness here his "Remonstrance." He has left us his own ennobling conception of Christ in the "Crystal." Nor was he content to preach this gospel of love simply. He also practiced it and lived it before others. It colored his very conception of beauty and art. Nay, he regarded love as inseparably linked with these. Probably no artist ever invested his calling with more sacredness than did he. Like the Hebrew seer of old, his soul was kindled

to ecstatic enthusiasm by the "beauty of holiness;"
and he loved these words, his biographer tells us,
and liked to reverse the phrase and speak of the
"holiness of beauty." In his glowing admiration of
this sentiment he reminds us of Milton and Ruskin.
Lecturing before the students of the Johns Hopkins
University, he said:

So far from dreading that your moral purpose will
interfere with your beautiful creation, go forward in
the clear conviction that unless you are suffused—soul
and body, one might say—with that moral purpose
which finds its largest expression in love; that is, the
love of all things in their proper relation; unless you
are suffused with this love, do not dare to meddle with
beauty; unless you are suffused with beauty, do not
dare to meddle with love; unless you are suffused with
truth, do not dare to meddle with goodness; in a word,
unless you are suffused with truth, wisdom, goodness
and love, abandon the hope that the ages will accept
you as an artist.

After a careful review of Lanier's poetry the conviction is irresistible that he was intensely in earnest. He was no "idle singer of an empty day," to
use Morris' phrase—a poet, by the way, with whose
conception of the poetic mission Lanier had little
sympathy. He looked upon the mission of a poet
as sacred a thing as the office of an ancient Hebrew
prophet. In answer to the question, What avails a
poet? he replies:

> "He beareth starry stuff about his wings
>   To pollen thee and sting thee fertile."

It was no doubt the man's intense earnestness of
purpose that led Stedman to tax him with magnifying his office as poet. But he took equally as serious
a view of the life of an artist. In the intensity of

the moral purpose of his message to mankind he reminds us of the nature-intoxicated Lucretius, whom he studied and ardently admired, or better still, perhaps, of the ancient Hebrew prophet, Isaiah. For, as Callaway has said, Lanier was something of a Hebrew in his love of righteousness and something of a Hellene in his love of beauty.

Such, then, was Lanier the poet. Not a great poet, assuredly, in the sense that any poem of his is entitled to rank with that class of literature which Goethe called *"welt litteratur;"* and yet a poet who interpreted life truly as far as he did interpret it, as far as his range extended. He possessed some of the elements of a great poet. He had a love of music as passionate as Milton's. But his genius, alas! was too much trammeled by the sad circumstances of his outward life, and this prevented him from becoming a great poet in utterance. Nevertheless, he is entitled to be classed with the very first American poets and is eminently worthy of a permanent place in the heart and affection of the American people.

LANIER

LIFE AND SONG

If life were caught by a clarionet,
   And a wild heart, throbbing in the reed,
Should thrill its joy and trill its feet,
   And utter its heart in every deed,

Then would this breathing clarionet
   Type what the poet fain would be;
For none of the singers ever yet
   Has wholly lived his minstrelsy,

Or clearly sung his true, true thought,
   Or utterly bodied forth this life,
Or out of life and song has wrought
   The perfect one of man and wife;

Or lived and sung, that Life and Song
   Might each express the other's all,
Careless if life or art were long,
   Since both were one to stand or fall:

So that the wonder struck the crowd,
   Who shouted it about the land:
His song was only living aloud,
   His work, a singing with his hand.

A BALLAD OF TREES AND THE MASTER

Into the woods my Master went,
   Clean forspent, clean forspent.
Into the woods my Master came,
Forspent with love and shame.

But the olives they were not blind to him,
The little gray leaves were kind to him;
   The thorn-tree had a mind to him
   When into the woods he came.

   Out of the woods my Master went,
      And he was well content.
   Out of the woods my Master came,
   Content with death and shame.
When death and shame would woo him last,
From under the trees they drew him last;
   'Twas on a tree they slew him—last,
   When out of the woods he came.

SONG OF THE CHATTAHOOCHEE.

   Out of the hills of Habersham,
   Down the valleys of Hall,
I hurry amain to reach the plain,
Run the rapid and reach the fall,
Split at the rock and together again,
Accept my bed, or narrow or wide,
And flee from folly on every side
With a lover's pain to attain the plain
      Far from the hills of Habersham,
      Far from the valleys of Hall.

   All down the hills of Habersham,
   All through the valleys of Hall,
The rushes cried *Abide, abide,*
The willful waterweeds held me thrall,
The laving laurel turned my tide,
The ferns and the fondling grass said Stay,
The dewberry dipped for to work delay,
And the little reeds sighed *Abide, abide,*
      Here in the hills of Habersham,
      Here in the valleys of Hall.

High o'er the hills of Habersham,
Veiling the valleys of Hall,
The hickory told me manifold
Fair tales of shade, the poplar tall
Wrought me her shadowy self to hold,
The chestnut, the oak, the walnut, the pine,
Overleaning, with flickering meaning and sign,
Said, *Pass not, so cold, these manifold*
Deep shades of the hills of Habersham,
These glades in the valleys of Hall.

And oft in the hills of Habersham,
And oft in the valleys of Hall,
The white quartz shone, and the smooth brook-stone
Did bar me of passage with friendly brawl,
And many a luminous jewel alone—
Crystals clear or acloud with mist,
Ruby, garnet, and amethyst—
Made lures with the lights of streaming stone
In the clefts of the hills of Habersham,
In the beds of the Valley of Hall.

But, oh, not the hills of Habersham
And oh, not the valleys of Hall
Avail: I am fain for to water the plain.
Downward the voices of duty call—
Downward, to toil and be mixed with main,
The dry fields burn, and the mills are to turn,
And a myriad flowers mortally yearn,
And the lordly main from beyond the plain
Calls o'er the hills of Habersham,
Calls through the valleys of Hall.

FROM THE FLATS.

What heart-ache—ne'er a hill!
Inexorable, vapid, vague and chill
The drear sand levels drain my spirit low.
With one poor word they tell me all they know;

Whereat their stupid tongues, to tease my pain,
Do drawl it o'er again and o'er again.
They hurt my heart with griefs I cannot name:
    Always the same, the same.

    Nature hath no surprise,
No ambuscade of beauty 'gainst mine eyes
From brake or lurking dell or deep defile;
No humors, frolic forms—this smile, that smile;
No rich reserves or happy-valley hopes
Beyond the bend of roads, the distant slopes.
Her fancy fails, her wild is all run tame:
    Ever the same, the same.

    Oh might I through these tears
But glimpse some hill my Georgia high uprears,
Where white the quarts and pink the pebble shine,
The hickory heavenward strives, the muscadine
Swings o'er the slope, the oak's far-falling shade
Darkens the dogwood in the bottom glade,
And down the hollow from a ferny nook
    Lull sings a little brook!

A SONG OF THE FUTURE.

    Sail fast, sail fast,
  Ark of my hopes, Ark of my dreams;
  Sweep lordly o'er the drown'd Past,
Fly glittering through the sun's strange beams;
    Sail fast, sail fast.
Breaths of new buds from off some drying lea
With news about the Future scent the sea;
My brain is beating like the heart of Haste;
I'll loose me a bird upon this Present waste:
    Go, trembling song,
  And stay not long; oh, stay not long:
  Thou'rt only a gray and sober dove,
But thine eye is faith and thy wing is love.

EVENING SONG

Look off, dear Love, across the sallow sands,
  And mark yon meeting of the sun and sea;
How long they kiss in sight of all the lands:
  Ah! longer, longer, we.

Now in the sea's red vintage melts the sun,
  As Egypt's pearl dissolved in rosy wine,
And Cleopatra night drinks all. 'Tis done:
  Love, lay thine hand in mine.

Come forth, sweet stars, and comfort heaven's
      heart;
  Glimmer, ye waves, round else unlighted sands.
O night! divorce our sun and sky apart—
  Never our lips, our hands.

SELECTION FROM THE MARSHES OF GLYNN

Oh, what is abroad in the marsh and the terminal sea?
    Somehow my sould seems suddenly free
From the weighing of fate and the sad discussion of
  sin,
By the length and the breadth and the sweep of the
  marshes of Glynn.

Ye marshes, how candid and simple and nothing—with-
  holding and free
Ye publish yourselves to the sky and offer yourselves to
  the sea!
Tolerant plains, that suffer the sea and the rains and
  the sun,
Ye spread and span like the catholic man who hath
  mightily won
        God out of knowledge, and good out of infinite
          pain,
        And sight out of blindness, and purity out of
          a stain.

As the marsh-hen secretly builds on the watery
    sod,
    Behold I will build me a nest on the greatness
      of God;
    I will fly in the greatness of God as the marsh-
      hen flies
In the freedom that fills all the space 'twixt the marsh
    and the skies:
    By so many roots as the marsh-grass sends in
      the sod
    I will heartily lay me a-hold on the greatness
      of God:
    Oh, like to the greatness of God is the great-
      ness within
    The range of the marshes, the liberal marshes
      of Glynn.

And the sea lends large, as the marsh; lo, out of his
    plenty the sea
    Pours fast; full soon the time of the flood-
      tide must be:
    Look how the grace of the sea doth go
    About and about through the intricate chan-
      nels that flow
        Here and there,
        Everywhere,
Till his waters have flooded the uttermost creeks and
    the low-lying lanes,
    And that marsh is meshed with a million veins,
    That like as with rosy and silvery essences
      flow
    In the rose-and-silver evening glow.
      Farewell, my lord Sun!
    The creeks overflow; a thousand rivulets run
'Twixt the roots of the sod; the blades of the marsh-
    grass stir;
    Passeth a hurrying sound of wings that westward
      whirr;
    Passeth, and all is still; and the currents cease to
      run;
      And the sea and the marsh are one.

How still the plains of the waters be!
The tide is in his ecstasy.
The tide is at his highest height;
　　And it is night.
And now from the Vast of the Lord will the waters of
　sleep
　　Roll in on the souls of men;
　　But who will reveal to our waking ken
　The forms that swim and the shapes that creep
　Under the waters of sleep?
And I would I could know what swimmeth below when
　the tide comes in
On the length and the breadth of the marvelous marshes
　of Glynn.

(The above selections are from "Poems of Sidney
Lanier," copyrighted 1884 and 1891 by Mary D.
Lanier and published by Charles Scribner's Sons.)

CHAPTER XV

WALT WHITMAN

Walter Whitman, familiarly called Walt Whitman, after his own practice of signing his name, is
an author whom the critic of American literature
cannot ignore, however vigorously he may reject
the Good Gray Poet's avowed poetic theory and
technique. No American writer has ever approached even remotely this bold iconoclast in utterly discarding all the time-honored literary traditions and conventions. For in his verse especially
Whitman set at naught all the canons of art and
poetic expression sanctioned by the ages and openly
debased the artistic and spiritual in his effort to
exalt the mere commonplace and physical. The
result was, he divided the critics into two hostile
schools and arrayed them against each other. The
one school set him up as a paragon of excellence,
bestowing upon him unstinted and indiscriminate
praise; the other went to the opposite extreme of
denying him all poetic gift and utterance. In consequence, Whitman has suffered in reputation, no
doubt, both at the hands of his admiring friends
and of his relentless detractors. But as the years
go by and the personal element is gradually eliminated, the scholarly world will come to weigh the
poet accurately and without prejudice or passion,
and estimate him at his proper worth.

Whitman came of mixed New England and Dutch
stock and was born at West Hills, Long Island, in
1819. His father, who was a carpenter, moved his
family to Brooklyn when Walter was only five years

old, but moved back again before the boy was out of his teens. But while he was living in Brooklyn, young Whitman had frequent opportunity to visit the scenes of his childhood; and he was always glad to return to his Long Island home and feast his soul upon the natural beauty of the country. The Long Island landscape made a deep and lasting impression upon the young poet's mind, and his imagination and perceptions were, no doubt, kindled and quickened by his close contact with nature.

His father having a large family to care for and only a meagre income, young Walter received merely a common-school education and had to shift for himself at an early age. When but thirteen years old he entered a printer's office and learned to set up type. Three years later we find him teaching school on Long Island and "boarding around" in the country. This afforded him ample opportunity to study human nature both in school and out. But he soon grew tired of this experience and sought a change. He then fell back upon his early occupation, and so, for the twelve years, he plied his trade as a printer. He also wrote for some of the New York papers and mingled freely with the people wherever he happened to be, entering fully into their everyday life. He made friends with all sorts and conditions of men and studied their character and manner of living at close range. From principle he became a frequenter of theatres and factories and a regular patron of the ferries and omnibuses, in order to gain a deeper insight into the life of the plain people, the masses. This, however, was no passing whim, but his chosen method of collecting material in his notebook and of obtaining a more thorough knowledge of the life of the common people which he was to undertake in due time to describe.

Whitman possessed a strong, burly physique and a nature which craved outdoor life, anyway, and he was resolved to gratify his desire. He reveled in sunshine and fresh air. His fondness for outdoor life he had inherited along with his robust constitution from his vigorous parents. In her youth, his mother—a Miss Van Elsor, of Dutch descent, as the name indicates—was "a daily and daring" horse-back rider, and spent much of her time in the open air; and his father, like his grandfather, a thrifty Long Island farmer, had by reason of his occupation always led an active outdoor life. The typical portrait of Walt Whitman also is that of a strong, healthy man clad in home-spun and an outing shirt with open collar, trousers stuffed down his boots and a slouch hat upon a bushy head of patriarchal gray locks. The figure itself is suggestive of the hay field and the meadow and is far removed from that ordinarily associated with urban life.

Notwithstanding Whitman's roving disposition and his habit of living outdoors, still he found some time for reading. He enjoyed no formal academic training, to be sure; yet he was fond of literature and had an appreciation for good books, which he read with intense interest and zest. He prized his few books all the more highly because his limited means made it difficult for him to obtain books, when a boy. It is interesting to note what books engaged the attention of this callow youth. As he tells us in his own words, "In the presence of outdoor influences, I went over thoroughly the Old and New Testaments and absorbed Shakespeare, Ossian, the best translated versions I could get of Homer, Aeschylus, Sophocles, the old German Niebelungen, the ancient Hindoo poems and one or two other masterpieces, Dante among them. As it happened, I read the latter mostly in an old wood."

Surely this young man was wisely directed in the choice of his books for reading, and his range was sufficiently wide to afford him no small acquaintance with the best literature.

Thus Whitman absorbed some of the world's masterpieces in literature, amid the outdoor influences, as he roamed over the fields and along the seashore of his beloved Long Island, or Paumanok, the Indian name, which he preferred. "I roamed, as boy and man," to quote his own language, "and have lived in nearly all parts, from Brooklyn to Montauk." His early life was so intimately identified with Long Island that, as he affirmed, he had practically incorporated it into his very being while he inhaled its atmosphere and mingled with its people. In his cross-country rambles he hobnobbed with the sturdy farmer folk and learned to look at life from their sober point of view. He liked also to roam along the seashore, talking with the plain fishermen, and to enter into their life. The unceasing moan of the sea itself and the myriad forms of life peculiar to it exercised over him a wonderful fascination and appealed very keenly to his responsive nature. He haunted the beach and saw the remains of many a wreck washed ashore. He used to run along for miles, naked, on the firm sand, declaiming Homer and Shakespeare to the surf and the sea-gulls. When a boy, he would spend day after day gathering the eggs of sea-gulls, digging clams, or spearing ells through the ice. He chronicled these early experiences in his "Specimen Days," and here he also tells us of his formative influences.

Whitman's career cannot be termed uneventful. He was successively printer, newspaper writer and editor. As a roving printer he traveled leisurely over the entire country east of the Mississippi—a trip of 8,000 miles about, made for the most part on foot. He worked his way along, relying upon his trade for his daily bread. At one time he was employed on the *Brooklyn Daily Eagle* and at another on the *New Orleans Daily Crescent.* But wherever he went, he made friends in the class of society called the common people. He always moved in obscure society throughout his whole life, for the matter of that. Yet during his *wanderjahre,* as in his later life, he had a warm, sympathetic heart and a quick, observant eye, and he took the pains to jot down his impressions for future use. He subsequently incorporated them into his famous "Leaves of Grass," or set them forth in his "Specimen Days."

Upon his return, Whitman took up his residence in New York and Brooklyn, leading a happy-go-lucky sort of life, and was a familiar figure about the hotels and theatres. His favorite resort was Pfaf's restaurant, on Broadway, where he would sip beer and chat with the literary lights of the day. Always an enthusiastic patron of the theatre and the opera, he declared that, as a boy and young man, he had seen all of Shakespeare's plays presented, at one time or another, "reading them carefully the day beforehand." He used frequently to hear Charlotte Cushman and the Elder Booth in their leading rôles, or listen to the soul-stirring notes of Jenny Lind. For music and the drama were with him a principle and a passion, and he depended upon these twin handmaids of culture to supplement in some measure the deficiency of his early training.

With the outbreak of the Civil War a change came over the current of Whitman's dreams. His brother, an officer in the Fifty-first New York Volunteers, being wounded near Fredericksburg, Vir-

ginia, Walt immediately left home and set out for
the camp hospital to nurse him. This was the
beginning of his work of mercy as an army nurse,
and from that time till well-nigh the end of the war
he was actively engaged in the camp hospitals in
Virginia and Washington. His ministries were of
unfailing tenderness and devotion to the sick and
wounded. He gave cheerfully of his own means
and solicited subscriptions from various sources to
contribute to the comfort of the needy sick. He
spent himself in relieving human suffering, now
supplying a dainty dish to tempt a languid appetite,
now dressing a wound, at one time writing a farewell letter for some doomed soldier, at another time
reading the Bible and giving spiritual comfort to
some dying one. He actually sacrificed his own
robust health in his untiring efforts to minister to
the sick and dying.

Whitman's war record is the finest chapter in his
life, and is a veritable inspiration. It furnishes
indubitable evidence of the humane and noble qualities of his heart—his abounding sympathy and his
absolute self-abandonment. It is this element in
his character which lends additional interest to his
biography and which inspired all that is really good
in his verse. For much of his verse did really spring
from the generous promptings of his noble heart,
and is marked by a broad sympathy with humanity.
But the poet was not happy in the manner of his
utterance and expressed his thought in a very blunt,
ungraceful and unattractive style.

The war made upon Whitman a profound impression. In his "Specimen Days" and in the posthumous volume of letters to his mother, the "Wound
Dresser," especially, he depicts with characteristic
graphic effect the horrors of war and the terrible
suffering it entailed. Although he had not seen

actual service upon the battle-field, still he had abundant opportunity as a nurse in the camp hospital to learn something of the frightful aspect of war in the thousands of wounded he saw; and he witnessed occasionally upon the near-by field a revolting scene of carnage and destruction. He noted two striking spectacles of different character furnished by the war. In his own language, they were "the general, voluntary, armed upheaval, and the peaceful and harmonious disbanding of the armies in the summer of 1865."

Whitman was greatly moved by the assassination of Lincoln, of whose strong, sturdy and noble character he was an ardent admirer. The news of the assassination was a tremendous shock to him, and he was so stunned that he was rendered unfit to attend to his ordinary daily tasks. He happened to be at home with his mother in Brooklyn at the time. Neither he nor his mother could eat a mouthful the entire day, he tells us. "We each drank a half cup of coffee; that was all. Little was said. We got every newspaper, morning and evening, and the frequent extras of that period, and passed them silently to each other." After the cruel shock was over, Whitman gave expression to his melancholy feelings in that pathetic burial hymn, "When Lilacs last in the Door-Yard Bloom'd," which ranks among his most beautiful poems.

Whitman's strenuous work in the hospitals imposed upon his splendid constitution a severer strain than nature could stand, and his health broke down. After the recovery of his health, his service as an army nurse was recognized in his appointment to a government clerkship in the Department of the Interior. But he held his new post only a brief while. The Secretary of the Interior, it is alleged, discovered after office hours a copy of

"Leaves of Grass" in Whitman's desk, and, believing that the author of that book was not a suitable person to hold a position in the public service, summarily dismissed him from the Department. However, the Attorney-General did not share this view and thought that there was no sufficient ground for Whitman's dismissal. He therefore re-instated him, giving him another position quite as good as that Whitman had filled in the Department of the Interior. Within a few weeks after this incident Whitman received at the hands of his enthusiastic admirer, William D. O'Connor, a complete literary vindication in the scathing pamphlet, "The Good Gray Poet." This was the origin of the poet's now familiar soubriquet and the inauguration of the era of Whitman worship.

"Leaves of Grass" was first published in Brooklyn, in 1855, the author himself setting up most of the type. Far from creating a sensation, the book came into the world still-born and made no impression. It is said that not a copy was sold. However, the contents of this slender volume of verse were original and startling enough to have attracted attention. For the book contained a new evangel—the doctrine of the equality of the body with the soul, which is sheer animalism. The author set himself the task of presenting a complete and adequate picture of typical humanity in this new country of ours, with its untold possibilities of material development, under democratic influences. His message is pre-eminently democratic, and he conceived his mission to be the poet of the people—the masses. But of this more anon. Not only was his evangel new and unique, but the poet felt that he must present it in a new form. He therefore rejected all the poetic traditions, discarding rhyme and all metrical restraints, in order to make his

practice square with his theory that he was the bard
of a free people in a great democratic country, untrammeled by Old World conventions. He actually
went so far as to eliminate all stock poetic phrases
from his verses, in order to present his system un-
impeded by metrical restrictions of any sort.

"Leaves of Grass," in the form in which the book
first appeared, contained only twelve poems. The
second edition, which was rather an expansion of
the first than a new issue simply, contained thirty-
two poems. Like its predecessor, it, too, met with
utter indifference on the part of the reading public.
It attracted more attention, however, from the
critics and was severely censured by those who
took interest enough in it to read the unique little
book. Indeed, some went to the length of threatening to prosecute the author for his coarse, indecent
utterances as they regarded them, and even the
publishers refused to sell the book. Whitman had
unquestionably expressed his new system of life
and thought with startling plainness and shocking
directness of speech. The question of sexuality in
his poems was the chief rock of offense. Consequently, there is small wonder that the reviewers,
almost to a man, indicated their unqualified dis-
approval of the poet's offensive treatment of unpoetic themes. They also objected to the egoistic
and blatant quality of his verse.

But the severe censure of the critics did not put
a quietus upon Whitman's muse or deter him from
his purpose of bringing out a third augmented edition of his "Leaves of Grass." However, he did
make a slight concession to the critics by culling
out all the offensive lines and grouping them under
the bizarre heading, *"Enfans d' Adams."* In vain
did Emerson expostulate with Whitman, in his
notable walk, upon his too plain and outspoken

treatment of sexual matters in the "Leaves." Whitman resolutely declined to remove the offending "Children of Adam" poems, and later affirmed that though Emerson's arguments for removal were unanswerable, he was nevertheless more thoroughly convinced that these poems must stand unaltered. In view of this later statement by Whitman we are forced to conclude that he was perfectly candid and sincere in writing "Children of Adam" in the interest of morality, whatever we may think of the poet's unpardonable lack of judgment and violation of the canons of art and good taste. Apropos of the apparent immorality of the "Leaves," some critic has made the witty comment that the book contains every kind of a leaf but the fig leaf.

In 1866 Whitman published his first volume of war poems, under the title "Drum Taps." These poems were, for the most part, descriptive, not lyrical, and grew out of their author's observations and experiences during the war. The tender and touching elegy upon Lincoln, "When Lilacs last in the Dooryard Bloom'd," was appended as a supplement. The strong, rugged personality of the great war statesman made a forceful appeal to Whitman's genius, and, somehow, seemed to inspire him to his noblest lyrical effort. His other ode to Lincoln beginning "O Captain, my Captain!" is a beautiful tribute to the martyred President, as stirring and passionate as it is simple and spontaneous. Whitman's war poems, unlike his "Leaves of Grass," were above reproach on the score of morality; and the offensive characteristics of the author, such as his egoism and his blatancy, are not here obtrusive, but are held in abeyance. "Drum Taps" therefore made a more favorable impression upon the reading public and was accorded a more cordial reception than the poet's maiden volume.

Whitman himself, however, esteemed the first product of his invention far more highly than any other product of his pen and bestowed upon it, first and last, more thought and labor than upon all his other achievements put together. For he regarded "Leaves of Grass" his *magnum opus,* as it no doubt was, and designed it to express his message to the world.

In 1873 Whitman sustained an attack of paralysis, which incapacitated him for work, and so he removed from Washington to Camden, New Jersey. At this juncture his mother died, to whom he was devoted. The future seemed very gloomy then to the invalid poet, now reduced to actual want. But his friends rallied to his support and provided for his needs. His critics, too, relented and became more sympathetic. His health soon improved and he was again able to travel and lecture. He signalized the year 1876 by a centennial edition of "Leaves of Grass," in two volumes, issued privately and containing "Democratic Vistas." This was the sixth augmented edition of the book, and its appearance was made the occasion, by the Whitmanites on both sides of the Atlantic, of the awakening of interest in the Camden bard. The seventh edition appeared five years later, in Boston, but was suppressed on account of a legal prosecution threatened against the alleged obscene passages in the book.

In 1882 Whitman published, in Philadelphia, his prose volume, "Specimen Days and Collect." This is chiefly interesting for its autobiographical value and as a commentary upon the sage's *rationale* of poetry. Here he reveals to the world a chronicle of the dark days he passed through when his health failed, and of his melancholy meditations.

In 1885 Whitman's health again became impaired. But he nursed it, and although the end seemed imminent, once at least in 1888, yet he rallied sufficiently to undertake his customary light work again. During the intervals of fitful work he succeeded in writing and publishing a volume of verse, "November Boughs," and a complete edition of his works, prose and poetry. He was much cheered and gratified with the hearty greetings which he received from almost all parts of the world upon the celebration of his seventieth birthday. This event he signalized by the issue of a limited edition of the "Leaves of Grass," which included an autobiographical sketch in prose and a small collection of verses entitled "Sands at Seventy." In 1891 the bard gave the world his swansong, "The Second Annex, Goodbye, My Fancy"; and in the same year appeared the tenth and definitive re-issue of the "Leaves of Grass." The following year the poet issued a complete edition of his prose works, uniform with the final edition of the "Leaves." On March 26, 1892, the venerable and patriarchal poet passed away, and his body was laid to rest in the massive and imposing tomb in the cemetery at Camden, which he had designed with his own hand.

No American writer has so sharply divided the world of scholars as Walt Whitman has by his writings, and even yet the reviewers have but little common ground to stand on in their criticism of his works. Swinburne and other English critics were eulogizing him before the Good Gray Poet's own countrymen awoke to an appreciation of his merits; and even now some eminent scholars decry his fame and assure us, on the contrary, that he wrote nothing to commend him to favor. Ever since the first appearance of "Leaves of Grass" virulent attacks have been made upon Whitman, directed especially against his egoism, his obscurity and his obscenity. But there was not wanting a host of warm friends and admiring defenders to repel the attacks of his detractors and to vindicate the poet's reputation completely from these damaging charges. Since his death the Whitman cult has spread and the coterie of his devotees has labored with unabated zeal to herald his praise far and wide. Nor has the propaganda been confined to our shores. For there are many Whitmanites in England and on the Continent. As a result of the unceasing activity of Whitman's disciples there are now Whitman Clubs, Whitman Fellowships, a Whitman literary organ and a formidable array of Whitman monographs and essays, an ever-increasing Whitman bibliography. While the zeal of the bard's followers may be commendable, their excessive and indiscriminate adulation has, no doubt, contributed to prejudice many, and thus has done positive injustice and injury to Whitman.

Any review of Whitman must concern itself primarily and mainly with his "Leaves of Grass," his greatest triumph. For this contains his message to the world, his philosophy of life, his ripest thought; and, as intimated before, upon it the author bestowed his best energy and unstinted pains. He elaborated and expanded it from the thin quarto edition of 1855 to the portly final edition of 1891. In it he sets forth his theory of life in its fullest and broadest sense,—physical, mental and moral,—but life of the individual as environed in a free, democratic country, the United States, and expressed in terms of absolute frankness and directness. But let the poet declare his purpose in his own words, in the preface to the "Leaves of Grass":

The theory of my "Leaves of Grass" [says the writer], is to thoroughly possess the mind, memory, cognizance of the author himself, with everything beforehand—a full armory of concrete actualities, observations, humanity, past poems, ballads, facts, technique, war and peace, politics, north and south, east and west, nothing too large or too small, the sciences as far as possible,—and above all America and the present,—after and out of which the subject of the poem, long or short, has been invariably turned over to his Emotionality, even Personality, to be shaped thence; and emerges strictly therefrom, with all its merits and demerits on its head. Every page of my attempt at poetic utterance, therefore, smacks of the living physical identity, date, environment, individuality, probably beyond anything known, and in style often offensive to the conventions.

The personal note is distinctive and dominant in the "Leaves of Grass." The very opening lines indicate Whitman's intense egoism, which is reflected in every page of the remarkable production. Whitman had a profound and abiding conviction, as every unbiased reader must admit, that this poem voiced his ripest thought and his conception of the philosophy of life. It is this conviction which made the poet so frank and courageous in the expression of his views. Moreover, he had the courage of his convictions and therefore positively refused to modify or alter the form and manner in which he first gave the poem to the world, however offensive to good taste and contrary to the accepted traditions of poetry. The form, too, of his unique evangel was quite as unconventional as the substance. Eschewing all the received forms of verse, he chose as the medium of his thought a free and lawless kind of dithyramb without rhyme or metre.

His poetic creed was in direct contravention of all the time-honored traditions.

Whitman's seriousness of purpose led him into a fundamental error. For he failed to realize that the poet must conform to certain well-defined principles of art in the representation of his creative imagination. He failed to see that there are certain things which from their very nature do not admit of poetic treatment, do not lend themselves to artistic representation. It is sheer folly to attempt to give these things poetic adornment. It is not in keeping with the eternal fitness of things and is contrary to every principle of art. Common sense ought to dictate this even if one's literary judgment and good taste should fail one utterly. So when Whitman, to cite a specific case, in his desire to exalt the body calls "the scent of the armpits aroma diviner than prayer," he simply shows that he has no sure sense of propriety or of the fitness of things, and he sins egregiously against the canons of art. He betrays, besides, a woeful lack of the aesthetic sense. Yet this cannot properly be regarded immoral as some of the critics assert. Whitman wrote many shocking things, but he was not really immoral.

The truth is, Whitman was wanting in due appreciation of good form, as a logical result of his plain breeding and Bohemian manner of life, and his aesthetic sense was not fully developed. His earnest desire to exalt the body as glorious and to combat the mediaeval notion that the body is base and unworthy serious consideration led him to take the indefensible position that the entire body is sacred and therefore all its functions and parts are proper subjects for poetic treatment. Of course this is manifestly absurd. Needless to say that it showed a conspicuous lack of the art instinct. In his free and unrestrained representation of the bodily functions Whitman furnishes unmistakable evidence of a biased sense of proportion. No exception, however, can be taken to some of his utterances as to the sacredness of the human body. For some of these are excellent of their kind, as for example, the following:

"If anything is sacred the human body is sacred, and
  the glory and sweet of a man is the token of manhood
  untainted,
And in man or woman a clean, strong, firm-fibered body
  is more beautiful than the most beautiful face."

Whitman is a difficult writer to classify with any degree of confidence. Nor can one speak with anything approaching assurance as to his ultimate place in American literature. His work is very unequal. There are dreary wastes of mere words which make the reader feel like closing the book in disgust. But turn one page more perhaps and you may find a superb passage of impeccable English and almost Hebraic in its earnestness. There is imagination, the thought is elevating, the rhythm musical, the diction well-nigh perfect, and the passage is excellent in every particular. But the interest is not sustained, and the inspiration is intermittent. Sometimes without warning the bard rises in an imaginative passage and carries the reader aloft, but only to descend again quite as suddenly as a spent rocket.

There is much in Whitman that smacks of cant. Indeed, there is in him so much of something akin to cant that he has been called by an eminent critic a victim of cant. His undue emphasis of the natural, including the human body, has been considered a form of cant simply, as likewise his con-

tinual harping upon the theme of equality, the un-
suitableness of European art to American needs
and his stress on originality. But this perhaps was
a mere accessory to his rôle as the singer of
American democracy, which he viewed with apparent complacency. No doubt, in the last analysis his
cant will be found to have sprung from his lack of
culture and balance. For had he possessed culture
and poise, these qualities would have saved him
from his egoism as well as from his crudity and his
shocking want of good form and propriety.

From affectation or some other reason, Whitman
appears to have depreciated culture and academic
training. Certainly this is a logical inference from
his writings. As far as his poetry is concerned,
even his staunchest defenders must admit that its
intellectual side is not so strong as its emotional.
Beyond all question, the author's emotional nature
was more fully developed than his intellectual. He
was passionately fond of music and lost no opportunity to cultivate his appreciation of it. Yet he
must also have attained a considerable degree of
intellectual development, as is evidenced by his literary achievement. But he was not a consecutive
thinker. His thought is not clear and it would be
an arduous task to deduce an orderly system from
his writings. His poetry is marred here and there
by carelessness and palpable errors in the use of
his mother-tongue. His tedious catalogues and his
affectation in the employment of foreign phrases
simply serve to parade and advertise his immature
scholarship. The effect of his grand "cosmic emotions" is frequently spoiled by his glaring defects
of style. Curiously enough, one of his mannerisms
was to interlard his diction with technical terms
and foreign expressions, when the pure Saxon word
would have been much more effective as being

readily understood. His rhetoric, too, is sometimes fearfully and wonderfully mixed; and incongruous figures are jumbled together, presenting no clear, distinct image.

Whitman is at his best, as a rule, in his brief descriptive poems. Parts of the "Passage to India" and the "Pioneers," and such poems as "Out of the Cradle Endlessly Rocking," "The Ox-Tamer," "Of that Blithe Throat of Thine," "A Clear Midnight," "On the Beach at Night," and his noble patriotic chants on Lincoln are well expressed and exhibit spontaneity and beauty, to a marked degree. He is especially happy in his poems describing the sea. The strictures upon his rhetoric and diction do not hold in the case of his best poems, which are generally above reproach in every detail. Here his conception is vivid and realistic, and his execution artistic and his language almost matchless. Here, too, his irregular dithyrambic verse, largely lawless and metreless, approaches to regularity and becomes rhythmical and highly musical. But here, to be sure, the poet is inspired and rises above his besetting faults of style. Here it is that he challenges our admiration and enchains our interest.

Was Whitman then a great poet? Some scholarly and eminent critics unhesitatingly affirm that he was and adduce a mass of evidence to establish their thesis. Yet others, again, quite as learned and cultured, maintain that he was not a great poet, and they produce abundant evidence in support of their position. Of course, in a question at issue like the present, much depends upon a definition of terms. If to be a great poet is primarily to voice adequately the ideals and aspirations of the human heart in a grand and inspiring song, then there is considerable ground for doubt whether Whitman measures up to the standard of a great poet. If,

moreover, to be a great poet implies the possession
of an innate artistic sense,—the art instinct,—so as
to express one's thought in an artistic manner, con-
formable to good taste, and to be perfectly natural
withal, then Whitman clearly does not deserve to
be classed among the world's great poets. For
Whitman has not, in the first place, produced any
grand and inspiring poem of sustained interest; nor
does he possess, in the second place, except to a very
limited extent, the art instinct. But if, on the other
hand, as some critics hold, to be a great poet is
simply to have "vision and voice, poetic conceptions
that are grand and high, and a masterful gift of
imaginative utterance," then Whitman may be regarded as a great poet. However, it can hardly be
expected that the present generation should satisfactorily settle this question. We are too near
Whitman's life and times to have the true perspective and to divest our minds of prejudice or passion.
We must leave the solution of this question to posterity. Yet we must admit that the Camden bard
was a poet in the received acceptation of that term.
For he possessed imagination, passion, insight,
faith and the gift of utterance.

WHITMAN

PIONEERS! O PIONEERS!

Come, my tan-faced children,
Follow well in order, get your weapons ready,
Have you your pistols? have you your sharp-edged
axes?
  Pioneers! O pioneers!

For we cannot tarry here,
We must march, my darlings, we must bear the brunt of
danger,
We the youthful sinewy races, all the rest on us depend,
  Pioneers! O pioneers!

O you youths, Western youths,
So impatient, full of action, full of manly pride and
friendship,
Plain I see you, Western youths, see you tramping with
the foremost,
  Pioneers! O pioneers!

Have the elder races halted?
Do they droop and end their lesson, wearied over there
beyond the seas?
We take up the task eternal, and the burden and the
lesson,
  Pioneers! O pioneers!

All the past we leave behind,
We debouch upon a newer mightier world, varied
world,
Fresh and strong the world we seize, world of labor
and the march,
  Pioneers! O pioneers!

We detachments steady throwing
Down the edges, through the passes, up the mountain
   steep,
Conquering, holding, daring, venturing as we go the
   unknown ways,
   Pioneers! O pioneers!

We primeval forests felling.
We the rivers stemming, vexing we and piercing deep
   the mines within,
We the surface broad surveying, we the virgin soil
   upheaving,
   Pioneers! O pioneers!

Colorado men are we,
From the peaks gigantic, from the great sierras and the
   high plateaus,
From the mine and from the gully, from the hunting
   trail we come,
   Pioneers! O pioneers!

From Nebraska, from Arkansas,
Central inland race are we, from Missouri, with the
   continental blood intervein'd,
All hands of comrades clasping, all the Southern, all
   the Northern,
   Pioneers! O pioneers!

O resistless restless race!
O beloved race in all! O my breast aches with tender
   love for all!
O I mourn and yet exult, I am rapt with love for all,
   Pioneers! O pioneers!

Raise the mighty mother mistress,
Waving high the delicate mistress, over all the starry
   mistress, (bend your heads all,)
Raise the fang'd and warlike mistress, stern, impassive,
   weapon'd mistress,
   Pioneers! O pioneers!

See my children, resolute children,
By those swarms upon our rear we must never yield or
  falter,
Ages back in ghostly millions frowning there behind
  us surging,
      Pioneers! O pioneers!

On and on the compact ranks,
With accessions ever waiting, with the places of the
  dead quickly fill'd,
Through the battle, through defeat, moving yet and
  never stopping,
      Pioneers! O pioneers!

O to die advancing on!
Are there some of us to drop and die? has the hour
  come?
Then upon the march we fittest die, soon and sure the
  gap is fill'd,
      Pioneers! O pioneers!

All the pulses of the world,
Falling in they beat for us, with the Western movement
  beat,
Holding single or together, steady moving to the front,
  all for us,
      Pioneers! O pioneers!

Life's involved and varied pageants,
All the forms and shows, all the workmen at their
  work,
All the seamen and the landsmen, all the masters with
  their slaves,
      Pioneers! O pioneers!

All the hapless silent lovers,
All the prisoners in the prisons, all the righteous and
  the wicked,
All the joyous, all the sorrowing, all the living, all the
  dying,
      Pioneers! O pioneers!

I too with my soul and body,
We, a curious trio, picking, wandering on our way,
Through these shores amid the shadows, with the ap-
paritions pressing,
        Pioneers! O pioneers!

Lo, the darting bowling orb!
Lo, the brother orbs around, all the clustering suns
and planets,
All the dazzling days, all the mystic nights with
dreams,
        Pioneers! O pioneers!

These are of us, they are with us,
All for primal needed work, while the followers there
in embryo wait behind,
We today's procession heading, we the route for travel
clearing,
        Pioneers! O pioneers!

O you daughters of the West!
O you young and older daughters! O you mothers and
you wives!
Never must you be divided, in our ranks you move
united,
        Pioneers! O pioneers!

Minstrels latent on the prairies!
(Shrouded bards of other lands, you may rest, you have
done your work,)
Soon I hear you coming warbling, soon you rise and
tramp amid us,
        Pioneers! O pioneers!

Not for delectations sweet,
Not the cushion and the slipper, not the peaceful and
the studious,
Not the riches safe and palling, not for us the tame
enjoyment,
        Pioneers! O pioneers!

Do the feasters gluttonous feast?
Do the corpulent sleepers sleep? have they lock'd and
bolted doors?
Still be ours the diet hard, and the blanket on the
ground,
> Pioneers! O pioneers!

Has the night descended?
Was the road of late so toilsome? did we stop discouraged nodding on our way?
Yet a passing hour I yield you in your tracks to pause
oblivious,
> Pioneers! O pioneers!

Till with sound of trumpet,
Far, far off the daybreak call—hark! how loud and
clear I hear it wind,
Swift! to the head of the army!—swift! spring to your
places,
> Pioneers! O Pioneers!

WHEN LILACS LAST IN THE DOOR-YARD BLOOM'D

1

When lilacs last in the door-yard bloomed,
And the great star early dropped in the western sky in
the night,
I mourned, and yet shall mourn with ever-returning
spring.
Ever-returning spring, trinity sure to me you bring,
Lilac blooming perennial, and drooping star in the
west,
And thought of him I love.

2

O powerful western fallen star!
O shades of night—O moody, tearful night!
O great star disappeared—O the black murk that hides
the star!

O cruel hands that hold me powerless—O helpless soul
  of me!
O harsh surrounding cloud that will not free my soul!

3

In the door-yard fronting an old farm-house, near the
  whitewashed palings,
Stands the lilac-bush tall-growing with heart-shaped
  leaves of rich green,
With many a pointed blossom rising delicate, with the
  perfume strong I love,
With every leaf a miracle;—and from this bush in the
  door-yard,
With delicate colored blossoms, and heart-shaped
  leaves of rich green,
A sprig with its flower I break.

4

In the swamp in secluded recesses,
A shy and hidden bird is warbling a song.

Solitary the thrush,
The hermit withdrawn to himself, avoiding the settle-
  ments,
Sings by himself a song—
Song of the bleeding throat,
Death's outlet song of life (for well, dear brother, I
  know,
If thou wast not granted to sing thou would'st surely
  die).

5

Over the breast of the spring, the land amid cities,
Amid lanes and through old woods, where lately the
  violets peeped from the ground, spotting the gray
  debris,

Amid the grass in the fields, each side of the lanes, pas-
sing the endless grass,
Passing the yellow-speared wheat, every grain from its
shroud in the dark-brown fields uprisen,
Passing the apple-tree blows of white and pink in the
orchards,
Carrying a corpse to where it shall rest in the grave,
Night and day journeys a coffin.

6

Coffin that passes through lanes and streets,
Through day and night with the great cloud darken-
ing the land,
With the pomp of the inlooped flags with the cities
draped in black,
With the show of the States themselves as of crape-
veiled women standing,
With processions long and winding and the flambeaux
of the night,
With the countless torches lit, with the silent sea of
faces and the unbared heads,
With the waiting depot, the arriving coffin and the
sombre faces,
With dirges through the night, with the thousand
voices rising strong and solemn,
With all the mournful voices of the dirges poured
around the coffin,
The dim-light churches and the shuddering organs—
where amid these you journey,
With the tolling, tolling bells' perpetual clang,
Here, coffin that slowly passes,
I give you my sprig of lilac.

7

(Nor for you, for one alone,—
Blossoms and branches green to coffins all I bring;
For, fresh as the morning, thus would I chant a song
for you, O sane and sacred death.

All over bouquets of roses,
O death, I cover you over with roses and early lilies,
But mostly and now the lilac that blooms the first,
Copious I break, I break the sprigs from the bushes,
With loaded arms I come, pouring for you,
For you and the coffins all of you, O death.)

8

O western orb sailing the heaven,
Now I know what you must have meant as a month
    since I walked,
As I walked in silence the transparent shadowy night,
As I saw you had something to tell as you bent to me
    night after night,
As you drooped from the sky low down as if to my side
    (while the other stars all looked on),
As we wandered together the solemn night (for some-
    thing, I know not what, kept me from sleep),
As the night advanced, and I saw on the rim of the
    west how full you were of woe,
As I stood on the rising ground in the breeze in the cool
    transparent night,
As my soul in its trouble dissatisfied sank, as where
    you, sad orb,
Concluded, dropt in the night, and was gone.

9

Sing on there in the swamp,
O singer bashful and tender! I hear your notes, I hear
    your call,
I hear, I come presently, I understand you;
But a moment I linger, for the lustrous star has de-
    tained me,
The star my departing comrade holds and detains me.

10

O how shall I warble myself for the dead one there I
  loved?
And how shall I deck my song for the large sweet soul
  that has gone?
And what shall my perfume be for the grave of him I
  love?

Sea-winds blown from east and west,
Blown from the Eastern sea and blown from the West-
  ern sea, till there on the prairies meeting,
These and with these and the breath of my chant,
I'll perfume the grave of him I love.

11

O what shall I hang on the chamber walls?
And what shall the pictures be that I hang on the walls,
To adorn the burial-house of him I love?
Pictures of growing spring and farms and homes,
With the Fourth-month eve at sundown, and the gray
  smoke lucid and bright,
With floods of the yellow gold of the gorgeous, indo-
  lent, sinking sun, burning, expanding the air,
With the fresh, sweet herbage under foot, and the pale
  green leaves of the trees prolific,
In the distance the flowing glaze, the breast of the
  river, with a winddapple here and there,
With ranging hills on the banks, with many a line
  against the sky, and shadows,
And the city at hand with dwellings so dense, and
  stacks of chimneys,
And all the scenes of life and the workshops, and the
  workmen homeward returning.

12

Lo, body and soul—this land,
My own Manhattan with spires, and the sparkling and
  hurrying tides, and the ships,
The varied and ample land, the South and the North
  in the light, Ohio's shores and flashing Missouri,
And ever the far-spreading prairies covered with grass
  and corn.

Lo, the most excellent sun so calm and haughty,
The violet and purple morn with just-felt breezes,
The gentle soft-born measureless light,
The miracle spreading, bathing all, the fulfilled noon,
The coming eve delicious, the welcome night and the
  stars,
Over my cities shining all, enveloping man and land.

13

Sing on, sing on, you gray-brown bird!
Sing from the swamps, the recesses; pour your chant
  from the bushes,
Limitless out of the dusk, out of the cedars and pines.

Sing on, dearest brother, warble your reedy song,
Loud human song, with voice of uttermost woe.

O liquid and free and tender!
O wild and loose to my soul—O wondrous singer!
You only I hear—yet the star holds me (but will soon
  depart),
Yet the lilac with mastering odor holds me.

14

Now while I sat in the day and looked forth,
In the close of the day with its light and the fields of
  spring, and the farmers preparing their crops,
In the large unconscious scenery of my land with its
  lakes and forests,

In the heavenly aerial beauty (after the perturbed
    winds and the storms),
Under the arching heavens of the afternoon swift pass-
    ing, and the voices of children and women,
The many-moving sea-tides, and I saw the ships how
    they sailed,
And the summer approaching with richness, and the
    fields all busy with labor,
And the infinite separate houses, how they all went on,
    each with its meals and minutia of daily usages,
And the streets how their throbbings throbbed, and the
    cities pent—lo, then and there,
Falling upon them all and among them all, enveloping
    me with the rest,
Appeared the cloud, appeared the long black trail,
And I knew death, its thought, and the sacred knowl-
    edge of death.

Then with the knowledge of death as walking one side
    of me,
And the thought of death close-walking the other side
    of me,
And I in the middle as with companions, and as hold-
    ing the hands of companions,
I fled forth to the hiding receiving night that talks not,
Down to the shores of the water, the path by the swamp
    in the dimness,
To the solemn shadowy cedars and ghostly pines so
    still.

And the singer so shy to the rest received me,
The gray-brown bird I know received us comrades three,
And he sang the carol of death, and a verse for him I
    love.

From deep secluded recesses,
From the fragrant cedars and the ghostly pines so still,
Came the carol of the bird.

And the charm of the carol rapt me,
As I held as if by their hands my comrades in the night,
And the voice of my spirit tallied the song of the bird.

Come, lovely and soothing death,
Undulate round the world, serenely arriving, arriving,
In the day, in the night, to all, to each,
Sooner or later, delicate death.

Praised be the fathomless universe,
For life and joy, and for objects and knowledge curious,
And for love, sweet love—but praise! praise! praise!
For the sure-enwinding arms of cool-enfolding death.

Dark mother, always gliding near with soft feet,
Have none chanted for thee a chant of fullest welcome?
Then I chant it for thee, I glorify thee above all,
I bring thee a song that when thou must indeed come,
*   come unfalteringly.*

Approach, strong deliveress!
When it is so, when thou hast taken them, I joyously
*   sing the dead,*
Lost in the loving floating ocean of thee,
Laved in the flood of thy bliss, O death.

From me to thee glad serenades,
Dances for thee, I propose, saluting thee, adornments
*   and feastings for thee;*
And the sights of the open landscape and the high-
*   spread sky are fitting,*
And life and the fields, and the huge and thoughtful
*   night—*

The night in silence under many a star,
The ocean shore and the husky whispering wave whose
*   voice I know,*
And the soul turning to thee, O vast and well-veiled
*   death,*
And the body gratefully nestling close to thee.

Over the tree-tops I float thee a song,
Over the rising and sinking waves, over the myriad
fields and the prairies wide,
Over the dense-packed cities all and the teeming
wharves and ways,
I float this carol with joy, with joy to thee, O death.

15

To the tally of my soul,
Loud and strong kept up the gray-brown bird,
With pure deliberate notes spreading, filling the night.

Loud in the pines and cedars dim,
Clear in the freshness moist and the swamp-perfume,
And I with my comrades there in the night.

While my sight that was bound in my eyes unclosed,
As to long panoramas of visions.

And I saw askant the armies,
I saw as in noiseless dreams hundreds of battle-flags,
Borne through the smoke of the battles and pierced
with missiles I saw them,
And carried hither and yon through the smoke, and
torn and bloody,
And at last but a few shreds left on the staffs (and all
in silence),
And the staffs all splintered and broken.

I saw battle-corpses, myriads of them,
And the white skeletons of young men, I saw them;
I saw the debris and debris of all the slain soldiers of
the war,
But I saw they were not as was thought,—
They themselves were fully at rest, they suffered not:
The living remained and suffered, the mother suffered,
And the wife and the child and the musing comrade
suffered.

16

Passing the visions, passing the night,
Passing, unloosing the hold of my comrade's hands,
Passing the song of the hermit bird and the tallying
    song of my soul,
Victorious song, death's outlet song, yet varying ever-
    altering song,
As low and wailing, yet clear the notes, rising and fall-
    ing, flooding the night,
Sadly sinking and fainting, as warning and warning,
    and yet again bursting with joy,
Covering the earth and filling the spread of the heaven,
As that powerful psalm in the night I heard from re-
    cesses,
Passing, I leave thee lilac with heart-shaped leaves,
I leave thee there in the door-yard, blooming, return-
    ing with spring.

I cease from my song for thee,
From my gaze on thee in the west, fronting the west,
    communing with thee,
O comrade lustrous, with silver face in the night.

Yet each to keep and all, retrievements out of the night,
The song, the wondrous chant of the gray-brown bird,
And the tallying chant, the echo aroused in my soul,
With the lustrous and drooping star with the counte-
    nance full of woe.
With the holders holding my hand nearing the call of
    the bird,
Comrades mine and I in the midst, and their memory
    ever to keep, for the dead I loved so well,
For the sweetest, wisest soul of all my days and lands
    —and this for his dear sake,
Lilac and star and bird twined with the chant of my
    soul,
There in the fragrant pines and the cedars dusk and
    dim.

O CAPTAIN! MY CAPTAIN!

O Captain! my Captain! our fearful trip is done;
The ship has weathered every rack, the prize we sought
    is won;
The port is near, the bells I hear, the people all
    exulting,
While follow eyes the steady keel, the vessel grim and
    daring.
            But O heart! heart! heart!
           O the bleeding drops of red,
              Where on the deck my Captain lies,
              Fallen cold and dead.

O Captain! my Captain! rise up and hear the bells:
Rise up!—for you the flag is flung—for you the bugle
    trills,
For you bouquets and ribboned wreaths—for you the
    shores a-crowding;
For you they call, the swaying mass, their eager faces
    turning.
            Here Captain! dear father!
            This arm beneath your head!
             It is some dream that on the deck
              You've fallen cold and dead.

My Captain does not answer, his lips are pale and still;
My father does not feel my arm, he has nor pulse nor
    will;
The ship is anchored safe and sound, its voyage closed
    and done,
From fearful trip the victor ship comes in with object
    won;
            Exult O shores, and ring O bells!
            But I with mournful tread,
             Walk the deck my Captain lies,
              Fallen cold and dead.

BIBLIOGRAPHY

The following works on American literature may be mentioned as especially helpful to the student:

American Literature (1607-1885). C. F. Richardson. 2 vols. 1887. Putnam.

A History of American Literature during the Colonial Time. M. C. Tyler. 2 vols. 1878. Putnam.

Poets of America. E. C. Stedman. 1885. Houghton, Mifflin and Company.

The Literary History of the American Revolution. M. C. Tyler. 2 vols. 1897.

Chronological Outlines of American Literature. S. L. Whitcomb. 1894. Macmillan.

American Literature. J. Hawthorne and L. Lemmon. 1892. Heath.

American Literature. Brander Matthews. 1896. Appleton.

A Reader's Handbook of American Literature. T. W. Higginson and H. W. Boynton. Houghton, Mifflin and Company.

Literary History of America. Barrett Wendell. 1900. Scribner.

America in Literature. George E Woodberry. Harper.

American Literature (in the "Literatures of the World" series). W. P. Trent. 1903. Appleton.

Literary Leaders of America. Richard Burton. 1904. Scribner.

History of Historical Writing in America. J. F. Jameson. 1891.

The New England Poets. W. C. Lawton. 1898.

A History of American Verse. J. L. Onderdonk. 1901.

A most excellent series is "The American Men of Letters," published by Houghton, Mifflin and Company, in which appear all the authors included in the present volume.

Those desiring to consult a good anthology may be referred to the *Library of American Authors* (1608-1889), edited by E. C. Stedman and E. M. Hutchinson, in eleven volumes. 1888-1890. Chas. L. Webster and Company. *American History Told by Contempories* by A. B. Hart (4 vols., 1897-1901), *American Prose* by G. R. Carpenter (1898).

Also worthy of mention are *An American Anthology* by E. C. Stedman (1900), *Southern Literature* by Louise Manly (revised, 1900), *Colonial Prose and Poetry* by W. P. Trent and B. W. Wells (3 vols. 1901).

The student is referred to the following special works for a detailed study of the authors included in the present volume:

FRANKLIN. The definitive edition of Franklin's works is A. H. Smyth's, in 10 volumes (1906), which also contains a biography. See also J. B. McMaster's *Benjamin Franklin* in the "American Men of Letters" series (1887).

IRVING. There are several editions of Irving's complete works. His *Life and Letters* were edited by P. M. Irving (4 vols., 1862-64). See Charles Dudley Warner's *Irving* in "American Men of Letters" (1881).

COOPER. There are various editions of Cooper's novels including his "Leatherstocking" and "Sea Tales." His miscellaneous writings are out of print. See T. R. Lounsbury's *Cooper* in "American Men of Letters" (1883).

POE. Among the early editions of Poe may be mentioned Griswold's (3 vols., 1850, vol. 4, 1856), Ingram's (4 vols., 1874-5), Stoddard's (6 vols., 1884); among the more recent editions are Stedman and Woodberry's (10 vols., 1894-5), Harrison's Virginia edition (17 vols., 1902), Richardson's Arnheim edition (1902). Among the biographies are Griswold's (1850), Gill's (1877-8), Ingram's (2 vols., 1880), and new edition (in 1 vol., 1886), Woodberry's (1885) in "American Men of Letters," Stedman and Woodberry's (1894), and Harrison's (1902).

PRESCOTT. The standard edition of Prescott's works is by John Foster Kirk (16 vols., 1870-74). Ticknor's biography appeared in 1864 and Rollo Ogden's in "American Men of Letters," in 1904.

HAWTHORNE. The standard edition of Hawthorne is the Riverside, in 12 vols. The biographies include Julian Hawthorne's *Nathaniel Hawthorne and his Wife* (2 vols., 1885), Henry James's *Hawthorne* in "English Men of Letters" (1879), Moncure Conway's *Hawthorne* in "Great Writers" (1890), G. E. Wood-berry's, in "American Men of Letters" (1902) and G. P. Lathrop's *A Study of Hawthorne* (1876).

EMERSON. The standard edition of Emerson is the Riverside, in 12 vols. The biographies include J. E. Cabot's *Memoir* (2 vols., 1887), Holmes's *Emerson* in "American Men of Letters" (1884), and Richard Garnett's, in "Great Writers" (1888). C. E. Norton edited the Carlyle-Emerson correspondence (2 vols., 1883). See Lowell's *Works,* vol. 1, and J. J. Chapman's *Emerson and Other Essays* (1898).

BRYANT. Parke Godwin edited Bryant's works, the *Poems* (2 vols., 1883) and the *Prose* (2 vols., 1884). His complete poetical works are published by the Appletons. Parke Godwin's *Life of Bryant* (2 vols.) appeared in 1883, John Bigelow's *Bryant* in "American Men of Letters," in 1890. See J. G. Wilson's *Bryant and His Friends* (1886).

LONGFELLOW. The standard edition of Longfellow is the Riverside, in 11 vols. Samuel Longfellow's *Life and Letters* (2 vols., 1886) and *Final Memorials* (1887) of his brother Henry Wadsworth Longfellow were collected in a *Life* (3 vols.), in 1891. E. S. Robertson's *Longfellow* appeared in the "Great Writers" series in 1887, G. R. Carpenter's *Longfellow* in "Beacon Biographies," in 1901, and T. W. Higginson's in "American Men of Letters," in 1902.

HOLMES. The standard edition of Holmes is the Riverside, in 13 vols. His *Life and Letters* (2 vols.) were edited by J. T. Morse (2 vols., 1896).

WHITTIER. The standard edition of Whittier is the Riverside, in 7 vols. His authorized biography is the *Life and Letters* by T. S. Pickard (2 vols., 1894). In addition, may be mentioned J. W. Linton's *Whittier* in "Great Writers" (1893), T. W. Higginson's, in "English Men of Letters" (1902), and G. R. Carpenter's, in "American Men of Letters" (1902).

LOWELL. The standard edition of Lowell's works is the Riverside, in 11 vols. His *Letters* were edited by C. E. Norton (2 vols., 1893). His biographies include H. E. Scudder's *Lowell* (2 vols., 1901), E. E. Hale's *James Russell Lowell and his Friends* (1899) and S. M. Crother's *Lowell* in "American Men of Letters." See also Howell's *Literary Friends and Acquaintances* (1900).

LANIER. Lanier's Poems were edited by J. H. Ward, and there is an edition of *Select Poems* with a *Life* by Morgan Callaway (1895). The *English Novel* and the *Science of English Verse* were published by the Scribners. A recent biography of Lanier is that by Edwin Mims in "American Men of Letters" (1906).

WHITMAN. The numerous editions of *Leaves of Grass* and *Complete Prose Works* (1898) have been superseded by the elaborate edition of Whitman, published in 1902. Among the biographies of Whitman are H. B. Binn's *Life of Walt Whitman,* Horace Traubel's *With Walt Whitman in Camden* and Bliss Perry's *Walt Whitman* (1906). The authorized biography of Whitman is Dr. R. M. Bucke's (1883). See also the special studies by J. A. Symonds (1893), John Burroughs (1896), W. N. Guthrie (1897), Stephenson, Dowden, Chapman, and *In re Walt Whitman* (1893).

The following books, though in a lighter vein as being reminiscential or anecdotal, are yet worth while, since they throw interesting sidelights upon our American authors:

T. W. Higginson, *Old Cambridge* (1899), and *Cheerful Yesterdays* (Houghton, Mifflin and Co.).

E. P. Whipple, *Recollections of Eminent Men* (Houghton, Mifflin and Co.).

M. A. DeWolfe Howe, *American Book Men* (Dodd, Mead and Co.).

Mrs. James T. Fields, *Authors and Friends* (Houghton, Mifflin and Co.).

W. D. Howells, *Literary Friends and Acquaintances* (Harper).

Mrs. Julia Ward Howe, *Reminiscences* (Houghton, Mifflin and Co.).